ESSENTIALS *of*
ENROLLMENT MANAGEMENT

CASES IN THE FIELD

AACRAO®
1 9 1 0

AMERICAN ASSOCIATION OF COLLEGIATE REGISTRARS AND ADMISSIONS OFFICERS

American Association of Collegiate
Registrars and Admissions Officers
One Dupont Circle, NW, Suite 520
Washington, DC 20036-1135

For a complete listing of AACRAO publications, visit www.aacrao.org/publications.

The American Association of Collegiate Registrars and Admissions Officers, founded in
1910, is a nonprofit, voluntary, professional association of more than 9,300 higher
education administrators who represent more than 2,400 institutions and agencies in
the United States and in twenty-eight countries around the world. The mission of the
Association is to provide leadership in policy initiation, interpretation, and implementation in the global educational community. This is accomplished through the identification and promotion of standards and best practices in enrollment management,
information technology, instructional management, and student services.

Library of Congress Cataloging-in-Publication Data

Black, Jim, 1959-
    Essentials of enrollment management : cases in the field / Jim Black and
    associates. p. cm.
    Includes bibliographical references and index.
    ISBN 1-57858-062-5
    1. Universities and colleges--United States--Admission--Case studies. I.
    American Association of Collegiate Registrars and Admissions Officers. II. Title.

    LB2351.2.B46 2004
    378.1'619--dc22

                                                        2004005647

**IN LOVING MEMORY OF
KINSEY BLACK JONES**
She filled my life with beauty and
laughter. Her unwavering grace
and courage, even in the face of
adversity, continue to inspire me.
Through her example, I have
become a more determined
person—always knowing I have
choices regarding how I respond
to life circumstances.

Jim Black and Associates

TABLE OF CONTENTS

ESSENTIALS *of* ENROLLMENT MANAGEMENT
CASES IN THE FIELD

PREFACE

Essentials of Enrollment Management: Cases in the Field is rich with stories of institutions that have adopted enrollment management concepts and practices. Though the case studies in this book are primarily focused on institutional successes, readers will identify with the struggles and even the failures described by the authors.

Perhaps the most valuable content in the entire book is the section for each case study titled, "Lesson Learned." For indeed, most us have learned enrollment management through a series of trial and error experiments. While we vehemently believe in the inherent value of using data for decision-making, the truth is that for much of what we do, there is no empirical data to support or guide our actions. Therefore, enrollment managers often resort to relying on gut intuition, following commonly held assumptions, or collapsing under the pressure to do something—anything--to get results.

With the recognition that virtually every enrollment management situation and campus culture is different, this book attempts to reduce the pain of trial and error by introducing some proven methodology and practices along with a dose of real challenges and obstacles facing enrollment managers. It is our hope that readers will glean from these case studies inspiration and ideas that can be applied on their respective campuses. At the very least, we hope to stretch the thinking of readers in "the art of what is possible."

STRUCTURE OF THE BOOK

With the exception of the first chapter, each chapter reflects a specific institutional case study. Chapter 1 provides an overview of themes and models that are fundamental to the field of enrollment management and are featured in a single case study or represent a pattern among two or more case institutions.

To ensure relatively broad coverage of the U. S. higher education landscape, cases include those from two- and four-year institutions as well as some that offer graduate and professional programs; public and private colleges and universities; and some diversity by institutional setting—urban, suburban, and rural. Represented among the case study institutions are commuter campuses, traditional residential campuses, institutions with national reputations and those that serve local communities. The cases range from relatively new to well-established, mature enrollment management enterprises. Some of the accounts of enrollment management journeys emphasize basic fundamentals while others reveal extreme or unique approaches.

Each case study includes three common elements—the institution's story or an overview of the evolution of enrollment management, results, and lessons learned. These common thematic elements provide a navigational map for the reader that is consistent throughout. Beyond these thematic elements, there are few similarities between the case studies. As illustrated in these cases, the diversity of approaches to enrollment management is seemingly infinite. Models, strategies, and templates are just that. There are no "silver bullets" or "one-size-fits-all" solutions in this book.

The case studies are not arranged in a particular order or designed to build one upon the next. They simply offer unique snapshots of real life experiences in enrollment management. Other than Chapter 1, there are only modest attempts to present theory. The chapters are intended to emphasize practice over theory.

ACKNOWLEDGEMENTS

The contributing authors to this book have been fervent in their efforts to accurately portray their institutions and enrollment management journey. They have openly shared the "good, the bad, and the ugly" for the good of the profession. For this, they are to be commended. And on an editorial note, I have never worked with a more dedicated group of authors. They remained punctual and highly professional throughout the entire process.

Special thanks to the American Association of Collegiate Registrars and Admissions Officers for their interest in contributing to the literature in the field of enrollment management. In particular, I want to express my appreciation to Amy Haavik for her assistance.

ABOUT THE AUTHORS

KATHRYN BAUGHER

Kathryn Baugher joined the Belmont University staff as dean of Admissions in February 1993. In 1996, Dr. Baugher was named dean of Enrollment Services, coordinating the work of all enrollment services areas at the university. Her work includes adapting Continuous Quality Improvement (CQI) techniques in many areas of enrollment and university administration. She also pursues research and improvement of the LEARN process and other applications of CQI to the classroom.

Dr. Baugher attended Samford University in Birmingham, Alabama where she earned the bachelor degree in education. She completed the master of arts degree in 1984 at Southwestern Baptist Theological Seminary in Fort Worth. She earned the Ed. D. degree at Peabody College of Vanderbilt University in 1993 in educational leadership.

JIM BLACK

Jim Black is currently serving as the associate provost for Enrollment Services at The University of North Carolina at Greensboro. His areas of responsibility include Undergraduate Admissions, Financial Aid, Registrar's Office, Student Academic Services (primarily responsible for advising and retention initiatives), Student Success Center, Evening University, and the student information system (SCT Banner).

Dr. Black is the founder of the National Conference on Student Retention in Small Colleges and cofounder of the National Small College Admissions Conference and the National Small College Enrollment Conference. He currently serves as the director of AACRAO's Strategic Enrollment Management Conference. Recognized as a leader in the field, he developed the first comprehensive evaluation tool for enrollment management operations and has conducted research into the status of the enrollment management profession. Dr. Black has published numerous articles and book chapters. Among his other published works are a monograph titled *Navigating Change in the New Millennium: Strategies for Enrollment Leaders* and two books, *The Strategic Enrollment Management Revolution* and *Gen Xers Return to College: Enrollment Strategies for a Maturing Population*. He has served as a consultant for more than seventy colleges, universities, professional organizations, and corporations and is currently serving on the board of two corporations. Dr. Black is one of only 23 IBM Best Practice Partners in the world, recognized as such for his institution's delivery of exemplary student services as well as his expertise in change management and human resource management.

Black earned a bachelor of arts in English education and a master's of education in higher education student personnel services with a cognate in counseling from the University of South Carolina. He holds a Ph.D. degree in higher education curriculum and teaching with a concentration in business administration from The University of North Carolina at Greensboro.

BOB BONTRAGER

Bob Bontrager is the chief enrollment officer for Oregon State University. During his 9-year tenure, Oregon State's freshman class has increased by more than 70 percent and overall enrollment has grown by nearly 40 percent. In 2001, he led the development of the Enrollment Management Division and took the new position of assistant provost, providing leadership to Admissions, Financial Aid and Scholarships, the Registrar's Office, pre-college programs, and Student Orientation and retention programs. He is also a faculty member in Oregon State's graduate program in college student services administration. Prior to joining Oregon State in 1994, Dr. Bontrager was vice president for Enrollment Management at Eastern Mennonite University in Virginia and was assistant registrar at Arizona State University from 1983-88.

Dr. Bontrager recently chaired AACRAO's Enrollment Management and Retention Committee and authored the monograph *Strategic Enrollment Management: An Introduction to Core Concepts and Strategies*, required reading for AACRAO's 2002 Strategic Enrollment Management Conference. He has written and presented frequently on the topics of enrollment management, business process reengineering, marketing, predictive modeling, and financial aid leveraging.

ROBIN K. HAMILTON

Robin K. Hamilton is the Student Affairs representative for Enrollment Management at the University of Missouri—Kansas City (UMKC). An alumna of UMKC, Hamilton has earned her master's in English literature and is currently pursuing a master's in library science. As student affairs representative, Hamilton coordinates, staffs, and reports on the progress of the university's enrollment management goals and objectives, while offering high-level support in the collaborative development of recruitment and retention strategies.

DAVID H. KALSBEEK

David H. Kalsbeek currently serves as vice president for Enrollment Management at DePaul University in Chicago, Illinois. In that capacity he leads the marketing and enrollment development strategies for the nation's largest and fastest-growing Catholic university enrolling 23,000 students in nine colleges and seven campuses throughout the greater Chicago region. His responsibilities at DePaul encompass Enrollment Management, Alumni Relations, Career Center and Employer Relations, University and Media Relations, and Marketing Communications. The innovative models he has developed at DePaul have been highlighted by CASE, by The Association of Governing Boards, and by The American Marketing Association Symposium for Marketing of Higher Education. Prior to joining DePaul in 1997, Dr. Kalsbeek served as the senior enrollment management administrator at Xavier University in Cincinnati, Ohio and before that at Saint Louis University in St. Louis, Missouri.

Dr. Kalsbeek is a frequent speaker on issues related to strategic enrollment management and marketing, net revenue planning, assessment and learning organizations. He has been a plenary speaker or presenter at most of AACRAO's eleven Strategic Enrollment Management conferences, as well as NASPA, NACUBO, AAHE, AIR, ACT, AACSB, and AMA conferences. He is on the Advisory Board for the American Marketing Association's Symposium on Marketing in Higher Education. He currently serves on the Editorial Board of the *Journal of College Student Retention* and previously served as Feature Editor for *About Campus* magazine. He has been a consultant to over twenty-five colleges, universities, and associations on issues related to strategic enrollment management.

Dr. Kalsbeek holds a Ph.D. in public policy analysis from Saint Louis University. He earned his master's degree in higher education administration at Ohio State University and a B.A. from Muskingum College in New Concord, Ohio, where he graduated summa cum laude with a major in philosophy.

CHRISTINE KERLIN

Christine Kerlin is currently the associate dean for Enrollment Services at Everett Community College, Washington. Prior to arriving at Everett in 1996, Dr. Kerlin served as director of Admissions and Records at Central Oregon Community

College and as the director of Admissions at The Evergreen State College in Olympia, Washington.

She is active in AACRAO, past president of PACRAO and past chair of NAFSA Region One, and often makes presentations at conferences held by these organizations. Among her contributions to the profession, she has chaired AACRAO's Task Force 2000, co-facilitated the AACRAO SEM Lite workshops, and authored a chapter in AACRAO's recent *International Guide*. Christine also has served as an adjunct faculty for Western Washington University's student personnel administration graduate program. Dr. Kerlin holds her master's from Western Washington University and her doctorate from Oregon State University.

JAMES LYNCH

James Lynch has been actively involved in student enrollment services for the past fourteen years. He has been the dean of Enrollment Management at Florida Gulf Coast University since 2000. In this position, Dr. Lynch is responsible for Admissions, Financial Aid and Scholarships, First Year Advising and Orientation, and Registration and Records. Prior to work at FGCU, he was the director of Graduate Recruitment and Marketing at The University of North Carolina at Greensboro.

Dr. Lynch's scholarly interests lie in multicultural education, college admission policies and practices, professional development of college admission officers, organizational culture on college and university campuses, use of technology in enrollment management, and innovative college marketing strategies and techniques. He has presented nationwide in a variety of conference settings, including the Florida Association of Collegiate Registrars & Admissions Officers, National Association of Graduate Admissions Professionals, the National Conference on the Adult Learner, and the National Association for Gifted Children.

Among his professional affiliations, Dr. Lynch serves on the Admissions Policies and Practices Committee of the American Association of Collegiate Registrars and Admissions Officers. Previously, he served on the International, Professional and Graduate Admission Committee of the Southern Association of Collegiate Registrars and Admissions Officers and the Human Relations & Diversity Committee of the National Association of Graduate Admissions Professionals.

ROBERT J. MASSA

Robert J. Massa has served as vice president for Enrollment, Student Life and College Relations at Dickinson College since July 1999. For ten years prior to joining Dickinson, he was the dean of Enrollment at Johns Hopkins University. Beginning in 1974 he held various positions in Admissions, Financial Aid and Student Affairs at Colgate University and Union College.

Dr. Massa has published widely in books and journals in the field of college admissions and enrollment management and is active as an instructor and journal editor in national organizations for admissions and financial aid professionals. His Aug. 28, 2000, New York Times op-ed "Who Needs the SAT?" on restoring the male/female balance at Dickinson and his January 2003 perspective piece in the NACAC Bulletin, "Early Decision – Fix It, Don't Kill It," have won him accolades from colleagues and inquiries from major national news organizations. He has also written and spoken extensively on the use of academic scholarships in student recruitment, tuition discounting and strategic enrollment management planning.

Massa received his bachelor's degree from the University of Rochester and a doctorate in higher education from Columbia University.

JANE A. MCGRATH

Jane McGrath, director of Enrollment Management at DePaul University, brings 21 years of higher education experience to her current duties in the division. Serving as an internal consultant, McGrath provides management of strategic initiatives that impact the Division of Enrollment Management. She provides focus for strategy development and implementation for division-wide organizational change efforts and is responsible for advancing the priorities for the division through the senior strategy team and departmental managers. Before joining the enrollment management team, McGrath served in several student affairs positions at DePaul including the director of the Career Center and director of Student Accounts.

Prior to joining DePaul in 1988, McGrath was at Creighton University in Omaha, Nebraska and worked in the areas of Residence Life, Admissions, Retention, and Alumni Relations. McGrath earned a bachelor of science in elementary education and a master's degree in counseling and student personnel services from Creighton University.

KEVIN POLLOCK

Kevin Pollock is the chief enrollment officer for West Shore Community College, located in Scottville, Michigan. During his three-year tenure at WSCC, enrollment has steadily grown and the concept of enrollment management and student success has come to the forefront of the college's vision and strategic plan. In 2002, Dr. Pollock became chair of the WSCC Strategic Planning Team, chair of the Michigan Association of Collegiate Registrars and Admission Officers (MACRAO) Enrollment Management Team, and in 2003, a board member of the Michigan Community College Student Services Administrators. He oversees Admissions, Registrar, Financial Aid, Career Counseling, Academic Advising, Women's Resource Center, and Student Activities at West Shore in addition to being an adjunct faculty member. Prior to joining WSCC in 2000, Dr. Pollock was director of Enrollment at Lake Superior State University and Admissions director at both Lawrence Technological University and Kettering University.

Dr. Pollock has spoken nationally on his dissertation topic, Undergraduate Student Recruitment: The Role of the Faculty. He has also presented on such topics as enrollment management, student success, vision and strategic planning. Dr. Pollock is considered an outstanding advocate for putting students first on his campus, and for developing a set of core indicators for performance measurement at West Shore Community College.

MELVIN C. TYLER

Melvin C. Tyler is assistant vice chancellor of Student Affairs for Enrollment Management and former director of Admissions for the University of Missouri—Kansas City (UMKC). Tyler is responsible for achieving and evaluating the strategic enrollment management plan for the university, which includes full oversight of enrollment services for Undergraduate Recruitment, Admissions, Registration and Records, Financial Aid and Scholarships, Retention and Student Success, and International Student Recruitment. He provides high-level direct support and expert advice to eleven academic deans, four vice chancellors, and the chancellor concerning the university-wide impact of enrollment management and is accountable for enrollment goals and objectives. Tyler has served as president of the Missouri Association for College Admission Counseling as well as chairperson of the Missouri ACT Executive Committee. He has recently presented UMKC's collaborative approach to enrollment management at the SEM XIII Conference held in Boston in November 2003.

x

JEFF ZELLERS

Jeff Zellers has been dean of Enrollment at Muskingum College (OH) since 1992. As dean, Zellers was integrally involved in Muskingum's re-pricing decision, where he was engaged in planning, research, modeling, marketing, and implementation of the plan.

Zellers holds a B.A. in economics from Muskingum College and an M.A. in college student personnel from Bowling Green State University. Prior to his appointment as dean he served as associate dean of Enrollment and director of Financial Aid at Muskingum from 1982-1992. Zellers has also held the positions of Financial Aid officer at Lebanon Valley College (PA) and Residence director at St. Mary's College of Maryland.

Zellers has served in the capacities of president and vice president for Training of the Ohio Association of Student Financial Aid Administrators (OASFAA), and was a member of the NACUBO Institutional Student Aid Advisory Group.

EMERGING THEMES AND MODELS

JIM BLACK

MYTHS about enrollment management are abundant, yet one truism has emerged from the case studies in this book: there is no single way to implement enrollment management. Indeed, the cases represented here are as diverse as the individuals and institutions from which they came.

Though no templates or one-size-fits-all solutions are forthcoming in the subsequent chapters, there are some common or fundamental themes and models that emerge in different ways in one or more case studies. In this chapter, those themes and models will be described in clusters according to their affinity with one another.

CAMPUS READINESS FOR ENROLLMENT MANAGEMENT

In some way, every case study author touches on the issue of campus readiness—the necessary ingredients for a successful adoption of an enrollment management model. One such ingredient is a compelling sense of urgency. A sense of urgency is often spawned from a precipitous dip in enrollment, the advent of a new presidency, the shifting of institutional aspirations, or the threat of some external force such as a new competitor. Regardless of the source, a sense of urgency is deemed necessary to alter the biorhythm of a college or university. Enrollment management is simply a means to achieve such a radical change in an organization that has been historically adverse to change. Few institutions have the organizational will to engage in significant change without a compelling sense of urgency.

Another ingredient is that of leadership. As many of the authors espouse, it takes bold leadership to support the radical changes to an institution's fabric that are required to implement enrollment management. Like the calculated risks taken by President Speck of Muskingum College, bold leadership propels an institution into a new operational paradigm and more importantly, a new mindset. Such leadership, exercised properly, can penetrate dense silos, overcome deeply ingrained patterns of behavior, and challenge the status quo. Rightfully, the enrollment managers who authored the case studies in this book give credit for leadership support of presidents, provosts, and others in positions of authority. Though the cases tend to focus on leadership by senior level administrators, leadership is needed throughout the organization to achieve optimal results. From the receptionist to the chief enrollment officer, leaders inspire others to excel and collectively create and sustain a high performing organization.

For leadership to be effective, there must be a clearly articulated vision. Generally, people will not follow even the most charismatic leader if they do not know where they are being led. Moreover, they must value the vision deep in their soul. The vision must be aligned with their own values and beliefs in order for them to be willing to sacrifice for it. And, like the vision established by Dr. Martha Gilliland, president of the University of Missouri-Kansas City, it must have a transformational quality. Perceptive leaders identify a vision that is consistent with the college's mission and its people's intrinsic beliefs while serving as a catalyst for institutional change.

PLANNING FOR ENROLLMENT MANAGEMENT

A common thread throughout the case studies is the use of data—for decision-making, for educating others, for evaluating effectiveness, for targeting efforts, and for planning.

The latter is fundamental to developing a plan grounded in reality. By using data to shape, and in some cases to restrain, institutional aspirations, planning objectives are more likely to be met. Virtually every college president aspires to grow enrollment, enhance the quality of the student body, expand diversity, and increase net revenue. The truth is that all four rarely happen concurrently, and in fact, the achievement of one can have a converse effect on another (e.g., increasing enrollments, quality, and diversity at the expense of net revenue—through increasing tuition discounts). Under some conditions, any one of these four may not be a desirable aspiration. For example, the campus that aspires to grow without the capacity and infrastructure to serve is headed down a perilous path. While aspirations should stretch a campus, unrealistic or counter-productive goals can demoralize faculty and staff and ultimately kill a change effort.

Applied insightfully, data can be used to avoid such pitfalls. Many of the colleges and universities featured in this book conducted an environmental scan, or, like Everett Community College, engaged in a SWOT (strengths, weaknesses, opportunities, and threats) analysis. The former considers a plethora of external factors that may impact an institution's future (e.g., demographic trends, economic indicators, workforce projections, competitor analysis). Too often such barometers of the external environment are glaringly absent from enrollment management plans or present but disconnected from strategies embedded in the plan. Similarly, the SWOT analysis can be omitted or not fully integrated into an enrollment plan. The SWOT analysis exposes internal strengths and weaknesses, usually through surveys, focus groups, and analysis of enrollment trends. It also is used to reveal external opportunities and threats, sometimes using environmental scan data or research such as an image study or demand analysis. Regardless of the methodology, the intent is to exploit institutional strengths that align with external opportunities and address internal weaknesses that may be exacerbated by some looming external threat. Of course, institutional strengths can be used to defend against environmental threats and conversely, weaknesses can be addressed to seize an opportunity, but these scenarios tend to occur less frequently.

Without data, enrollment management plans can only be tactical, not strategic. Even at the tactical level, the absence of data results in a plan predicated on intuition and wishful thinking with a low probability of success. At the strategic level, the pursuit of forward thinking is particularly precarious devoid of data. Uninformed predictions and strategic planning are akin to striking the bull's eye on a dartboard wearing a blindfold without knowing where the target is located. The chances of accurately guessing the future without data are statistically insignificant.

4

Strategic planning occurs at many levels within a college or university. The enrollment management plan should be integrated into the institution's strategic plan, and be driven by the academic direction outlined in the plan. Other linkages with the enrollment management plan include the institution's facilities and budget plans as well as the plans from the other divisions. Such an integrated plan is imperative to garnering campus-wide buy-in and overcoming obstacles to implementation.

Although implementation obstacles are not typically identified overtly in an enrollment management plan, they are recognized by the savvy enrollment manager and addressed indirectly. Examples of implementation obstacles include a lack of leadership support, budget constraints, institutional politics, space limitations, or a technology infrastructure that is inadequate. Whatever the constraining force, the enrollment plan must provide solutions for overcoming such obstacles.

Every institution has resource limitations that can prevent or retard implementation. Case studies for Belmont University, DePaul University, The University of North Carolina at Greensboro, and Everett Community College speak specifically to the issue of managing limited resources. If data are analyzed and incorporated into the planning process, institutional aspirations are derived for the data analysis, the plan is strategic in nature, and constraining forces have been identified, available resources can be deployed to maximize results. Ideally, the planning process will yield a sharpening of focus and lead to the allocation of precious resources, human and financial, on the basis of their potential impact on the institution's vision, not historical patterns, politics, or even knee-jerk reactions to a crisis.

STRATEGIES FOR ENROLLMENT MANAGEMENT

Among the case studies are various examples of strategies, most of which can be described under the rubric of core business functions: marketing, recruitment, financial aid, student services, and retention. These core business functions represent the building blocks of enrollment management. Strategies related to these core business functions are the DNA of the enrollment management organization—they define who we are at a given point in time. But unlike DNA, strategies are malleable and replaceable. As a rule, strategies must evolve or be replaced; otherwise, they lose their competitive advantage, if not their effectiveness, with a particular audience.

MARKETING

Strategies under the core business function of marketing focused on integration, branding, and market position. Institutions like DePaul and Florida Gulf Coast University have invested considerable effort, and in some cases money, to define their market position. Knowing a university's relative position in the higher education marketplace as well as among its competitors endows an institution with leverage—leverage to exploit competitor weaknesses and capitalize on institutional strengths. By identifying institutional and program niches, marketing efforts can be targeted to particular market segments and presented in a way that differentiates them from others in the same market space.

Several of the case study institutions have engaged in branding their institutions. Most notably, Dickinson College has adopted a brand statement, "Engage the World." As Robert Massa's case study conveys, the brand statement is a "promise." It is a covenant between the institution and the students (as well as other constituent groups) it serves. The notion of branding is not some marketing gimmick but rather a commitment to live the brand promise every day. Dickinson, for example, has integrated their brand promise into nearly every facet of the academic and student life experience. With this approach to marketing, the expectations prospective students develop from their interactions with promotional efforts are congruent with the experience they have as enrolled students. When incongruence exists between student perceptions and reality, conditions are right for attrition to occur.

Having the brand promise extend to every corner of the campus is consistent with the notion of integrated marketing. Most often integrated marketing is described as having a consistent message, design, and, when referring to the Web, navigation. While consistency of promotional materials, signage, business cards, tour guide scripts, and chancellor speeches is an important facet of integrated marketing, it is not the only dimension of integration that matters. Integration of products (e.g., academic programs, student services, internships, service opportunities, residence hall environments) with the message is imperative. Failure to integrate product and promotion, and in some instances price and place (the four P's of marketing), results in the incongruence described above.

RECRUITMENT

All of the case studies in this book touch on some aspect of recruitment. Two reoccurring areas of recruitment in many of the cases are the use of technology and communications flow. In particular, The University of North Carolina at Greensboro, Florida Gulf Coast University, and Dickinson College cite the use of technology as critical to their ability to communicate with prospective students by leveraging the power of segmentation and customization. No case study institution, however, indicates that technology replaced more traditional modes of communication (e.g., face-to-face, phone calls, direct mail). Rather, technology is seen as a tool to enhance communication—making it more relevant and personal. Technology also is used to manage student information (e.g., enterprise systems, document imaging, portals); provide services anytime, anywhere (e.g., Web services, electronic forms, Web chat options); target efforts and resources (financial aid leveraging, geodemographics, predictive modeling); and evaluation. Regardless of the use, it is clear that the modern-day enrollment management operation is highly dependent upon technology to work smarter and more efficiently.

Part of the increasing reliance on technology stems from the need to communicate more effectively in an increasingly competitive market. Students today are under assault from commercial marketers attempting to stake a claim to a portion of their spending power. When college marketers enter the mix, the result is overflowing mailboxes and inboxes. Teenagers, initially flattered by the attention, over time become numb, if not indignant. This presents an interesting challenge to college marketers. How do we influence the decision-making of a seventeen-year-old when they are bombarded by thousands of images and perhaps hundreds of sales pitches every day?

The answer most enrollment managers gravitate to is one of improving communication and the flow of that communication to targeted audiences. Often a communication flow has several objectives. One such objective is to have relevant information delivered to an individual in a timely basis. Timely means precisely in the decision-making process when a decision can be influenced by the communication. Other than immediate responses to requests, it is impossible to pinpoint the exact moment when a communication can have the most impact. But, we do have a general sense of when the majority of traditional students move through the stages (i.e., awareness, interest, action, and commitment) of decision-making. For nontraditional and graduate students, the decision drivers are different, but the stages are the same. The stages for these populations tend to be condensed into a shorter timeframe than the nine to eighteen months typical of their younger counterparts.

A related objective of a traditional-aged prospect communications flow is to move content delivery from general to specific, gradually adding volume as the prospect student interest increases. In fact, each communication is designed to synergistically build upon the last driving interest. Again, nontraditional undergraduate and graduate prospects tend to want specific information at the onset of the inquiry process and generally desire large quantities of information all at once. Because of the compressed recruitment cycle for these older students, the communication flow has fewer touch points, an initial packet with an application and other enrollment and academic information, followed by six to ten cultivation and informational communications. Regardless of the length or level of specificity of a communication flow, each contact typically has a "call to action"—a response mechanism designed to measure interest and engage the prospective student, theoretically increasing his or her commitment to the institution.

In recent years, a third objective for a communication flow has emerged. The objective incorporates a multi-channel approach to communication—mixing mediums (e.g., e-mail, Web, video, CR-ROM, print media, radio, television, direct mail, telephone, face-to-face communications) and varying the author (e.g. Admissions staff, current students, alumni, the president, parents of current students, faculty). Common wisdom suggests that the multi-channel approach is more effective, though little research has been conducted to validate this.

FINANCIAL AID

Financial aid and pricing issues are much more dominant in the case studies from private institutions than from publics. The nationally publicized story of Muskingum College's lowering tuition costs and Dickinson's approach to discounting are particularly noteworthy, but surprisingly, two public universities, the University of Missouri-Kansas City and Oregon State, write about their forays into financial aid leveraging. Not surprising, however, the community colleges did not focus on financial aid or pricing from a strategic perspective.

The strategic use of financial aid and pricing in higher education can take many forms: differential pricing, tuition payment plans, tuition freezes, preferential packaging, gapping, vanity awards, merit awards, frontloading, and the like. But, for the purpose of this chapter, the focus is on the two dominant strategies discussed in subsequent chapters, discounting and financial aid leveraging. Nonetheless, note that the two are not mutually exclusive from one another or from some of the others previously listed.

Discounting usually refers to the practice of earmarking institutional dollars for the purpose of supplementing other aid sources, in essence lowering the net price for eligible students. Eligibility requirements are determined by the institution and most often are awarded on the basis of documented need. However, many colleges and universities have elected to provide discounts to certain populations in order to achieve institutional objectives. For instance, an institution may want to improve their academic quality, geographic diversity, representation of first generation college students, or fill empty seats in a low demand academic program through preferential packaging of institutional aid dollars. There are as many variations to the standard, need-based methodology as one can imagine.

Many institutions, mostly private, have attempted to become more scientific in their approach to discounting and aid packaging by adopting a financial aid leveraging strategy. Leveraging applies a matrix principle that typically considers on one axis an individuals ability to pay (e.g., no need, low need, moderate need, high need) along with their willingness to pay on the other axis. The willingness to pay may be determined through academic indicators such as standardized test scores, geographic proximity, ethnicity, or any other variable where reliable and valid yield rate differences exist. The premise behind leveraging is that yield rates can be influenced by manipulating the type and amount of aid offered in each cell of the matrix.

STUDENT SERVICES

Whether it is the "students first" philosophy at West Shore Community College, the "student-centered" vision at The University of North Carolina at Greensboro, or the commitment to "student success" at the University of Missouri-Kansas City, the student is at the heart of many of the enrollment management case studies in this book. A student focus helps to anchor an enrollment management effort to a common purpose that most in higher education can embrace. Decisions, priorities, strategic directions, organizational behavior, the culture, and the like are shaped by an institution-wide commitment to a student-centered purpose.

One natural outgrowth of such a shared purpose is the desire to streamline processes. The goal of streamlining may be to improve efficiencies or simplify the work of staff. However, in a student-focused environment, the primary goal would be to make the processes of the institution as intuitive and invisible as possible to students. To accomplish this goal, processes must be viewed through the students' eyes. How do they see and interact with campus processes? Typically, they do not view student processes through hierarchical organizational structures but rather as a means to an end. Consequently, organizational boundaries need to be invisible and processes that cross those boundaries should be integrated into a seamless whole.

This so-called "seamlessness" can be achieved by organizing the Web by student process rather than department or division where a particular process is housed; by reorganizing to group like functional processes together (e.g., Student Accounts and Financial Aid translate to paying for college from the student perspective); or by creating a student services one-stop. Belmont University's, Belmont Central, is an excellent example of clustering like processes together and cross-training individuals to respond to a variety of student needs. Like Belmont, The University of North Carolina at Greensboro has a one-stop, Information Station, but they have also added a no-stop, Virtual Information Station, where students can get questions answered via live Web chat and transact business with the university.

Apart from the mechanism through which student services are provided, true integration of services will not occur without reengineering the process with the students' needs in mind. Reengineering processes begins with understanding the existing process, usually through process mapping or flowcharting. Once the existing process has been defined, the next step is to imagine the ideal process. A common mistake here is to create the ideal without asking students what they need. While the intentions are good, such an approach is likely to fall short of a student-centered outcome. The ideal process is mapped to the existing process in order to identify gaps, and work begins to bridge the gaps where appropriate.

RETENTION

Though retention is mentioned generically by a number of the case study institutions, only Supplemental Instruction and the support provided by student success centers, like the one at West Shore Community College, were mentioned as retention strategies with any frequency. Most student success centers provide tutorial services, academic counseling, and academic skills workshops. Some also provide placement testing, skills assessment, courses designed to teach learning skills, and programs like Supplemental Instruction.

The founding institution for Supplemental Instruction (SI), the University of Missouri-Kansas City, provides a description of a campus-wide implementation of SI. This retention strategy uses experienced upperclassmen and graduate students as SI leaders. In coordination with the instructor, the SI leader attends class (usually a 100 or 200 level course with a high proportion of Ds, Fs, and Ws) and works with class members to facilitate learning. Students voluntarily attend SI sessions where the SI leader engages participants in learning class content and more importantly, in understanding how to successfully navigate the learning process.

IMPLEMENTATION OF ENROLLMENT MANAGEMENT

As alluded to earlier in this chapter, strategies can be easily replicated, and they tend to lose their effectiveness over time. Hence, the only sustainable competitive advantage we have is in how well we execute strategies, not the strategies themselves. Execution depends upon people, so an investment in human capital—staff learning—combined with motivation yields a high performing enrollment management organization. The University of North Carolina at Greensboro's focus on staff learning is an excellent example of a corporate learning model applied to a higher education environment. Similarly, the generalist model applied in Belmont Central improves staff performance as well as service to students.

For most of the institutional case studies presented here, execution of enrollment strategies was not limited to members of the enrollment management team. In some cases, implementation literally involved the entire campus as well as some external constituent groups such as alumni and corporate sponsors. Perhaps, the most difficult constituent group to engage is faculty, but they can have more impact over recruitment and retention than any other group of individuals outside of the enrollment management enterprise. Faculty must be involved. Yet, many are reluctant participants until they understand enrollment dynamics (e.g., factors influencing choices to enroll or persist, external forces impacting enrollment, the rationale for institutional aspirations); their role in recruitment and retention; and the value added due to their participation. Regarding the latter, faculty need to understand the value they add to the institution's efforts but also to their own lives as faculty. They may ask, "How will this affect me?" For example, more students could equate to larger class sizes, more papers to grade, more time with advisees, less time for research, etc. Why would anyone support an effort that intuitively appears to make their life more difficult? It is the job of the enrollment manager and senior leadership to answer this question as well as other such legitimate concerns.

Involving others is just one facet of managing complex change necessary in the implementation of enrollment management. As in the case of DePaul University, change associated with the implementation of enrollment management often includes organizational restructuring. Or like Everett Community College (EvCC), the implementation of enrollment management can be a long-term process with incremental changes along the way. Elements of change at EvCC include, among other things, restructuring, a marketing campaign, and a series of planning exercises. At Oregon State University, the evolution of enrollment management consists of a number of structural changes as well as organizational realignments, leadership transformations, and efforts to win staff loyalty and buy-in.

Change takes many forms, but all successful change efforts require management of barriers to implementation, such as power struggles, institutional silos, resource constraints, leadership voids, or lack of a shared vision. The enrollment leaders featured in this book, each in their own way, have managed to overcome such obstacles. They have seized opportunities, taken risks, leveraged knowledge to inform decisions, and most importantly, led people to become more and accomplish more than anyone imagined they could. They thrive on all the uncertainty and possibilities that accompany a journey to a place no one has been. They tend to be systems thinkers and consequently, see the layers of complexity associated with enrollment management implementation. Intuitively sensing how all the parts should fit together, they lead others to do what Kathryn Baugher so aptly described as managing the "spaces in-between."

EVALUATION OF ENROLLMENT MANAGEMENT

Too often, so much time and energy is invested in planning and implementation that evaluation is neglected. The aimless perpetuation of strategies that are ineffective or have costs that far exceed the benefits are rampant throughout enrollment management operations. When asked, "What works?", many enrollment managers have no evidence to justify their priorities other than their own intuition, vague anecdotes, general claims made in the literature, and what peers are doing. In the absence of data, they cannot accurately access return on investment (ROI).

At the risk of sounding like an enrollment management zealot, proselytizing to the masses unwashed, ROI is the single most important factor in determining long-term success. Few enrollment managers have the luxury of having "a blank check" or a staff that is larger than what is needed to accomplish existing enrollment objectives and serve students effectively. In fact, the vast majority of enrollment management operations are woefully under funded and the staff feels stretched cellophane thin. Consequently, it is imperative that we know what works, what return we are receiving on our investment of scarce human and financial resources, and what strategies are most likely to yield the highest ROI. This knowledge transforms a floundering enrollment management operation from using a scattershot approach to one that has laser point accuracy. Honing strategies using a ROI filter will produce optimal results. Other kinds of evaluation appropriate for the field of enrollment management include ability to benefit (how many people will be impacted), audience-need evaluation (did the strategy reach the intended audience and meet their needs), and objective-based assessment (did the strategy meet stated objectives). An example of the former is found in the case study presented by The University of North Carolina at Greensboro in their use of key performance indicators (KPIs).

Regardless of the type of evaluation conducted, it must be ongoing. Dynamics such as audience preferences, competitor strategies, technology advances, and institution aspirations are fluid, so what works today may not work tomorrow. Evaluation should be formative as well as summative. Formative evaluations are conducted during various phases of implementation to inform mid-course revisions or enhancements to the implementation process or the strategy itself. Typically, summative evaluations are administered at the end of an implementation to determine program or strategy viability or effectiveness.

CONTINUOUS IMPROVEMENT IN ENROLLMENT MANAGEMENT

Both formative and summative evaluations are needed to guide the continuous improvement of enrollment management efforts. Several of the case study institutions (West Shore Community College, Belmont University, and Florida Gulf Coast University) refer directly to their commitment to the concept of continuous improvement. Others (Muskingum College, Everett Community College, DePaul University, Oregon State University, and The University of North Carolina) write obliquely about continuous improvement by referring to combating complacency and continuing to innovate and reinvent themselves.

In their own way, the case study institutions have excelled. Partly due to their successes, expectations placed on their operations have increased and, in some cases, escalated beyond their capacity to deliver the desired results. Internal pressures associated with ever-changing expectations compel enrollment managers to constantly be in the continuous improvement mode. Of course, external pressures, such as competition, an upsurge in the number of high school graduates entering the higher education system, or legislative accountability related to retention and graduation rates, have a similar effect on enrollment managers. Admittedly an arguable point, but the natural tension produced by internal and external pressures is what makes enrollment management an exciting profession.

To successfully respond to such pressures, enrollment managers must straddle the awkward chasm between constantly reinventing their operation and staying the course.

The inherent challenge in the former, besides using evaluation to guide the direction, is ensuring that the adoption of new strategies occurs with the necessary antecedents for success in place—infrastructure, space, technology, staff skills, funding, and the like. Without the necessary antecedents, even the best strategies and the best enrollment managers will fail.

The apparent paradox between reinventing the enrollment management operation and staying the course assumes the two are mutually exclusive. They are not. Change of strategies and direction can and should occur within the parameters of an immutable vision. Furthermore, the basic tenets that guide operational practices and organizational behavior should be constant as well (e.g., core values, the brand promise, a customer focus, a commitment to excellence). To engage in continuous improvement in a rapidly changing and highly competitive marketplace, enrollment management organizations must be incredibly nimble but grounded and singularly focused at the same time. The capacity to stay the course in the midst of a storm is paramount to successful enrollment management operation.

MODELS IN ENROLLMENT MANAGEMENT

Though the following is not an exhaustive list of enrollment management models, it does reflect those at the case study institutions and as such, is illustrative of some of the best models in the profession.

* DePaul University views its evolution in enrollment management through three lenses: structural, tactical, and strategic. Embedded in the DePaul model is also the notion of integration or alignment. The DePaul case study addresses the integration of offices, functions, services, and communications, along with marketing and academic program development.
* Everett Community College engages in an incremental approach to enrollment management.
* West Shore Community College adopts a student success core value that drives its enrollment management model.
  * A reoccurring model throughout the book is that enrollment management is a continuum from initial inquiry of a prospective through the life of an alumnus. Each interaction along the continuum is perceived to be an opportunity to cultivate or manage a relationship between the individual and the college or university.
* Another prevailing model in many of the cases is the focus on changing the culture.
* While many of the case study institutions reference collaboration, the University

of Missouri-Kansas City embraces collaboration as its dominant model for enrollment management.

* The University of North Carolina at Greensboro invests in a staff learning model.
* Dickinson College uses institutional branding to drive its enrollment management model.

The diversity of models represented here is further evidence that there is no single model or "best way" to implement enrollment management. Models are institution-specific and should be defined by the institution's mission, vision, enrollment objectives, and campus culture. Once defined, models should influence organizational structure and address institutional priorities such as resource allocation, staffing patterns, professional development opportunities, etc.

FINAL THOUGHTS

The case studies in this book are chocked full of useful strategies and models that have application in a variety of institutional settings. However, it is incumbent upon the reader to translate, and where necessary, to modify the strategies and models presented here to fit a unique circumstance. Even though some adaptation may be required, the stories told are powerful evidence that enrollment management can and does transform a campus. Read the following chapters with this in mind. Derive from each case the best strategies and models for your institution. But, perhaps more importantly, be inspired by the perseverance and ingenuity of the individuals featured in these case studies. And, believe in yourself.

2

RISK MANAGEMENT
IN HIGHER EDUCATION

JEFF ZELLERSJEFF ZELLERS

RISK management is not a process widely used in higher education and was a concept almost foreign to Muskingum College. It is probably fair to say that the decision to reduce price did not follow an intentional strategy to engage in a risk management effort to strengthen the institution, but that is what happened. And, to the surprise of many both within the institution and among the larger higher education community, the endeavor has been very successful. Risk management can be a useful component to any business enterprise. It has benefited Muskingum College in the case study described here, and will be a necessary tool for future strategic thinking if the college is to remain viable for another 160 years.

PREFACE

In November 1995 the Muskingum College Board of Trustees voted to reduce the tuition charges for full-time students who would enter the college in the fall of 1996 by the amount of $4,000, a 29% reduction. This decision culminated following nearly five years of pondering this significant topic, and led to an outcome that significantly changed the course of history for the 160-year old institution.

Risk management is not a process widely used in higher education and was a concept almost foreign to Muskingum College. It is probably fair to say that the decision to reduce price did not follow an intentional strategy to engage in a risk management effort to strengthen the institution, but that is what happened. And, to the surprise of many both within the institution and among the larger higher education community, the endeavor has been very successful.

Risk management can be a useful component to any business enterprise. It has benefited Muskingum College in the case study described here, and will be a necessary tool for future strategic thinking if the college is to remain viable for another 160 years.

MUSKINGUM COLLEGE—OVERVIEW AND HISTORY

Muskingum College is a liberal arts and sciences institution affiliated with the Presbyterian Church, USA, located in the village of New Concord, Ohio. Though small, somewhat remote, and modestly endowed (approximately $50 million at present), the college has successfully produced graduates of high quality who have contributed greatly to society. Among the more notable alumni are former astronaut and U.S. Senator John Glenn and his wife, Annie, late actress Agnes Moorehead, zoo and television personality Jack Hanna, and Philip Caldwell, former CEO of the Ford Motor Company.

For most of the first 125 years of existence, Muskingum's enrollment had been below 1,000 students. Then, in the "hey-days" of the 1950s and 1960s, enrollment grew to about 1,400, leaving the college in a relatively stable financial position. As the decade of the 1970s rolled around, however, Muskingum experienced a precipitous enrollment decline that saw full-time student numbers drop below 1,000, bottoming out at 850 in 1978. As a typically enrollment-driven institution, this decline placed enormous hardships on the college, so much so that immediately after the installation of President Arthur DeJong in 1978, Muskingum placed itself in the state of financial exigency. Things improved shortly thereafter, with the help of fairly extreme crisis management measures, and by the early 1980s Muskingum was back on its feet with a balanced budget and enrollment up to 1,000 students.

During the decade of the 1980s, Muskingum experienced consistent enrollment in the 1,000-1,100 range with entering freshman classes of about 300 students. This stability occurred despite negative demographic trends, largely due to increased numbers of high school graduates choosing to attend college. Another change had also occurred. Students coming from distant states—particularly the East Coast—had all but disappeared from the scene. As such, Muskingum had become a very regional institution, with 85% of its students coming from Ohio compared with about 65% in the late 1960s.

Deeply ingrained in the challenge of enrolling potential students was the continuing issue of lack of name recognition. This concern had plagued Muskingum for generations, and no solution had ever been discovered. Up until the 1950s the identity issue was somewhat mitigated by the college's very strong ties to the United Presbyterian Church, a conservative branch of the larger Presbyterian denomination. While the UP denomination was not large, it was loyal and many families in the region sent their children to either Westminster College (PA) or Muskingum, the only two United Presbyterian colleges in the region. Until the mid 1960s, over 50 percent of Muskingum's students were Presbyterian by faith. In 1958 the United Presbyterian Church was absorbed into the larger Presbyterian Church, USA, and in the years following, the identity Muskingum enjoyed as the regional United Presbyterian college disappeared. The impact of this was not strongly felt until a few years later, after the student deferment era of the sixties had passed. The little name recognition Muskingum had was gone, and it has since been in a battle for students with the more-than 70 four-year colleges and universities in Ohio.

Throughout the decades of the 1970s and 1980s, student dependency on student financial aid increased at Muskingum as it did across the nation. The fact that increased percentages of students were choosing to attend college, largely from "needy" families, contributed to this challenge. By the late 1980s, the issue of financial aid had become an increasing concern to the Muskingum leadership, despite enrollment stability.

It is important to mention that the decision-making culture at Muskingum had always been quite conservative and was perhaps even more so following exigency. Risk-taking was not a concept that often made it to the table. One exception to this, however, was

18

the decision to add a program for learning-disabled students in 1984. Having had positive experience with students with learning disabilities, the college determined that it could perhaps distinguish itself in this area by establishing a formal program to attract students of this type. The program met with immediate success, due to a combination of a rapidly growing recognition of learning disabilities within the educational community and the fact that few colleges anywhere had developed programs to meet the needs of these students. Within only a few years Muskingum's PLUS Program held national distinction, and enrollment in the program grew to approximately 100 students by the late 1980s. The PLUS Program was an instrumental factor in the college's enrollment growth to 1,100, and buffered years in which an enrollment decline could have been more painful. The PLUS Program also brought a clientele of students whose families were of significantly stronger financial means, which served, for a while, to soften the impact of growing financial needs on the part of most students.

"TRUTH HAPPENS TO AN IDEA"

By the late 1980s, PLUS Program enrollment had reached capacity, and financial aid became a growing concern. Though enrollment was stable, Muskingum was experiencing erosion in the growth of net tuition revenue. In the discussions that ensued, a casual comment was made by a member of the president's staff regarding the possibility of reducing tuition. It can probably be stated that "off-the-cuff" remarks such as these had been made at many institutions across the country, only to be dismissed as ridiculous thinking. For whatever reason, Muskingum's president at the time, Dr. Sam Speck, was intrigued by the idea and thought it appropriate to study it further. He set up a task force that included members of the board of trustees in addition to faculty and staff for the purpose of seeking solutions to the net revenue dilemma. President Speck wanted the price reduction idea to be on the table as an option for the leadership to consider.

The goal of the college's decision to study pricing and financial aid was to find a way to increase net tuition revenue. A variety of ideas were explored, and consultants were brought in for their opinions. The tuition reduction idea, while viewed as quite sexy, was not embraced by most because of its extreme departure from convention. One of the consultants believed Muskingum could achieve increased enrollment and tuition revenues through improved marketing initiatives, and strongly advised against a price cut. Some of these higher education experts were concerned that a decision this extreme would send a very loud signal of distress that would generate doubt in the minds of consumers about the viability of the institution.

Essentials of Enrollment Management | CASES IN THE FIELD

The task force prepared a report for the Muskingum leadership in 1991 that included the tuition reduction as one of three options, along with a tuition freeze and the creation of new scholarships and awards as a method to attract additional students. The decision was made to pursue the third option—the marketing of additional discounts with the hope of creating interest in the college, which would result in increased enrollment and tuition revenues. At the time of this decision President Speck remarked privately that he believed the college would have to revisit the price reduction strategy down the road. He was correct.

In the immediate term, the strategy of increased discounts worked well. The 1993 freshman class of 375 was the largest in a decade, and overall enrollment, which had been 1,020 in 1992, grew to over 1,100. When the dust settled two years later, however, the picture was not quite as bright as first envisioned. Freshman classes reverted to normal levels of about 300, and overall enrollment dipped just below 1,100. The new financial aid programs had also eaten significantly into the tuition revenues. While things were better than before the 1991 decision, darker clouds were once again looming on the horizon.

In late 1994, President Speck decided it was time to take another look at an old idea. Quoting Milton, Sam stated, "Truth happens to an idea." He believed that Muskingum needed to take a different path to achieve a higher level of institutional stability, comfort and image; pursuing the status quo was not the answer. As such, work was resurrected on the tuition reduction idea.

BUILDING THE CASE

The idea of making the case for reduced tuition was never envisioned as one that needed institution-wide consensus. President Speck, while sensitive to faculty concerns (he had been a member of the faculty, on and off, for many years prior to assuming the presidency), realized that it would be difficult to move the analytical and decision-making processes forward using an academic approach. Therefore, he brought together a small group of people—the assistant director of Development and executive assistant to the president for Planning, the dean of Enrollment, the director of Admission, and the director of Public Relations—to build the case for re-pricing.

This process, which was sometimes referred to as a "commando effort," was both strategic and tactical in nature. Most of the analytical work, including the significant task of model-building, was undertaken by members of the enrollment office staff.

Similar work had been done three years earlier when the tuition reduction idea was first considered, so it was not necessary to design the entire analytical structure from scratch. Paramount in this process was discovering a way to determine the "break-even" point -- that is, the number of additional new students who the college would have to enroll in order to achieve the same aggregate "net tuition" level.

The science utilized in performing the analysis was not particularly complex. Using an assumption that the economic profile of a new applicant pool would be similar to that of recent years (even though there was hope that the idea might attract students with a greater ability to pay), the new pricing and financial aid awarding schemes were applied against the cohort of students who entered Muskingum the prior year to determine a net tuition revenue result. Models were constructed at three levels of price reduction—$3,000, 4,000 and 5,000—and an effort was made to determine the level of reduction which would be significant enough to be marketable, yet modest enough to not result in reduced net tuition revenue from the majority of the entering class. In the 1995 entering class, nearly 95 percent of students received Muskingum-funded financial aid, with 88 percent demonstrating financial need. The average amount of Muskingum-funded gift assistance to these needy students was approaching $8,000. It was understood that for many students, a reduction in price could be offset by a like reduction in institutional gift aid. While Muskingum would not be any less expensive for these students, it would remain as "affordable" as before. Other students who paid more and received less assistance would pay less, and the college would therefore receive less tuition revenue. The expectation was that additional new students would cover the loss in tuition revenue, and the goal was that it would do even more than that.

It is important to note here that members of the planning group, and others who understood the concept of tuition discounting, were comfortable with the concept that, for most students, the Muskingum education would not really be less expensive. It was believed that the needy students who made it through the financial aid process and ultimately enrolled were being treated as reasonably as they were being treated at most institutions. The goal was to attract more of these kinds of students, who were not even considering Muskingum or other private colleges because of the initial price tag. Another objective was to entice students who might not need as much financial aid, perhaps none at all, who were succumbing to "sticker shock" and choosing to attend one of Ohio's many fine public universities. The overriding goal was to increase interest, and subsequently admission applications. The net cost to many families would be much the same as before, with the net cost to those paying the most perhaps being reduced. This did not present a philosophical obstacle.

The plan had always considered keeping returning students at the old tuition levels, though as time went on it became apparent that there might also be a cost of retaining some of these students. Considering costs related to both new and returning students, the models suggested that a figure of $4,000 was a reasonable reduction of tuition. That amount represented 29% of tuition—an unimportant number—but the $4,000 amount brought new student tuition from $13,850 in 1995 to $9,850 in 1996, sneaking below the psychological $10,000 barrier.

The pricing models were constructed with the objective of determining the number of additional new students that would be needed to cover the cost of lost tuition revenue to a portion of the entering class. Again, no assumption of a greater ability to pay was included. Factored in, however, was the consideration of needing to spend additional financial aid resources on a small pool of returning students who received little or no financial aid. A particular challenge was determining the base number of entering students to use in the break-even analysis. Muskingum's first-year classes over the previous ten years had averaged 306 students, though there had been the exceptional year of 375 (in 1993), and the 1995 entering class numbered 284. Using the 306 number as a base figure, it was estimated that a $4,000 tuition reduction would need to generate twenty-eight additional new students (a first-year class of 334) to break even. This number, rounded to thirty for purposes of the proposal, was a pivotal statistic in the discussions that ensued.

While the leadership believed that a formal campus debate regarding the reduced tuition proposal was not necessary or practical, significant efforts were made to educate the community at various stages of the planning process. A Pricing Task Force consisting of faculty and staff members was formed to lend input to the development of the proposal, and this group backed the leadership's position to not put the proposal to a vote and justified this decision. There was much general support for the proposal within the task force, but also strong opposition from a few individuals. Primary concerns ranged from questions about how lower tuition could possibly increase revenues to perspectives about how this move might be perceived by the public. The most common position held by members of the faculty on the task force was not altogether surprising—"... we're behind you if it works!"

The task force proved to be more helpful in process than in substance, inasmuch as the plan received a type of hearing and was not going to catch the internal professional community off-guard. It was accepted that the decision, however, would rest with the leadership. In one area, however, the task force provided useful insight. There was great concern about how continuing students might respond to the price reduction since it would not affect them. This had always been an issue, not so much for those students who received significant financial aid but for those who did not. A faculty member on the task force was responsible for developing a "we'll meet you half-way" approach with returning students who received less than $4,000 of institutional gift aid. He proposed that these students, for the remainder of their stay at Muskingum, would receive a "Transition Grant" which amounted to one-half of the difference between the $4,000 price reduction and the amount of Muskingum gift aid they were currently receiving. Using this model, students who previously received $2,000 of Muskingum aid would get an additional $1,000; those with no aid would get $2,000. These students were identified, and a budget for the Transition Grants through the "out years" was built.

President Speck retained the responsibility of educating members of the board of trustees on the proposal. Having discussed the concept only a few years previous, many of the board members were familiar with the idea. This time, the proposal was not going to be presented with a variety of options. As with many college boards, there were a few key members whose support it was necessary to gain. Among these were Board Chair Hal Burlingame (at the time vice president for Human Resources at AT&T), and Finance Chair Bill Dentzer (retired CEO of the Depository Trust Company).

Dentzer, a thoughtful and fiscally conservative trustee, was particularly important to the proposal's success as no major financial decisions were made without his support. Fortunately, he followed the development of the proposal closely, including intense review of the models. The efficacy of these forecasts, combined with his concern about the status quo of shrinking increases in net revenues, contributed significantly to earning his eventual support.

Additionally, in a move that would prove to be critical in the marketing success of the price reduction, President Speck chanced to meet with the two editors of the *U.S. News and World Report Annual Guide to Colleges*, Mel Elfin and Al Sanoff. During the meeting he mentioned that he and Muskingum were seriously considering a reduction in tuition as a way of combating the spiral of high tuition and high financial aid. The two *U.S. News* editors found the idea quite intriguing and encouraged Speck to call them first if the idea were to move forward. He eventually did.

A formal proposal was developed and presented to the board of trustees for its April 1996 meeting. The proposal was quite well received this time around, in large part because of growing concerns with the status quo. For the trustees, the key elements supporting the proposal were present:

* The college had substantial excess capacity and could absorb growth.
* The vast majority of students were being "discounted," most to a sizeable degree.
* The break-even number of thirty new first-year students (10% of the current entering class size) seemed achievable, and the overall goal of growing Muskingum's enrollment from 1,091 to 1,200 within five years seemed reasonable.

The major question that troubled board members was that of how the public might perceive such a decision. They were unwilling to move forward without an answer, or at least some valid information, about how the external world might respond. Would prospective students and families become excited about such an initiative, or would they be turned off by what they perceived as an act of desperation from a college in trouble?

With that, the board charged the leadership with conducting market research and presenting the results at the October 1995 Board meeting, at which point a decision might be made. The leadership contacted the Gallup Corporation, which had performed previous research for the college, and engaged that corporation in a modest study to gauge public opinion on the high cost of college and the possibility of an institution actually reducing tuition.

After consultation with professionals in the Gallup Corporation, a survey instrument was designed with the purpose of determining how parents of college-bound students might react if a college with which they were even remotely familiar decided to reduce the price it charged for tuition. Several questions were included in the instrument, which were meant to introduce the parents to the issue of paying for college, and the issue of a price reduction was handled toward the end of the survey. Additionally, a similar survey was designed for a small group of guidance counselors to assess their reaction to such a move. This research was funded in part by a grant from the Student Loan Funding Corporation.

The survey was specifically designed as a telephone instrument, because of the need for a significant response as well as because of the nature of the questions and the subject matter. The sample to be queried was drawn from Muskingum's inquiry pool of rising high school seniors. The survey was conducted in August 1996, just prior to the student's senior year. No institutional names were divulged, and since students were prospects or inquiries at several colleges, it is likely that Muskingum remained anonymous. Six hundred twelve respondents completed the survey.

The results of the Gallup Study proved crucial to Muskingum's decision to move forward with the price reduction initiative. From the outset it was evident that the topic of college costs caught the attention of prospective student parents; most continued through the duration of the survey (12-15 minutes) and remained engaged. Presented here are the primary results from the Gallup study, prepared in September 1995:

1. Cost was the most important concern parents had about attending a private college, by a 4:1 margin. Quality of education in major field of study was next.

2. Cost was also the most important concern parents had about attending public universities, but by only a 3:2 margin over safety, quality of education in major field of study, and size (too big).

3. Where cost was concerned, parents were worried about the total cost, amount of debt incurred, and their ability to pay the required amount. Few were concerned the value may not be worth the price.

4. Slightly more than half of parents surveyed were confident that they would qualify for financial aid at both public and private institutions. The remainder thought they would qualify for little or no aid, or didn't know. Patterns of income level were similar for both public and private institutions.

5. Only 10% of families thought they could afford a private college without financial aid, compared with nearly half believing they could afford a public university without aid. With aid, perceived affordability exceeded 80% for privates and 90% for publics.

6. Nine percent of the group sample indicated that they were able and willing to pay the full cost of a typical private college education. Twelve percent said they were able but unwilling to do so.

7. Nearly half the families indicated they were able and willing to pay the full cost of a public university education.

8. For those families not able or willing to pay the full cost of either a private college or a public university, the average yearly dollar amount parents were

able and willing to pay was about $7,300, though the responses varied widely within income ranges.

9. Comparing private colleges with total costs of $14,000, $18,000 and $22,000, of similar size, program and general quality, parents would be more likely to express interest in the $14,000 school by a 3:1 margin.

10. A scenario was presented where a college costing $18,000 reduced its price by $4,000, and based its financial aid on the lower amount:

    * 61% indicated this move would increase their level of interest in the college;
    * 82% believed a decision to reduce price was either a responsible move or a wise marketing decision; 15% saw it as a move of desperation; and
    * 93% viewed this initiative as either positive or very positive.

    A vast majority of the guidance counselors surveyed (n-29) also responded very positively to the price reduction idea.

As an interesting aside, the survey included a question to parents of whether they would prefer a scenario of a $10,000 college where they received no financial aid, or an $18,000 institution which offered them $8,000 of gift assistance. By a 3:1 margin they preferred the latter case, equating higher cost with higher quality. It is reasonable to assume that this preference would be valid in cases where the financial aid is known at the time of the search. Since financial aid does not work in that fashion, their response to the earlier question (#9 above) might indicate that they would never make it to the point of receiving gift aid at the higher priced college. The parents' response to this question did not deter their positive reaction to the price reduction scenario, which was asked later in the survey.

Muskingum officials were struck by the overwhelmingly positive response to how the marketplace might react to reduced price. Whether or not it would really be the case, consumers viewed lower price as more affordable to them. "Sticker shock" was indeed an issue. Many families did not understand how financial aid works, and often would make early choices which eliminated higher-cost schools from consideration. And, the issue of desperation was not at the forefront of consumer thinking—perhaps that concern rested primarily with those in academe.

With the information gleaned from the Gallup report, the Muskingum leadership had as much information as they were going to get, and realized that a decision was imminent. An overall summary was presented again to the board of trustees at its

October 1995 meeting, along with a marketing plan that included publication materials in the design stage. The trustees realized two important facts:

1. There would probably be a distinct advantage to being the first college to go this route (at least in recent years).
2. There might be a bigger risk to maintaining the status quo than to moving forward with the bold price reduction initiative.

The board approved the price reduction action in principle, desiring to wait until the marketing plans were in place and ready to be engaged before taking a final vote, which would occur by phone in late November. There was a concern that word would leak out before the college was ready. The voice vote by phone, which occurred just before Thanksgiving, was unanimous and enthusiastic. The announcement was just a few days away.

ROLLING IT OUT

President Speck's decision to share Muskingum's decision with the *U.S. News and World Report* editors well in advance of a final decision proved to be a stroke of genius. Dr. Speck kept the editors aware of Muskingum's progress, and it was agreed that the public announcement of the tuition reduction would be timed with a *U.S. News and World Report* weekly magazine article. The article was scheduled to hit the newsstands on Monday, December 4, 1995, the day Muskingum students returned to classes after the Thanksgiving break. Muskingum officials had prepared both external and internal public relations strategies, designed to break on the same day. The external strategies included the following:

* News releases to all conceivable media outlets—press, radio, TV;
* A specially designed price reduction publication for various constituencies. Copies were sent to all prospective students in the inquiry pool, and to all high schools on the institutional mailing list;
* Letters explaining the tuition reduction plan were sent to admission and financial aid directors at all Ohio colleges; and
* Purposeful contacts were made to "experts" in the college-financing field in the event that they might be queried by the media about Muskingum's move.

As the news hit the streets, a full-page article was published in *U.S. News and World Report* entitled "New Fare Wars at College. Muskingum College tries something rad: a $4,000 price cut." This coverage made Muskingum a national story—a rare event for a regional college —and major newspapers and media outlets immediately picked up the story

Internal marketing approaches would prove to be just as important. Since continuing students would not be affected by the price reduction, there was a good chance that the plan could play well externally but backfire within the Muskingum community. In an effort to minimize that potential downside, several steps were taken:

* President Speck held a Sunday night meeting—just as students were returning to campus from Thanksgiving break—with approximately 150 student leaders. This group included Student Senate members, club and organization officers, resident advisors and members of the various student media. He wanted to be able to explain how the program was designed to work and how current students might benefit.
* Letters explaining the same issues were sent to all students on campus.
* Similar letters were sent to parents of current students at home.
* Meetings and interviews were arranged with the student newspaper, radio and TV stations where the program could be described in greater detail.
* A public announcement was sent to all Muskingum alumni.

THE IMMEDIATE AFTERMATH

One of the goals of the price reduction initiative was to create name recognition, and that outcome was instantaneous. Following the lead of the *U.S. News and World Report* article, the story was picked up by all the major news outlets, including *The Washington Post* and *The New York Times*. CBS News came to campus for a visit and did a news segment. Regional and local papers, radio and television stations picked up the story. The regional/local coverage across Ohio and into western Pennsylvania, in communities large and small, may have been the most valuable because of those areas being Muskingum's primary recruitment area.

President Speck became an immediate celebrity in higher education circles, speaking at conferences, testifying to Congress, appearing in many media events. The fact that Dr. Speck understood both the global problem and Muskingum's approach to dealing with it made him a credible spokesperson.

Interest in Muskingum from an admission perspective was nearly as immediate. While there was not a deluge of phone calls and visitors in the admission office, unlike the public relations areas where the phone did not stop ringing for several days, business picked up and remained steady throughout the winter and spring months. The expectation was that any major admission application and enrollment growth would occur in the second year, since the price reduction announcement came well into the college search cycle for seniors. That assumption proved to be wrong; the admission impact was immediate.

Also somewhat surprising was the lack of "backlash" from current students and recent alumni, who did not (or perceived that they did not) benefit from the price reduction. In total, the number of complaints reaching college officials numbered fewer than fifteen, though it is likely that there were others who did not express their concerns to the college. Most of the Muskingum family—current students, parents, alumni— seemed to rather enjoy their day in the limelight, even though the plan did not affect them directly.

EARLY RESULTS

Though the primary intent of the re-pricing initiative was to grow enrollment, the goals were modest ones. There was a desire to have full-time undergraduate enrollment reach the 1,200 level by the fall of 2000, by entering first-year classes consistently falling in the 330-340 range. The 1,200 enrollment target depicted a figure at which Muskingum officials believed the college could operate comfortably. The tuition reduction plan was not designed as a "yield" activity, so most of the entering class growth would result from an increased number of applications. The objective here was to increase the first-year application numbers from approximately 950-1,000 per year to 1,100-1,150.

 The admission application growth began almost immediately. First-year applications for the fall 1996 term totaled 1,348, an increase of 357 (36%) over the previous year. With such a large increase, there was an assumption that a portion of these applications would be "soft"—just applying out of curiosity with no real interest in Muskingum— and that there might be a drop in the yield rate, which had ranged from 35-40% in recent years. As it turned out, the yield rate came out at the low end of the historical range—35.5%—but the size of the entering first-year class was 394. This was much higher than the goal of 335, and represented an increase of 110 students over the size of the Fall 1995 class. Transfer numbers grew as well, from thirty-five to fifty-seven. When the dust settled at the beginning of the 1996 fall semester, full-time undergraduate enrollment stood at 1,208, up from 1,091 the year before (+10.7%). The institutional leadership was both elated and puzzled by these results; the target for fall 2000 was 1,200 students and that figure had already been surpassed. What did all this mean? Fortunately, Muskingum had been operating with excess capacity for many years, both academic and residential. Some scrambling was required, but the college was able to address the issues connected with the size of the entering class with relative ease. The unknown, however, was whether this pattern would continue, and, if so, for how long. There was reasonable confidence that the institutional notoriety gained from the tuition reduction would have some degree of staying power, so it was expected that Muskingum would be able to enroll large entering classes for at least one or two more years. It was also recognized that the large class of 1993 would be exiting the pipeline in 1997, so there were limited expectations for growth in the second year. After that, with two small classes exiting, the potential for more significant enrollment growth was much greater.

GROWING PAINS

Muskingum was able to accommodate enrollment growth in the initial year, but future increases were going to stretch the institution, particularly with respect to housing. During this time, an informal group of administrators began gathering to discuss other steps that should be taken to ensure that enrollment growth would be handled effectively in a variety of ways. The Planning for Success group (consisting of the vice president for academic affairs, the associate academic dean, the executive director of development, the executive secretary of the faculty, the dean of students, the dean of enrollment and the controller) tackled and made recommendations on a number of issues, including housing, class availability and course distribution, first-year program, staffing and parking. At this point in time there was considerable hesitation to making significant financial investments based on anticipated future growth, with only one year of history. There was strong sentiment that one year's experience did not serve as an adequate predictor of the college's enrollment future. Therefore, some of the smaller endeavors were dealt with, but no permanent investments were made, including to the size of the faculty or staff.

In the second year, first-year application numbers grew to 1,441, an increase of nearly 100 from the prior year, and efforts were made to limit the size of the entering class because of housing limitations. Despite this restraint, the final first-year class numbered 415, and overall enrollment grew to 1,267, even with the replacement of the large graduating class. By this time, plans were undertaken to construct additional residence units, and townhouses with seventy additional beds were online by the fall of 1998. Even so, it was necessary to limit the subsequent 1998 entering class, and with the new student number of 446 first-years and transfers, the college entered 1998 fall with 1,365 full-time students.

This enrollment growth continued each year at a fairly rapid pace through the 1999-2000 academic year. By that time full-time enrollment was 1,468, an increase of 35%

in just four years. It was expected that this growth would not continue, however, since all of the small classes had made it through the pipeline, and new classes would be replacing graduating classes of approximately the same size. The fact that there had been four consecutive years of large entering classes had given the institution confidence that the enrollment growth was not a "spike," but something more long-term. Future growth, however, was uncertain. The growth had also put enough pressure on the institutional infrastructure that it had become necessary, and possible, to invest in the educational program.

Despite projecting to the contrary, Muskingum's enrollment continued to grow, reaching 1,606 full-time undergraduate students for the Fall 2002 term. Even with replacement of large classes, admission applications continued to grow and efforts were made to maximize enrollment to the extent possible.

NOTHING BUT NET

It is important to note that during this rapid period of growth, revenues from tuition grew substantially as well. The impact of net tuition revenue growth, enhanced by additional auxiliary revenues from more residential students, cannot be overstated. As a resource-challenged small college, the re-pricing decision had everything to do with the bottom-line financial health of the college.

Muskingum was reasonably successful in predicting the outcome of financial aid expenditures under the tuition reduction model, so there were no surprises resulting from net revenue shortfalls. In fact, since full-time enrollments exceeded expectations in each year since the pricing plan was implemented, net tuition revenues came out better than anticipated. Net tuition revenue has grown by approximately $6.4 million in the six-year period of 1996-97 through 2002-03, an increase of nearly 95%. This compares with a net revenue growth of less than fifteen percent in the six years prior to 1996.

This revenue factor is not widely understood, or, in some cases, even believed. The substantial growth is a combination of both enrollment growth and the fact that net tuition revenue per student did not change much from what it was prior to the price cut. The pricing model projected a loss of as much as about $500 per student in the initial years, with the hope that the gap could be narrowed over time. That result did occur, and while it is impossible to accurately predict what financial aid expenditures and resultant per student net revenues might have been under the status quo, projections indicate that actual per student net revenues are probably within plus-or-minus five percent of what they would have been had the price reduction not been implemented. As a result, most of the net revenue derived from additional students was indeed additional revenue—very little was used to cover the loss in per student revenue caused by discounting.

One ancillary benefit to the price reduction and related financial aid model was that Muskingum's financial aid discount rate declined. This was primarily a reflection of the math used in the rate calculation, but the college was nonetheless able to demonstrate a decline in the unfunded aid discount rate from 42% in 1995 to 33% in 2002.

It is reasonable to attribute some of this ability to control student aid expenditures to the robust economy of the late 1990s. In fact, it is very possible that some of the enrollment growth, though not fifty percent, would have occurred without the price cut. The bottom-line effect of enrollment growth and controlled student aid expenditures has proved to be quite a benefit to the college.

It should be mentioned that while much restraint was shown in protecting financial resources in the first few years of rapid enrollment and revenue growth, a few wise decisions were made. The first was to immediately begin reducing the "spending rate" from the endowment. In the early 1990s this rate had been increased to 7.5%, in order to pay expenses related to running a fund-raising campaign but also to handle increased annual budget demands. With the financial benefits of enrollment growth, the Muskingum leadership began to ratchet down the spending rate by one-half percent per year until the desired five percent figure was reached. Instead of taking five years, this process was completed in four. Additionally, other budgetary items that in normal years would have been problematic, including increasing health care and energy costs, were handled with relative ease. The beginning stages of a faculty salary plan were underway, and a technology plan was developed and approved by the trustees. With end-of-year positive balances, significant physical plant capital projects and improvements were undertaken which would otherwise have been added to the list of growing deferred maintenance concerns.

INVESTMENT IN PROGRAM
In early 1999, President Speck accepted an invitation to join the cabinet of Ohio Governor Bob Taft as director of the Department of Natural Resources. His departure was quick, and following a period of interim presidency, Dr. Anne C. Steele was appointed as Muskingum's twentieth president beginning in January 2000. President

Steele immediately assessed the need for ramped-up investment in the college's educational program in order to better ensure continued success—enrollment and otherwise—for the future.

One of President Steele's first moves was to assess the size of the faculty and staff relative to the current enrollment model. During the period of enrollment growth, Muskingum had shifted from a marginally overstaffed community (particularly on the faculty side) to one that was understaffed in many areas. This contributed to the beginnings of erosion in program quality. In the past three years the number of faculty positions has been increased by 20%, and staff positions have been added at both professional and support levels. In addition, aggressive improvement was made with faculty and staff salaries, on top of adequate increases in the late 1990s. Recent improvements have allowed Muskingum salaries, which had lagged behind for many years, to become competitive with those at comparable institutions.

Muskingum, under President Steele's leadership, has energetically pursued the addition of new campus facilities. Within a year of the beginning of Dr. Steele's presidency, a decision was reached to construct a new Communication Arts Complex, the college's first new academic building in nearly thirty years. The facility, nearly complete, will open during the 2003-04 academic year. Two other major facility projects and several smaller initiatives are slated for completion during the next five years.

Despite continued enrollment growth, the decision was made not to construct additional on-campus housing. An analysis of the admission environment did not reach the conclusion that further enrollment growth was imminent. In the short-term, a variety of ingenious methods were used to create "just-in-time" housing to accommodate annual residential growth, and Muskingum has operated at nearly 100% residential capacity for the past few years. The college will continue to pursue strategies which increase admission applications, and, based on that outcome, will determine whether the application pool justifies a need for housing with a reasonable assurance that all residential spaces will be filled.

Several new programmatic initiatives have also been undertaken. New interdisciplinary academic programs have been added or strengthened. A significant effort has been made to increase the racial/ethnic diversity of the student body. Collaborative student/faculty learning projects have been expanded greatly. All of these require resources, and are now viewed more as investments in the college's future than as luxuries. It is unknown how much of this would have occurred without enrollment and revenue growth.

Another area of extreme growth for Muskingum has been in the area of graduate programs. The college instituted a master of arts in education program in the late 1980s, and the program was quite modest in enrollment for many years. In the mid 1990s, however, almost coincidentally paralleling the undergraduate enrollment experience, the graduate numbers grew dramatically. In recent years the MAE growth has stabilized, but a new program—a master of arts in teaching—was added last year. Other non-traditional programs are in the planning stages.

CAPACITY PLANNING

With the start of the 2002-03 year, Muskingum's full-time undergraduate enrollment had grown to just above 1,600 students, and the college is now at capacity, both residentially and program-wise. This represents a growth of over fifty percent from the average enrollment of the two decades before the price reduction, and it has occurred in a seven-year period. The task facing the college is now perhaps more difficult—managing enrollment at capacity. The goal is maintaining an institutional equilibrium that allows for the continued improvement of program in an environment of relatively stable undergraduate enrollment.

In late 2001, President Steele engaged her senior staff in serious discussions regarding capacity planning. In this planning context the term capacity was defined broadly to include academic, administrative and residential components. Academic capacity issues involved the size and deployment of faculty, teaching and programmatic space limitations, and overall program considerations. Administrative areas included staffing and scope of programmatic efforts. The residential component involved both housing and dining facilities and the college's commitment to the village of New Concord that residential enrollment growth would be accommodated on campus.

The college leadership approached this task under the premise espoused by Tom Williams, former president and CEO of Noel-Levitz, that it is often more difficult to manage enrollment and related resources at capacity than it is to grow enrollment. By the fall of 2002, the college had benefited from significant revenue growth resulting from substantial undergraduate and graduate enrollment increases over a seven-year period and was now faced with the possibility that undergraduate enrollment had reached its limit. After studying demographic and market outlooks, considering the state of the economy, and evaluating the cost of new housing, the decision was reached to try to maintain full-time undergraduate enrollment at about 1,600 students, with a desired tolerance of plus-or-minus two percent.

It was understood that this decision would result in a change in the revenue flow for the institution, and that both internal and external pressures would not allow for revenue stagnation. President Steele and her financial advisors had engaged in significant long-term planning to enable the college to maintain and even modestly grow operations over a period several years into the future. It had become apparent, however, that Muskingum would have to seek other revenue means, most likely from non-traditional sources. Efforts are currently underway to actively explore alternative revenue sources for the college, which may include additional graduate programs, programs for non-traditional students, and programs for constituencies with particular needs. In developing new programs, priorities beyond revenue generation include being consistent with the institutional mission and providing services to people in the region. Program development, however defined, is an integral part of the strategic planning for Muskingum's future.

SHAPING CONSIDERATIONS

When the re-pricing plan was introduced, possible outcomes were articulated. These included improving the academic profile of the student body, improving the relative financial strength of students (reducing dependence on financial aid), and increasing racial/ethnic diversity. It was soon realized that these considerations represented "goals in conflict" and expectations were modified. The objectives that Muskingum settled on were to grow the size and diversity of the student body while maintaining academic quality.

The economic profile of students did change somewhat, as measured by dependency on financial aid. The class entering Muskingum in 1995 had 88% of its students demonstrating financial need. In years following the tuition reduction, that percentage fell into the mid-seventies. As stated previously, the improved economy probably contributed to this, just as the current downturn has pushed the relative financial needs of students back up. This modest economic profile improvement, however, was an instrumental factor in allowing the per-student net revenues to be comparable to the per-student figures, both prior to the price reduction and what they likely would have been had the tuition reduction not taken place.

The improved financial situation of the college allowed for investments to be made in seeking increased diversity, which are now beginning to pay off. There have been increases in the numbers and percentages of both domestic minority students and international students, and further growth is expected. There have also been modest changes in geographic diversity. While remaining a "regional" institution, the college has experienced an increase in the number of students from more distant parts of the region, particularly northeast and western Ohio.

LESSONS LEARNED

To wonder if Muskingum would have done things differently had the outcome of the tuition reduction been known at the time of the decision is to engage in "twenty-twenty hindsight." The lessons learned, therefore, are not about what might have been done differently, or better, but rather how the college uses the experience in future planning and decision-making.

First, it has become imminently apparent that the price reduction plan is not a "silver bullet" solution for all colleges. It was a specific strategy for a specific time at Muskingum. Is it replicable? Yes, depending upon an institution's circumstances and challenges. But it is not a universal solution.

It has become very apparent that rapid change for an organization requires great agility and responsiveness. Since the outcomes are unknown, the institution must be flexible enough to adapt to new and different circumstances that can occur, at least on a relative scale, almost instantaneously. Understanding the need for this agility has helped Muskingum deal with the "domino effect" of decisions that followed the first one. As an organization, Muskingum has learned that innovation is progressive, that moving forward is a way of life, and that being comfortable with the status quo is not an option.

Finally, through this experience it has become better understood that it is not possible to move Muskingum forward while maintaining a "constancy of philosophy." The people who may initiate an idea are not necessarily the same persons who must deal with the outcomes. Muskingum experienced a leadership change and learned that it is not always possible, or even appropriate, to "marry" the philosophies and styles of leaders who perhaps have differing perspectives and visions. Decision-making must be done in a way that makes it possible for future generations of leaders to move forward, using their own methods of agility and responsiveness to deal with the new opportunities and challenges of their time.

WHY TUITION REDUCTION WAS IMPORTANT

It is very important to take note of the fact that it is not possible to measure the outcomes of the price reduction plan in a vacuum. It is important to understand that the price reduction was not a controlled experiment—it was real life and happened in real time. Other variables entered in. There have been measurable outcomes since the price reduction was implemented which have been viewed as positive, yet it is presumptuous to assume that all the positives and negatives which have come to bear upon the college since 1996 are due to that initiative. Is there a relationship? Certainly. But many other factors, both internal (the huge success of graduate education, for example) and external (the robust economy of the late nineties) have contributed greatly to Muskingum's well-being. As with most other periods of change, whether positive or negative, it is the convergence of many factors that influenced the progress Muskingum College has made in recent years.

As an effort is made to try to assess the long-term outcome of the decision to reduce tuition, it is important to determine who has benefited from the decision. The first response is that students benefited. All Muskingum students now have the benefit of a higher quality educational product than was available before the price reduction, as a result of investing new resources into the educational program. Faculty and staff are better paid, facilities are improved, programs are expanded and new ones have been added, all at no additional cost to students beyond what would be expected from reasonable annual tuition increases.

Families who were paying perhaps more than their relative fair share of tuition costs received a price break, but not to the detriment of other families less financially capable. Perhaps most importantly, students who may have never considered, or even heard of, Muskingum College became interested because of the attention surrounding the price cut and chose to attend. Their world was changed, hopefully much for the better.

Muskingum College has benefited greatly from this endeavor. The college's reputation has been both broadened and improved. There is much greater financial stability, which has allowed for enhancement of the educational program in a variety of ways—upgraded salaries, improved and expanded programs, enhancements to the physical plant and the addition of new facilities. The respect and attention Muskingum gained were appreciated by alumni and friends. All of this was reflected recently as the college received an unqualified re-accreditation from North Central, with a committee report that was far more positive than the one prepared a decade ago.

The higher education community has also gained something through the Muskingum experience. A handful of institutions have implemented price reduction plans mirroring Muskingum's, and several have experienced very positive results. But perhaps most importantly, the higher education industry has witnessed a successful example of managerial risk-taking that worked.

The decision to reduce price certainly contributed to these successes and was also in part responsible for some of the challenges that arose. But nothing happened independently.

THINKING BACK AND AHEAD

Reducing tuition is not every small college's answer to enrollment and revenue problems. It would not work at many places and did not even work at some schools that tried it. It has been successful at Muskingum because it was designed to attack Muskingum's specific set of challenges. Tuition reduction is not the "be-all, end-all" for the challenges that do and will face Muskingum. Is Muskingum better off having made this significant decision eight years ago? Certainly. Is it something that will carry the college into the future? Probably. But successes will be limited unless the college continues to move forward assertively.

In many ways the re-pricing initiative went to the very core of enrollment management. Conventional methods to boost enrollment and generate financial resources had met with varying degrees of success or failure, and the outlook for improved results under the status quo was not seen as particularly bright. Throughout the planning, decision and implementation processes members of the Muskingum leadership team became enrollment managers, and the enrollment unit was a vital partner in the endeavor. Much of the plan's infrastructure, including idea generation, concept development, numerical and financial modeling, report writing and presentation, and subsequent marketing of the initiative, was carried out by those in positions of leadership on the enrollment staff. And, while it was essential for the entire enrollment unit to continue fundamental recruitment and processing efforts, it was incumbent upon members of the admission and student financial services staffs to be able to view the plan from a broader perspective, with a sense of institutional vision. Years later, it is still necessary for members of the enrollment unit to think beyond the scope of their operations, and it is just as important that all who work at the college see themselves, at least to some degree, as enrollment managers.

It has become increasingly apparent that the basic expectations of the re-pricing plan were correct. The plan was primarily a marketing initiative designed to gain exposure for

Muskingum that would result in increased interest from prospective students. This happened; applications increased, generating higher enrollments. Revenues after consideration of institutional financial aid grew substantially, and those resources helped stabilize the college's financial base and were used to strengthen the educational program.

The price reduction program also addressed issues of affordability and accessibility, though to a lesser degree. Some students benefited financially, either by the full $4,000 or by some lesser amount, and no student was worse off than they would have been under the status quo. It can perhaps be argued that the improvement of the college's financial situation also made it more possible to continue to offer acceptable financial assistance to needy students, who still make up most of Muskingum's population. The fact remains that finding ways to make college affordable continues to be a monumental challenge.

As the tuition reduction plan was being unveiled, the news director of the campus radio station, having heard the explanation of the plan, suggested, "So this is all about marketing." The response made at the time, which remains true today, is that the tuition reduction was certainly about marketing, but not all about marketing. Many students have attended Muskingum over the years since the price reduction who would not have done so had the status quo been maintained. The lives of these students were shaped forever, just as all colleges shape the lives of their students. Those experiences add up to something much greater than marketing.

The tuition reduction plan and its outcomes have helped to make a difference in the lives of students, and in the well-being of Muskingum College. This is what the program is ultimately about. That project of providing a more affordable education for students is still on the list for Muskingum and many other institutions.

Muskingum's experience with the tuition reduction plan will also help to serve as an example for future decision-making. For a college that, from its recent financial history, had developed a posture of "hunkering down and weathering the storm," the re-pricing decision was a monumental change. The idea was not rocket science - the challenging aspect was moving an institution suffering from recent decades of identity crisis to one that decided to take control of its own destiny. Whether this occurred because of forward-thinking leadership or the realization that the status quo was a more precarious route, or some likely combination of the two, is unimportant. The fact that an environment was created that allowed for a decision to be made was very important. Muskingum's recent success has contributed to a more forward-moving culture. The decision to reduce price is by no means the only factor in this cultural change, and this outlook could change over time if allowed to do so. The present leadership will not permit that stagnation or complacency, however, and creativity and innovation are now integral aspects of the planning process. Success is now an expectation rather than a hope, and the future of Muskingum College requires that philosophical perspective.

Ideas are important, if carried forward. Sometimes, "Truth happens to an idea." In Muskingum's case, it did.

3

COLLABORATIONS FOR SUCCESS

MEL TYLER AND
ROBIN K. HAMILTON

UMKC The University of Missouri—Kansas City challenges higher education to redefine the standards regarding collaboration in strategic enrollment management. More and more, higher education is playing a numbers game—will enrollment provide enough net revenue to support the programs and services needed to compete in today's economy and tomorrow's society? For many institutions, the numbers are coming up short, but few have created the culture to effectively adapt to change.

INTRODUCTION

The University of Missouri—Kansas City (UMKC) challenges higher education to redefine the standards regarding collaboration in strategic enrollment management. More and more, higher education is playing a numbers game—will enrollment provide enough net revenue to support the programs and services needed to compete in today's economy and tomorrow's society? For many institutions, the numbers are coming up short, but few have created the culture to effectively adapt to change. Such an environment is described succinctly by Frank Rhodes, president emeritus of Cornell University:

> *The university is the most significant creation of the second millennium. From modest beginnings over nine hundred years ago, it has become the quiet but decisive catalyst in modern society, the factor essential to its effective functioning and well-being. ... In a millennium in which knowledge has become the new economic capital, the universities—the traditional providers of knowledge—face both extraordinary challenges to which they must adapt, and extraordinary opportunities they must seize.*

The challenges are acute in Missouri, a state that has traditionally allowed the cost of higher education to fall on the students and their families in order to contain taxes. An economic decline over the past three years has resulted in additional state cuts in allocations to higher education, which has forced universities to raise tuition and drop under-enrolled programs. UMKC is no exception, and it has faced these recent challenges by redefining its role in educating tomorrow's leaders.

INSTITUTIONAL OVERVIEW

UMKC is an urban institution offering undergraduate, graduate, and professional degrees currently serving 14,000 students in twelve distinct academic units. Chartered as the University of Kansas City (UKC) in 1929, the Kansas City Chamber of Commerce created a board of trustees, whose first task was to raise initial capital and endowment funding during the Great Depression. The board persisted, recognizing their growing city's need for a university to serve its citizens. In 1933, UKC started classes with 17 faculty members and 264 students in one building.

The university's impetus for growth was provided by the affiliation of several local professional schools. In 1963, UKC became part of the University of Missouri System, joining campuses in Rolla, Columbia, and St. Louis. The system designated UMKC as its campus for the health and life sciences, performing arts, and urban affairs. With a strong civic connection and dedication to the community, the independent professional schools that originally merged with UKC created a unique profile for UMKC as a public institution consisting of nationally recognized professional programs.

A COMPELLING NEED FOR CHANGE

As happens at many large institutions over time, silos developed across the campus—made especially easier at UMKC because of a structure of academic units, each with its own

> **University of Kansas City**
> College of Arts and Sciences EST.1929
>
> **Existing Institutions Merging with UKC**
> Kansas City School of Law, 1938
> Kansas City Western Dental College, 1941
> Kansas City College of Pharmacy, 1943
> Kansas City Conservatory of Music, 1959
>
> **Academic Units Established**
> Henry W. Bloch School of Business, 1953
> School of Education, 1954
> School of Graduate Studies, 1964
> School of Medicine, 1970
> School of Nursing, 1980
> School of Biological Sciences, 1985
> School of Computing and Engineering, 2001

mission, that led to an image of UMKC being "less than the sum of its parts." These silos prevented any unified recruiting efforts, and retention levels declined. Admission to the university became an inward-focused process that concentrated on shuffling paperwork rather than connecting to people, and the lack of personal engagement with the campus actually encouraged students to transfer elsewhere. UMKC suffered from a lack of a positive public image, and its relationship with the city of Kansas City slowly declined. As a result, few Kansas Citians recognized that a nationally ranked public institution of comprehensive higher education existed in the heart of the city. Rather, UMKC was viewed primarily as a graduate school; the Kansas City commuter campus for UM-Columbia.

Only within the past 10 years has UMKC initiated concerted recruitment and retention efforts to target new undergraduate students. The university started by conducting analysis reports on market positioning, financial aid leveraging, and student services; as a result, the Office of Admissions was restructured to include recruiting staff who actively visited area high schools and college fairs. Recruitment publications—viewbooks, degree program fact sheets, and scholarship brochures—were printed and distributed. Additionally, the university purchased Noel-Levitz products and services to manage its prospective student database. Academic advising, a function of the Admissions Office, was identified as a key point of contact with prospective and current students; and in order to more actively engage these students, the academic units assumed advising services in an effort to increase retention rates.

These incremental changes were steps in the right direction, but they could neither attain nor sustain increased enrollments without an engaged campus. Marketing was approached with a laissez-faire attitude, and recruiting was viewed as a function of the Office of Admissions and not an activity in which the deans or faculty participated. The prevailing attitude across campus was one of doubt and passivity: "Students will enroll in our programs because of the convenient location and commuter-friendly campus," and "Why would academic units want more students when the increased enrollment would only strain their budgets more?" The campus was content with the status quo; and change is impossible to ignite unless the campus is willing to take the risk.

At the beginning of a slowing enrollment trend, faced with mediocre recruitment results and surrounded by staff, faculty, and administrators entrenched in their silos, UMKC needed, more than ever, to take that risk and create a bold vision for itself and the future of higher education. In the spring of 2000, the UMKC community welcomed a new chancellor, Dr. Martha Gilliland, who brought with her a vision for revitalizing the university and its relationship with the city. As Kansas City's only comprehensive research university offering a wide array of degree programs for all levels of students, it only made sense that UMKC needed to be the community's leader in higher education. In her inaugural speech, Dr. Gilliland proclaimed:

> These times call for new standards for higher education. We accept the fact that the measures of success are changing; the old criteria will not sustain us. A few universities will have the courage to respond to the times. UMKC will be one of those. Right now, at this university, at this time, nothing else is worth doing.

Not only did UMKC need to refocus attention on its role as educator of Kansas City's future leaders, but it had to do so under continual decreases in state budget allocations. Taking a grassroots approach, the Chancellor utilized the resources at hand—the university's own faculty, staff, students, alumni, and Kansas City community leaders—to collaboratively design what UMKC now calls **Our Emerging Future.**

INSTITUTIONAL STORY

Our Emerging Future is centered on the vision of UMKC being a community of learners making the world a better place. Creating this vision, however, required a "quantum transformation"—a process by which the entire UMKC community shapes our university with the idea that individuals want to be and will be part of something bigger than themselves. Such a bold initiative required bold strategic planning; no longer would the "business as usual" paradigm fulfill our needs. The traditional hierarchical leadership model too easily

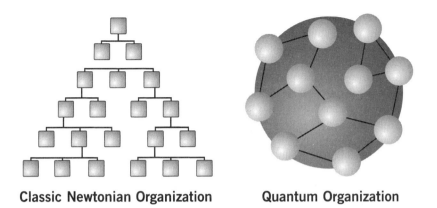

Classic Newtonian Organization   **Quantum Organization**

Figure 3-1 illustrates the inherent differences between a hierarchical relationship, commonly referred to as a Newtonian model, and the quantum model. UMKC strove to replace the linear, top-down model with a living and dynamic set of relationships, knowing that only by changing our campus culture can a future be envisioned.

results in stagnation, possessiveness, and redundancy. UMKC elected to break out of the outmoded and create something entirely new—a breakthrough into a quantum leadership model wherein the complexity and diversity of relationships are actively encouraged. In other words, the collective wisdom of the university drives the decision-making process. Though the results are inherently unpredictable, they are remarkable.

The challenge was in shifting the campus culture to accept a radical change in organizational theory by moving from a Newtonian to a quantum paradigm. It began with eighty people—a diverse group of students, staff, faculty, and administrators—who gathered together in a series of retreats to develop the university's vision. During the next three years, eighty expanded into a 170-member extended cabinet whose members represented a broad range of university affiliations and interests. The purpose of the extended cabinet is to network and build collaborative relationships across the campus and to provide multi-faceted feedback to the chancellor and central administration. More than 1,000 university and community leaders participated in "transformation workshops" that provided the forum for shaping UMKC's future and shifted a silo culture into one of collaboration, passion, and accountability. Quantum transformation instills ownership and pride in the future—that we as a university have the courage and the drive to fulfill our expectations and unleash human potential to transform UMKC and realize its vision of being a community of learners making the world a better place. Such a transformation is not an easy process. Roadblocks to success were frequently encountered, including facing the doubt, mistrust, and cynicism of many university personnel. One conversation at a time, however, the group of dedicated and passionate dreamers grew; and slowly, the entire university aligned itself to a vision of possibility. The "network of conversations" consistently identified enrollment management as one of the key Breakthrough Projects that would help us live this vision. As a university, a commitment was made to focus attention on enrollment as a means of shaping the future of its community, and to do so, the concepts of strategic enrollment management needed to be implemented across the entire campus.

To meet the challenge of creating a community of learners, Chancellor Gilliland commissioned a task force in the fall of 2000 to develop a university-wide enrollment management plan that would encompass marketing, recruitment, and retention. Chaired by Dr. John Cleek, a respected faculty member of the Henry W. Bloch School of Business and currently serving as dean of the School of Education, the task force set the stage for enrollment management efforts at UMKC. To create focus, the task force adopted Don Hossler's definition of enrollment management as an integrated systems approach that focuses on student enrollment from the time of their inquiry through graduation and post-graduation. An effective enrollment management system alters and improves the institution's frame of reference about itself and its prospective students, community members and business partners. (Hossler, 1986)

The task force asserted that enrollment management is an intrinsic process that revolves around students. As a holistic and comprehensive effort, enrollment management must be everyone's business. In a quantum leadership model, Dr. Cleek reveals, "We need all the right people who could make it happen—not only the chancellor and the provost, but also the deans, faculty, and staff." Only when everyone participates do breakthrough results happen.

The task force made recommendations to the chancellor regarding university-wide marketing, recruitment, and retention strategies. These strategies were driven by the unifying need to attract new students, retain current students, and graduate successful alumni. In order to measure our successes, the task force calculated two sets of percentage-based student headcount enrollment projections. In Figure 3-2, the blue line represents the "business as usual" paradigm in which moderate enrollment gains are produced by simply doing more of the same. The gold line represents the goal that an energized and collaborative enrollment management program can accomplish—to serve at least 17,172 students in the Fall Semester, 2006. These figures were determined by

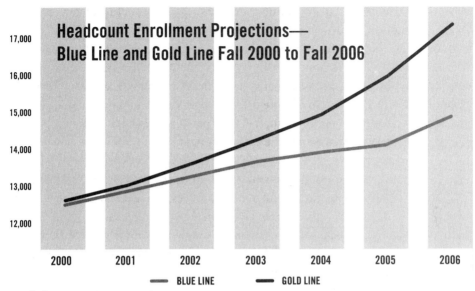

**Headcount Enrollment Projections—
Blue Line and Gold Line Fall 2000 to Fall 2006**

BLUE LINE   GOLD LINE

Figure 3-2

an aggressive across-the-board increase, automatically assuming that some academic programs would grow faster than others. For example, the professional schools (Medicine, Dentistry, Law, and Pharmacy) have capped enrollments based on their accreditation standards, and thus would not be able to contribute significantly to the university's enrollment growth. Other units, however, would be able to compensate by developing new degree programs (for example, the School of Nursing started their highly popular BSN program and the College of Arts and Sciences opened an Urban Design and Planning program along with a Film and New Media Studies program).

The academic units were only asked to submit strategies on how to improve marketing, recruitment, and retention in their own units. Ironically, they were not asked to submit projected enrollments, as the task force relied instead on percentage-based numbers. Despite working toward shared goals, there was a disconnect between the units' input and the task force's recommendations. UMKC's first enrollment management plan, while outlining innovative strategies, reinforced the fact that quantum transformation is not a smooth road.

Another roadblock was full-fledged campus action. Despite having a shared vision, a clear mission, and the number 17,172 on a chart, it was more convenient to just go about one's business—and less expensive, too. The academic units saw no incentive to reach for that gold star. More students, in the deans' eyes, did not equal more money for their programs. Thus, the task force recommended the creation of a shared revenue incentive plan that rewards the units with increased enrollments and supports those units whose enrollments are capped by their accreditation rules. The task force convinced all the deans that such a plan would have a monetary benefit and they would in fact be able to support the increase in students. As Dr. Cleek asserts,

> *Enrollment management will create the means for increased revenue; and the funds that are not returned directly to the academic units will contribute to the good of the whole. In other words, even units with capped enrollments will benefit.*

With an incentive plan underway, the academic units could concentrate on their enrollment plans as well as encourage members of the faculty and staff to participate in the transformation process.

As more and more university and community personnel actively contributed to the design of UMKC's future, the "network of conversations" became the momentum for change and innovation. This new campus culture—a culture in which "the university" became "we" instead of a faceless institution—identified our core values and set bold goals that the entire institution must work together to achieve. Collectively, the three-year process resulted in the creation of **Our Emerging Future,** and the strategic enrollment management program has been concurrently aligned with the vision, mission, values, and goals, shown in Figure 3-3.

In the spring of 2002, the Strategic Enrollment Management Team (SEMT) spearheaded the transformation of enrollment management into a collaborative paradigm accountable for the university's leading goal: attracting, nurturing, and developing responsible community leaders. Under the leadership of Mel Tyler, newly appointed assistant vice chancellor of Student Affairs for Enrollment Management, SEMT expanded the network of conversations necessary for fostering collaboration and ownership. The core Enrollment Management Cluster for the Division of Student Affairs, which consists of the Office of Admissions, the Financial Aid and Scholarships Office, the Office of the Registrar, and the International Student Affairs Office, developed a bold goal statement that creates an environment that encourages collaboration:

> *In 2006, our strategic enrollment management program has produced break-*

Figure 3-3

Vision, Mission and Goals:
UMKC 2006 *Our Emerging Future*

UMKC—A University with a Bold VISION

* A Community of Learners Making the World a Better Place

* Creating New Standards in Higher Education

* Academic Excellence

* Campus Without Borders

* Unleashing Human Potential

Which Is Manifested through Our MISSION

* Lead in Life and Health Sciences

* Deepen and Expand Strength in Visual and Performing Arts

* Develop a Professional Workforce; Collaborate in Urban Issues and Education

* Create a Vibrant Learning and Campus Life Experience

Through Processes That Have Us Living Our VALUES

* Education First

* Discovery and Innovation

* Integrity and Accountability

* Diversity, Inclusiveness and Respect

* Energized Collaborative Communities

To Achieve Our GOALS

* In 2006, we attract, nurture and develop responsible community leaders.

* In 2006, we are a national leader in scholarship and creative activity.

* In 2006, we are an essential community partner and resource.

* In 2006, we are a workplace of choice.

* In 2006, we have the resources to fuel our vision.

50

through results in student enrollment with a unified university enrollment management plan that supports and fuels the Bold Goals. The strategic enrollment management program has forged a university-wide partnership within the Divisions of Student Affairs, Academic Affairs, University Advancement, and Administration and Finances, the academic units, faculty, staff, students, and community members. This partnership will achieve the gold line standards in marketing, recruitment, and student success, thereby stimulating a rich environment for attracting and nurturing our community's future leaders while being an active community resource.

As part of the charge, SEMT would create a truly university-wide strategic enrollment management plan.

In order to engage more faculty and staff members in creating their vision for enrollment management, the academic units were encouraged to form their own enrollment management committees to develop strategies and action plans to reach their enrollment goals. This strategy is relatively uncommon in enrollment management circles, but has proven to be an effective tool for generating more feedback and involvement from faculty, staff and students within each unit regarding their future goals and how those goals align with our university's bold goals. We consider it a huge success of this new collaborative process that the student headcount projections submitted by each unit currently exceed the original 2006 goal of 17,172 by over a thousand students. A goal initially met with trepidation is now a touchstone due to SEMT's commitment to our community of learners and to our future. The team seized the opportunity to set aggressive goals within a framework of collaboration and campus support.

A unique factor contributing to the success of the Strategic Enrollment Management Team was its makeup. Members of the team represented all twelve academic units and all four administrative divisions (Student Affairs, Academic Affairs, Administration and Finance, and University Advancement). Additionally, the academic liaison structure served as the foundation upon which SEMT was built: a liaison was appointed by each unit to serve as a formal connection with the Division of Student Affairs to help coordinate communications and student services. In this structure's original conception, the liaisons served as consultants and had little ability to affect real change within their units. In SEMT, the academic liaisons are integral to building their units' strategic enrollment management planning, and receive full support from their deans and the chancellor.

Another important aspect of SEMT was its scope. Not only did the team concentrate on university-wide undergraduate recruitment and retention, but members also chaired sub-committees focused on more specific aspects of enrollment; for example, the Minority Recruitment Sub-committee, Graduate Recruitment Sub-committee, Student Success Sub-committee, Learning Technologies Sub-committee, and Distance Education Sub-Committee. These groups encouraged more people—faculty, staff, and students who have first-hand knowledge of each issue—to be involved in identifying shortfalls and in devising solutions and strategies to overcome the imbalance.

RESULTS

The resulting strategic enrollment management plan—created in collaboration with all the units—is fully aligned with the UMKC's vision, mission, values, and goals. The plan is action-oriented and results-driven with clearly defined accountabilities and with university-wide support. In the first two years of implementation, UMKC has exceeded expectations by reporting record student enrollments—higher than our original gold line projections. Not only has the campus succeeded in recruiting new students, the student demographics profile shows that more students are returning to UMKC to continue their education and our retention rates are improving. These results are wholly due to SEMT and the quantum transformation process working in conjunction to spark the momentum fueling breakthroughs in campus communications and ownership, university-wide and community partnerships, and specific accountabilities for realizing our future.

The transformation from linear to quantum was a challenge to dream and to achieve what can be possible for our future. Figure 3-4 below illustrates the phases of transformation. Phase I, which the original "Group of Eighty" initiated, focused on building the foundation that now supports our strategic enrollment management program. After working through roadblocks and learning from breakdowns, we—as a university community—were able to move into Phase II and create the environment wherein results happen. "Breakthrough Projects" that were originally designed to be quick fixes have evolved into long-term strategic programs that directly help us achieve our goals. For example, our goal of attracting, nurturing and developing responsible community leaders has made academic service-learning (AS-L), once just an idea about which a small breakthrough team felt passionate, into a significant component of our commitment to life-long learning. Phase III of the process will allow UMKC to stabilize what it has achieved so quickly and to evaluate where its dreams and passions can take it for the next six years.

52

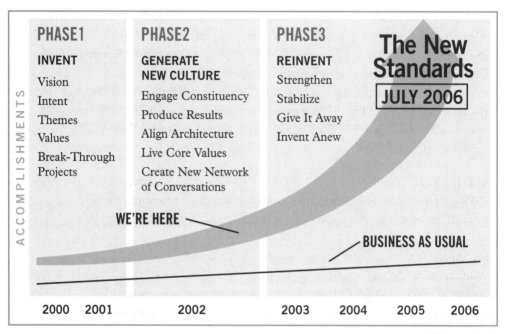

Figure 3-4

Enrollment management could not have happened at a better time for UMKC; nor could it have happened without the leadership and commitment of our people. We were able to develop the plan and implement its strategies despite several missing pieces that, in all reality, should have prevented us from accomplishing anything. UMKC lacks a comprehensive and dedicated marketing plan for public relations and advertising. The most important yet unpredictable piece missing is a strong and overflowing budget. UMKC is also still in the process of developing benchmark data for measuring successes. Rather than being data-driven and perhaps bogged down by numbers, the transformation process and enrollment management plan was based on an overwhelming intuitive need to fulfill our vision.

Despite these missing pieces, the enrollment management program at UMKC has sustained successes, not the least of which is a comprehensive, four-year university-wide strategic enrollment management plan. The plan includes university-wide marketing, recruitment, and student success strategies as well as unit-specific strategies, which were created by each unit's enrollment management committees.

Most important, the plan is a working document. Although it serves as the blueprint for achieving goals in 2006, as strategies are refined and new collaborations created, those are also incorporated into the plan in annual updates. In Dr. Cleek's assessment, the plan's collaborative spirit stems from the campus community's willingness to persist and to evaluate efforts:

> *The plan is a breakthrough because it is a working document—continuing to expand, modify, develop and implement—and as long as it stays a dynamic process, it'll work.*

With the shift in campus culture that the transformation process has generated, the UMKC community drives the enrollment management program: SEMT and the sub-committees have taken accountability for ensuring the success of their efforts.

The main section of the plan consists of university-wide strategies developed in conjunction by SEMT and the Enrollment Management Cluster. Nearly all of our marketing and recruitment strategies require collaborations between the academic units, the divisions of university administration, and with the university community at large.

HIGHLIGHTS OF UMKC'S UNIVERSITY-WIDE MARKETING AND RECRUITMENT STRATEGIES

Perhaps the most impressive feat of collaboration is the annual *Discover UMKC* Open House, first held in October 2002. The open house is UMKC's opportunity to throw open its doors to the community. During the day, the academic units showcase various degree programs and research opportunities, demonstrate experiments, and hold mock lectures. Faculty, staff, administrators, and students all work together to ensure that the community's questions are addressed and to provide an environment that welcomes community participation. Response to the open house has been very positive with even greater collaboration taking place for the 2003 event.

Not only was UMKC successful in rallying internal resources for the open house, it has also been successful in partnering with external groups. An important collaboration exists between UMKC and several area colleges and community colleges to recruit and support transfer students. For example, UMKC and The Metropolitan Community Colleges of Kansas City, Missouri (MCC) have signed articulation agreements in which MCC students are dual enrolled at UMKC and have access to advising services. These articulation agreements assure a seamless transfer process when students are ready to pursue their studies at a four-year institution. Dr. Wayne Giles, chancellor of The Metropolitan

Community Colleges, is very optimistic about the partnership: I believe these articulation agreements provide wonderful opportunities for the students we serve in Kansas City. Students and their families are the beneficiaries. These agreements also represent a level of cooperation among educational institutions that is what the Kansas City community expects from its public community college and public university.

UMKC and MCC have joined with Missouri Western State College in St. Joseph to offer an innovative 2+2+2 program. Students at MCC transfer into Missouri Western for undergraduate coursework taught at UMKC's Northland campus. After graduation, these students enroll in a master's program offered by UMKC at the Northland campus. Collaborations with these colleges further strengthen a commitment to students and to educating the future leaders in the Kansas City metropolitan area.

UMKC's International Student Affairs Office initiated a cooperative recruitment partnership with MCC and Rockhurst University, a private Jesuit university located in the heart of Kansas City, Missouri. This unique collaboration resulted in a view piece developed for international student recruitment in which the focus is on higher education options in Kansas City, whether for first-time freshmen new to the country or for international students wishing to transfer institutions. Joint recruiting efforts better serve the interests of international students and their educational goals, and serve to enrich Kansas City as a whole. This partnership helps the International Student Affairs Office become the community resource for international student regulations, policies, and programming.

Another partnership for UMKC serves our students across the state line. The Metro Rate program allows undergraduate students residing in the four contiguous Kansas counties (Johnson, Leavenworth, Miami, and Wyandotte counties) to pay in-state tuition while attending UMKC. This program has saved many students thousands of dollars each semester while allowing UMKC to be the affordable institution of choice. The Metro Rate has proven to be an effective recruitment tool—from Fall 2001 to Fall 2003, the number of Kansas residents receiving the Metro Rate at UMKC has increased by 105%—affirming a commitment to providing world-class education to the Greater Kansas City community, no matter which side of the state line.

HIGHLIGHTS OF UMKC'S UNIVERSITY-WIDE STUDENT SUCCESS STRATEGIES

Not only focusing on university-wide recruitment, SEMT redefined retention as

"Student Success" to emphasize a goal to attract, nurture, and develop responsible community leaders. Student Success became a priority for SEMT, and a sub-committee formed to develop strategies and ideas to encourage student engagement. As a university, UMKC defines student success to encompass the following:

> UMKC is committed to student success, enabling our students to:
> Expand the bounds of knowledge;
> Become wiser & more compassionate;
> Discover their true potential;
> Develop as individuals, able and committed to making a difference.

Using this statement as a guide, the SEMT developed a pilot New Student Welcome Day, a second part to the summer freshmen orientation program scheduled for the day before classes start. This day will give freshmen further opportunities to engage the campus, their faculty, and their peers. Additionally, orientations for international students have been expanded, featuring more community involvement, networking opportunities, and social activities in Kansas City and on campus.

Other exciting facets of Student Success encourage more student engagement with the campus community. The UMKC Day of Learning is one such activity that promotes campus-wide engagement and student-faculty interaction outside of the classroom environment. Held in conjunction with Convocation, the Day of Learning celebrates UMKC accomplishments and sets the tone for the year, what College of Arts and Sciences dean, Dr. Bryan Le Beau, calls:

> ...[T]he passion about life that opens the world of opportunities; and UMKC
> is about unleashing human potential to explore these passions and opportunities.

The Day of Learning is directly connected to the first-year experience seminar program, generally called "A&S 100" even though more academic units are partnering together to offer the course. Each seminar is tailored for first-year students in a particular major (i.e., health sciences, business, or education) and creates a sense of community among these students and their faculty mentor. The Day of Learning includes a campus-wide directed reading which is the core text for the seminar. Such a structure promotes a community culture among students and faculty engaged in pursuing life-long learning while easing first-year students into university student life at UMKC.

We hope to expand the concepts of the Day of Learning into the new residence hall currently under construction. The 560-bed facility will create an environment that will facilitate living-learning communities and co-curricular programming. These communities, developed with direct involvement of faculty members, will provide the support network that first-year college students so often need but are unable to find. UMKC has long been perceived as a "commuter campus" with few resources available for traditional students; the new residence hall is a giant step toward actively engaging these students in their educational and personal successes.

Personalized quality advising is a top priority for UMKC student success, as advisors serve as mentors to a broad range of students: those who are new to the university as freshmen or transfers, students who are continuing their coursework here, those who have changed majors and career paths, and prospective students who are still in the decision-making process. SEMT works closely with the academic advisors, and sponsors the Advisors' Forum and Handbook to give advisors the resources and support they need to help students succeed.

One critical student resource at UMKC is the internationally known Supplemental Instruction (SI) program, developed at UMKC in 1973. Supplemental Instruction serves as the "foundation for student success" according to Dr. Glen Jacobs, director of UMKC's Center for Academic Development. Hundreds of universities around the world have taken the SI program as the foundation for their students' success as well, recognizing that the innovative support service increases pass-rates on historically challenging courses. Led by student peers, SI groups develop strategies for studying and succeeding in these courses. These students perform better in their other coursework, as well, benefiting from the study skills and strategies learned in SI.

Other resources designed for student success involve campus life, not just academic life, at UMKC. Along with the new residence hall, which will provide social programming opportunities, the Student Life Office is UMKC's source for student engagement with campus life. Several programs sponsored by the Student Life Office encourage personal and professional development, including the Emerging Leaders, Talent Scholars, and Scholars 4 Success programs. Dr. Zauyah Waite, director of the Student Life Office, explains that these programs,

> ...[C]ommunicate to students that we care about them; that we are
> committed to giving them as many opportunities as possible to develop their

skills and talents to contribute back to their community. [These programs]
challenge them from the start to think about their future, to start planning
now in order to gain maximum experiences that will help them succeed.

These programs target specific groups of students and provide a forum to explore their career aspirations, the tools they will need to achieve their goals, and the support network of like-minded individuals with a keen eye for success. Also incorporating the expertise of other university personnel, including the Career Services Office and the Counseling, Health, and Testing Office, these high-profile collaborations promote student success in a very positive environment for students.

Strategic enrollment management has also affected intra-office collaborations within the UMKC administration, improving many business processes that indirectly promote student success. These changes make it easier for students to cut through red tape in order to concentrate on their studies. For example, the Financial Aid and Scholarships Office revisited the academic progress policy to make it more efficient and student-friendly. Recently approved, the new academic progress policy clarifies how students receiving financial aid remain eligible to continue receiving their aid. The next steps for this policy are to collaborate with the academic units to develop advising plans for students who are placed on probation for failing to achieve acceptable academic progress. Also recently approved, the new student e-mail account policy actively promotes student engagement with their peers and helps streamline university communications. Our next step is to encourage the faculty to also utilize students' e-mail accounts for course-related communications.

Another business process that has been streamlined is the new short-term loan policy, which is now tightly and smoothly operated for greater student convenience. The collaboration between the Financial Aid Office, University Cashier, and the Student Loan Office has set a precedent that the Division of Student Affairs and the Division of Administration and Finance can successfully work together to accomplish great things for UMKC students and to further enrollment management goals.

HIGHLIGHTS OF UMKC'S UNIT-SPECIFIC STRATEGIES

UMKC's enrollment management plan would not be complete without input from the academic units. Each unit submitted its own strategies for marketing, recruitment, and student success. These strategies were developed from within the unit's own ranks of faculty and staff to create a wholly unique and targeted plan. Each unit's enrollment management committee aligned its strategies with UMKC's goals to create a document more powerful in its unification behind a shared vision. As previously mentioned, this collaborative atmosphere produced breakthrough results in that the units' projected enrollments totaled more than the original gold-line goal of 17,176 students. More than that, each unit challenged their silo-mentality to create innovative strategies that work towards the good of the whole rather than just their own unit.

Two particularly unique recruitment strategies deserve to be highlighted here. One strategy involves three academic units who were not working together to recruit students before the quantum transformation occurred at UMKC. The School of Biological Sciences and the College of Arts and Sciences had a long and understandable history of competing over the same pre-health students. Instead of working against each other, these academic units decided to combine forces with the School of Dentistry, which had not previously heavily recruited undergraduate UMKC students for its programs. These three units together began an academic advising program for pre-health undergraduates interested in pursuing dentistry as a career, and the School of Dentistry initiated a Reserved Seat Program for qualified undergraduates at UMKC. In addition, the units developed a pre-dentistry brochure that highlights the advantages of each route an undergraduate student could take—either through the School of Biological Sciences or the College of Arts and Sciences—to be admitted into the School of Dentistry as a graduate professional student. This collaboration demonstrates that units working together contribute to the overall enrollment—that the university is greater than its parts.

The second recruiting strategy is marvelously simple and has quickly become a university-wide initiative. The Office of Admissions concentrates on undergraduate recruitment, leaving graduate and professional recruitment to the units. SEMT hoped to remedy this situation with the development of a Graduate and Professional Recruitment Sub-committee to provide support for these activities. The academic units volunteered to join together to help each other cover the expenses and travel time to participate in recruitment fairs across the country. This initiative requires cross-training and dedication to UMKC as a whole, not just a particular unit affiliation. Motivated first by budget cuts, the sub-committee recognized the common desire to provide wide recruiting coverage for all professional and graduate programs at UMKC. What began as a survival instinct turned into a breakthrough in collaboration.

Such strategies as these are testament to the change in philosophy at UMKC. We live in a culture of collaboration and innovation, and the benefits not only help us reach our goals, but also make us a stronger university whose primary function is to serve our students.

LESSONS LEARNED AND UNEXPECTED OUTCOMES

In retrospect, although quantum transformation has been a rough road, it continues to be a very rewarding one. An enrollment trend analysis shows that not only is UMKC recruiting more freshmen and transfers, but our existing students are staying here, too. This combination of numbers obviously equals a successful increase in student enrollment; but it also signifies our success in aligning enrollment management as a university priority—it is truly everyone's business. Whereas strategic enrollment management began as an administrative priority, SEMT was able to engage the campus. Though SEMT had the chancellor's support, it was up to the individual members to take accountability for getting things done—for developing strategies, engaging the units, and promoting ownership.

We learned some valuable lessons along the way, especially the importance of actively listening—of going out into the academic units and understanding their situation and their needs. Learning to really listen takes time and effort, especially learning to hear all the complaints and criticisms without becoming defensive or angry. Listening, UMKC found, is the essential factor to establishing relationships built on trust and empathy. Such relationships solve problems rather than generate excuses. Another lesson learned is the value of persistence and commitment; as Dr. Cleek reveals: "Enrollment management wasn't going to go away—persistence and follow-up kept it on everyone's minds. This plan is not a shelf document." Campus-wide "buy-in" to recognizing that strategic enrollment management is a cornerstone for UMKC did take time. Working through breakdowns, however, SEMT proved that, with listening and persistence, enrollment management can, in fact, be a unifying force that promotes collaboration.

We also learned that taking risks can be rewarding. An unexpected outcome of the entire process at UMKC was watching one vision expand as more and more people shared in **Our Emerging Future**. Enrollment management was first an idea, then it was a number on a gold line, and finally it became a very personal goal of attracting, nurturing, and developing responsible community leaders. Strategies designed to meet this goal are more powerful than any strategy used simply to increase numbers—after all, we are in the university environment to promote life-long learning, and people are at the heart. Taking the initiative to define new standards in how higher education meets challenges is, admittedly, a risky and ambitious venture. But with strategic enrollment management, only by taking risks can the rewards be so fulfilling.

Another unexpected outcome was that with these bold risks and gold-line goals, community supporters appear who are willing and able to fuel the momentum. The UMKC Board of Trustees has become an active supporter of our transformation, aligning its goals with the university's vision. To help us meet our goal of attracting, nurturing, and developing responsible community leaders, the board established the Trustees' Scholars Program, which provides ten full scholarships to outstanding entering freshmen. These students not only receive monetary support, they also receive mentoring and internship opportunities from Kansas City's most successful business and community leaders. Hugh Zimmer, UMKC Trustees chair and chairman of The Zimmer Companies, assembled the support of the business community's leaders, who are integral to the success of the program. Mr. Zimmer reveals:

> The goal of the UMKC Trustees' Scholars Program is to bring together the best and the brightest students from our area and match them with the support and involvement of the key Kansas City-based firms. The result will be great job opportunities for these future graduates and access to this excellent employee pool for our Kansas City companies. Everyone is a winner in this fine program.

The Trustees' Scholars Program is a key recruitment tool that has student success at its heart, success that will directly affect the Kansas City community.

Recognizing that a high-profile marketing image is a valuable asset, the Trustees initiated a project in which nationally renowned marketing and communications firms in Kansas City, many with an international clientele, together with key community leaders, have volunteered to help us tell our story to the world. With so much talent joining forces to support our university, Dr. Pat Long, vice chancellor of Student Affairs and Enrollment Management, believes that this collaboration is truly groundbreaking:

> They [the marketing and communications firms] know UMKC, they know what we have to offer to Kansas City and to the world. Lending us their expertise, we can develop a marketing and communications plan that sets standards for a truly community-wide partnership that will change the way people interact with this university.

Great things are happening at UMKC, and with such strong community support, higher education in Kansas City will reach a whole new level.

CONCLUSION

The outcomes of implementing strategic enrollment management at UMKC are impossible to fully measure at this point. Counting its successes, UMKC can affirm that momentum is indeed building, that enrollment management is a uniting force on campus. Quantum transformation is an organic process, one that facilitates growth and collaboration; the evolution from idea to number to goal to success is indeed gratifying.

Enrollment management can either be a shot in the dark, a last-ditch effort at increasing numbers and revenue, or it can be a part of a conscious, university-wide strategic decision to change a culture of passive acceptance into one of passionate ownership. UMKC has chosen to forge its own future and set the standards for collaboration in higher education.

REFERENCES

Hossler, D. (1986). Creating Effective Enrollment Management Systems. New York: The College Board.

Rhodes, F. (2001). Creation of the Future: The Role of the American University. Ithaca, New York: Cornell University Press.

University of Missouri—Kansas City (2002). Our Emerging Future. Kansas City, Missouri.

4

STUDENT SUCCESS: A CATALYST FOR CHANGE

KEVIN POLLOCK

WSCC For the first thirty years, West Shore Community College, a small, rural, community college, grew steadily and improved its offerings of educational programs and services to its community, but with respect to students, it lacked a solid commitment to student success. Over the past six years the college has been transformed into an institution with a vision and strategic plan that is sharply focused on student success. Teams have been formed to implement goals to move the college forward.

Established in 1967, West Shore Community College, located in Scottville, Michigan, is one of the smallest community colleges in the State of Michigan. The college's district is composed of all or part of four counties: Mason, Manistee, Lake and Oceana. Within the college's service area there are fifteen separate school systems, ten of which fall within the college's in-district tuition and fee structure. These school systems produce between 850–900 high school graduates each year, with a yearly average of 20% of the graduates attending WSCC.

Of the approximately 1,400 students that attend West Shore each semester, nearly two-thirds are women. Sixty percent of the students are classified as part-time students with an average age of twenty-seven.

Since its inception, West Shore has experienced a slow, steady growth in enrollment, peaking in the fall of 1995 at 1,617 students. After experiencing three years of enrollment decline, enrollment has steadily climbed since the 1998–99 academic year. The overall student headcount has increased a total of 12.6% and the total number of credit hours has risen 10.8% since that year. Summer semester has shown the largest increase in student enrollment. Both the number of students and credit hours for summer has nearly doubled from 1998 to 2003.

In the 2001–02 academic year, 46% of the student body was identified as first generation college students. In the fall of 2002, 5.5% of West Shore's students self-reported their ethnicity as Hispanic, African-American, or Native American. While this percentage may seem low, it closely mirrors that of the college district population. Nearly 42% of the students at West Shore Community College are eligible for aid and can be considered economically disadvantaged.

There are four divisions on the campus, each reporting to a vice president. The academic side consists of the Arts and Sciences, and the Occupational divisions. One non-academic division is Administrative Services, which consists of such areas as the Bookstore, Cafeteria, Business Office, and Maintenance.

The other non-academic division at WSCC is the Student Services area, which consists of Admissions, Registrar, Financial Aid, Career Counseling, Academic Advising and the Women's Resource Center. However, other student support services are fragmented and spread around the campus. These additional services, including Supplemental Instruction and testing services, housed in the College Learning and

Testing Center, report to the vice president of Arts and Sciences, and the STaRS (Support, Tutoring and Resource Services) Program, which works predominately with at risk students, reports to the vice president of Workforce Development.

STATEMENT OF THE PROBLEM

For nearly the first thirty years of its existence the concept of student success, or putting students first, was not a driving force on the campus. While there was a quality improvement movement on the campus, it was operating "under the radar" and without strong support from the community college. Even though West Shore experienced a slow steady growth in its enrollment, it was not until the past five years that issues such as quality improvement, enrollment management, and student success became the driving forces they are today.

Over the past five years there have been two main events that sparked the movement toward a more student-oriented campus. The first event happened in 1998 with the hiring of a new president with a commitment to teamwork, continuous improvement, strategic planning and putting students first. His first two years at West Shore Community College were marked by attempts to change the culture on the campus. There was the inevitable opposition to change involving some members of the faculty, staff, and even the board of trustees. By 2000, three of the four deans on the campus had been replaced. This time also marked the start of the board of trustees focus on an open atmosphere, with putting students first as its highest priority, and a commitment to the new direction of the president.

Thus began a time of a cultural shift on campus and a push toward the alignment of the vision, mission, strategic plan, and budget in an effort to have all facets of the on-campus community working in concert. With limited resources, both in people and funding, the college could not afford to waste time or effort on initiatives that were not moving the college forward. The president espoused a simple motto: "Do the right thing for the right reason and when in doubt, lean toward the student." At this point, the campus reached a cultural turning point and began the movement toward becoming an institution that puts students first.

In 1998, an Enrollment Development Task Force met and reviewed the current population of students and potential market segments in an effort to understand the driving factors behind the enrollment at WSCC and to then utilize the information to increase enrollment. The task force determined that there were seven identifiable market segments:

1. Students age 60 and over
2. Recent high school student graduates (age 18–22)
3. Current high school students
4. Former WSCC students
5. Recent high school graduates (age 23–29)
6. Non-traditional students (age 30–60)
7. Retention of current WSCC students

In addition, the task force reviewed factors for students selecting a college that distinguished WSCC from its competitors. Among the positive aspects were: cost, small class size, curriculum, close proximity to home, and an open door policy for admissions. The negative aspects included: too close to home, a limited curriculum, transportation problems, no sports, and no residence halls. Strategies that were recommended to help increase enrollment included open houses, focus groups, increased visits to high schools, and the development of new programs and distance learning offerings.

In late spring of 1999, a final report was issued by the team. In addition to the earlier recommendations came a call for an increase in reviewing enrollment statistics and data collection. The team suggested that the college work closer with its Tech Prep partnership, increase the number of scholarships available to students, and develop an Honors Program to attract superior students. An additional new concern revolved around the need for creative scheduling ideas to maximize student enrollment. Among the suggestions were Friday classes, weekend classes, weekend blocks of classes, on-site classes for local companies, on-line classes, rotated times of class offerings, and late evening classes.

Unfortunately, by 1999, due to personnel changes, and shifts in philosophy, many of the strategies were not initiated. A new president was leading the campus, the dean of Student Services had left, a new director of Admissions was in place; all were positions critical to implementing any of the strategies suggested by the team. Four years later, many of the ideas and suggestions made by the team were still being debated on the campus. For example, the same concerns about class scheduling that were raised in 1999 have been raised in 2003, resulting in the creation of a task force to create a more student-friendly class schedule.

THE FIRST STRATEGIC PLAN
Over the past three years WSCC has moved forward by linking its vision and strategic plan directly to the concept of student success. How did a college with fragmented

support services for students, no enrollment management plan, and a history of not implementing student-friendly changes, move to such a step?

The first step toward the creation of a more comprehensive strategic plan started in 2000 with the initiation of a campus-wide team approach to deal with issues that crossed over traditional management lines. Each team comprised a mix of faculty and staff, and occasionally students. One of the teams created was an Enrollment Management Team. During its first year of existence, the Enrollment Management Team concentrated on such enrollment issues as recruiting, retention, and marketing. While there were numerous discussions concerning enrollment, no concrete plans were made by the team to bolster the enrollment through the implementation of new recruiting or retention activities.

The second step began in 2001 when the president initiated the strategic planning process by creating a campus-wide team charged with reviewing and updating the institution's vision and strategic plan. The team consisted of the four campus deans, faculty members from the two academic divisions on the campus, and various administrators, staff, and student representatives. The team was asked to create broad opportunities for campus participation in the process, tie all campus funding into the plan, keep the plan relatively simple, connect existing and new teams into the process, and make each goal it created measurable.

After nine months, the initial strategic plan was completed and delineated five priorities that challenged the college to increase the admission of students and improve retention, enhance the college infrastructure and resources, support diversity and global awareness, promote economic development, and provide cultural and social opportunities for community enrichment. Predominately due to concerns over future budget needs, the Strategic Planning Team agreed that the number one goal for the campus was student recruitment and retention.

When presented to the WSCC Board of Trustees in late spring, however, several concerns about the plan were raised. The board felt that the plan lacked a clearly defined, inspiring vision. In addition, there were concerns over alignment, community input, the measurability of the plan's goals, the lack of a strong economic development component, and the burden of too many details. Overall, board members did not feel that the process resulted in a plan in which they could take ownership.

This initial strategic plan was simply not driven by a vision; therefore, it was not truly strategic. Without a clear picture of a desired future state, no plan can claim to be moving an institution in any intentional direction. In addition, the goals seemed too simplistic and easy to attain. For example, when dealing with the enrollment issue the strategic planning team set a goal of an overall enrollment increase of three percent in the student population. By the end of the year, enrollment had grown nearly six percent, without new strategies or programs having been implemented. Was the goal then completed?

There was fallout over the board's rejection of the initial strategic plan, much of it dealing with the Strategic Planning Team itself. While some team members were able to look at the board's concerns as constructive criticism, others were deflated by the comments. Before the start of the summer, the Strategic Planning Team chair had resigned, and the president had taken over the team on an interim basis. The change in the team structure as a whole was minimal, due to the timing of the board's comments in relationship to the start of a summer break. However, this also caused the team members, who thought their work was completed, to continue working throughout the summer in order to have a plan in place for the fall semester.

THE NEXT STEP
Running along a parallel track during the time the strategic plan was written, several events moved the concept of student success to the forefront of the college's plans. The first was a simple step of renaming the Enrollment Management Team the Student Success Team. The Enrollment Management Team had been created the previous year to review the college marketing plan, create new recruiting activities, and identify and eliminate barriers that hindered students from attaining their educational goals. The Student Success Team concentrated primarily on the elimination of barriers and the concept of retention and the success of students. Whereas some on the campus, particularly faculty, could state that the enrollment situation was not tied to any of their roles, the concept of student success was one that could be embraced by all.

The second was the creation of the college's first institutional climate survey. The survey was given to all faculty and staff on campus and covered such areas as campus values and ideals, general working conditions, communications, and training. The response rate was excellent, with approximately 75% of the full-time faculty and staff responding. The survey consisted of thirty-eight questions, or opinion statements, divided into seven categories. Respondents answered the questions using a five-point scale ranging from number one, "strongly disagree", through number five, "strongly agree". The overall average for the survey was a 3.8 indicating that most employees, by agreeing with the questions and opinion statements on the survey, supported the direction in which the college was headed.

One specific question asked if the college should embrace a "students first" philosophy. The response to the question had the highest rating of all items on the survey; 93% of the respondents "agreed" or "strongly agreed" with the students first philosophy. The overwhelming response to the question demonstrated strong support for a student success movement on the campus. In essence, this gave the "silent majority" on the campus a stronger voice over the typical doom and gloom voice of a more vocal minority. It was a turning point for the college that resulted in a major cultural shift on the campus, for now the silent majority could be comfortable in speaking out as advocates for students. It also provided a strong push for the student success initiative on the campus.

In 2002, a year with state funding cuts in higher education and a resulting budget crisis, the survey was given to the employees for the second time and the overall score rose from a 3.8 to a 4.0, indicating that employees were even more in agreement with the direction in which the campus was moving.

In the summer of 2002, the strategic planning process began anew. The change in the team chair and team members provided a different direction for the team. The team was asked to start the process by "dreaming" of the future of the college and writing down all of their ideas on post-it notes. The notes were collected, grouped, and three specific areas rose to the surface: student success, serving the community, and pursuing greatness.

Another driving and intervening force, also on a parallel track during the same year, was the Academic Quality Improvement Program (AQIP), the new North Central Accreditation (NCA) model. The AQIP model was adopted by West Shore as its new accreditation model because it promoted annual continuous improvement and focused on measurable results. West Shore was one of the first 40–50 colleges to join the new accreditation model; currently there are approximately ninety colleges in AQIP, including nine from Michigan.

The old accreditation model relied on a team of evaluators conducting an audit every ten years. The AQIP model requires that the college create a series of action projects that must be measured and reported each year. Every three years, the college is required to submit a "systems portfolio" which provides a comprehensive review of the improvements made by the plan and how the college's operations align with the AQIP model. One of the action projects must make some aspect of student learning a top priority. WSCC selected improving the success of at risk students as its project to address this priority. The other two AQIP projects adopted by the college addressed other needs: the collection and dissemination of data and the institutional climate survey. AQIP action projects now automatically had to become high priorities within the strategic plan.

Over the course of the summer of 2002 a new vision was written for the college that put student success at its forefront. The new vision statement read:

Our vision is to be one of the premier community colleges in America, driven by a passion for
* Assuring student success;
* Serving our entire community; and
* Pursuing greatness.

In order for the vision and strategic plan to be successful it was critical that there was "buy-in" by the faculty. Faculty members had representation on each of the campus teams, including the Strategic Planning Team and had a strong voice during the creation of the new vision and strategic plan. During the creation of the new plan, the faculty perspective raised several points that needed to be recognized.

For example, faculty members, concerned with maintaining high classroom standards, had to recognize the community college's open enrollment and its impact on learning. Because of open enrollment, students in the classroom would have a broad range of academic skills.

The need to gather data that supported new initiatives was considered critical. As part of the new strategic plan the college was to move to a learner-centered environment. At the heart of the learner-centered environment are two principles: student learning should be the central focus, and learning should be enhanced through increased connections with the students. Faculty needed to buy into the new concept and they required training and input as the college moved toward the new system.

In addition, faculty members were asked to work more closely with local K-12 teachers to develop a better working relationship with the local community. The new strategic plan would have an impact on the faculty in various ways: class scheduling, course offerings, and remediation needs of students, to name a few.

During academic year 2002–03, a new permanent strategic planning chair replaced the president and the updated strategic plan was completed. Over the course of the two years it took to complete the final vision and strategic plan it became obvious that the college was sorely lacking in the area of data collection. This was apparent when the board reviewed the first attempt at the strategic plan and noted that one component that was missing was the measurability of the plan's goals. To compensate for this problem the strategic planning team adopted the Core Indicators of Community College Effectiveness as a guideline for the gathering of data. The college would begin gathering data related to student goal attainment, persistence, degree completion rates, and placement rates in the workforce, among other areas.

To finalize the process for improving the data collection at WSCC, the college made one of its AQIP goals a critical goal in the strategic plan: improve stakeholder assessment, data gathering, and the data dissemination process. To assist in this task, a new administrative position was created, and the college hired its first director of Institutional Research in the summer of 2002.

A total of twenty-eight goals were created that were tied to the vision, core values and mission of the institution, many focusing on student success. Among the goals directly related to enrollment management and student success were:
* Improving the success of at risk students;
* Optimizing course offerings;
* Creating substantive learning-centered change in all student settings;
* Removing financial barriers for students; and
* Developing a comprehensive advising model.

Seven teams were created and staffed with representatives from both faculty and staff, and charged with the implementation of the goals. The teams were: Academic Excellence, Community Service, Cultural Awareness, Institutional Effectiveness, Infrastructure and Resources, and Student Success. A matrix was created and attached to the strategic plan that showed each goal's relationship to the vision, mission, and core values of the college. The teams each had two members as part of the Strategic Planning Team and had to present mid-year and end-of-year reports on the progress of the teams' goals.

In May of 2003, the board of trustees accepted the new vision and strategic plan. It was noted that the strategic plan needed to be a fluid document, one that would, through the use of an environmental scan, be reviewed and updated yearly. The accepted new plan also created new roles for many on the campus. For example, AQIP requires a board of trustee member to be actively involved in the AQIP process. The president was now required to share the plan with the community and seek public comments and input. The faculty and the staff now served on various teams seeking to complete goals set forth by the plan.

In 2002, the Student Success Team defined student success as, "Students attaining their educational goals in the most efficient manner." One of the strategies then to enhancing student success was the elimination of barriers that could hinder students from accomplishing their educational goals; it was NOT the lowering of academic standards. The Student Success Team immediately identified several areas on the campus that needed to be addressed. Among them:

* The need for a comprehensive advising model;
* A review of class scheduling and a call for a "student-friendly" schedule;
* A review of historical snapshot of classes with high "failure" and/or withdraw rates; and
* A student survey to determine student needs.

ADDITIONAL AREAS

Other initiatives occurred on the campus, many of which were tied directly to the concept of student success. In 2002, a new administrative position, director of College Relations, reporting directly to the president, was created and filled to assist in the creation and implementation of the college's marketing and outreach plan. The new director, working with the director of Admissions, and the Student Services area, began work on the first comprehensive marketing plan for West Shore Community College. The plan, currently undergoing revisions, will include a combined enrollment management and marketing plan designed to funnel students from prospect to enrollee. The plan, tailored to different niches of students, will reach students through various means, including a direct mail campaign, brochures and publications, electronic e-mail, ads, and contact with prospective students' parents.

The Student Services area also began to support students through more advanced uses of technology. In the spring of 2002, Web registration for students was available for the first time. Today, nearly seventy percent of the students that register for classes at WSCC do so through the Web. In 2003, online orientation for students also became available for students via the Web. As a major goal for 2004, the Student Services area had dedicated itself to the implementation of new Web resources for students, including such things as transfer guides and on-line degree audits.

In 2001, The Women's Resource Center opened on the campus. The center works closely with an advisory team that includes community members. Created to assist students in need, the center has had nearly 400 students visit in its first two years. The center has held thirty-seven campus seminars on varying topics to over 1,000 students. In addition, the center has referred 102 students to local agencies, held classroom presentations to a total of 1,900 students, and presented to thirty-eight community groups, reaching 1,576 people.

In 2003, a report concerning the success rate of students in the college's developmental math classes, revealed that, over a five year period, 77% of all students enrolling in math courses at WSCC were enrolled in one of four developmental courses. The developmental courses, Basic Math, Introduction to Algebra, Intermediate Algebra, as well as the non-developmental Trigonometry course, traditionally had high numbers of students receiving either grades of D or F, or withdrawing. With this data as a basis for action, the college administration determined that a new developmental math faculty position would be created. The faculty member would not only teach developmental math but would assist in creating a program that would be tied to the available support mechanisms on campus to increase the success of students.

NEW INITIATIVES

One new initiative on the campus came from the need for data. In 2002, a report was created that showed the D, F, and W (withdraw) rate for each course offered on the campus. The report delineated the total number of students attending all class offerings for each course. For example, over a five-year period 761 students had taken the college's Introduction to Algebra class. During that timeframe 17.7% of the students taking the class withdrew, 10.0% received an "F", and 5.0% received a "D", showing that a total of 32.7% of all students did not succeed in the class.

The report, a common tool used nationwide in Supplemental Instruction, became a lightning rod for discussion for faculty on the campus. Some faculty were concerned that, because of the limited number of faculty teaching the same course over the five years, that individual faculty members might be identified. While the strategic plan emphasized maintaining the highest class standards possible, another concern was that faculty would be asked to lower standards to improve the success rates of students in certain courses. Many faculty members, despite the negative comments, looked at the data as a possible means of improving the success of their students by adjusting Supplemental Instruction, content delivery, and tutoring options. If nothing else, the data initiated a discussion on earlier intervention with students that were failing courses.

Another new campus initiative is the college's partnership with several other Michigan colleges in the Michigan Total Quality Improvement Project (MiTQIP). This group was formed to assist other colleges interested in joining AQIP, to share best practices, and develop training activities in quality methods and tools.

One of the MiTQIP projects was a course in strategic level quality training called the Gateway to CQI (Continuous Quality Improvement). West Shore Community College, working with five other Michigan colleges as benchmarking partners, developed five strategic level quality measurements that can be shared and compared with other participating colleges. The five areas include enrollment trends, continuance, student success, student satisfaction, and financial performance. The project will be piloted in the fall of 2003, and if successful, will be expanded to include all of the other Michigan community colleges.

West Shore's involvement with MiTQIP and the Gateway to CQI will have a dramatic impact on the WSCC Strategic Plan as areas of measurement for the plan's goals will have to align with the project. This will result in the need for the college's various teams to determine what data needs to be collected in order to measure success. It will be important for the college to be able to connect effectiveness and performance.

Two areas critical to student success received increased exposure due to the goals created during the strategic planning process. Because one of the goals for the strategic plan was also a main goal for the AQIP accreditation the success of at risk students became a greater priority on the campus. An At Risk Task Force was created by the Student Success Team and given the goal of first defining at risk, and then creating new methods to support the students that fell under the definition. The definition was not easy to come by for the team. The question that arose was what intangibles made a student at risk? Should the college use the definition suggested by the state, the definition used by Perkins Funds, or a definition created by the college? In addition, should students themselves be defined as at risk, or should courses be defined as at risk? Should any student struggling in any class, or in danger of leaving the college, be defined as at risk? To complicate matters, members of the task force discovered that there was already another ad hoc team on campus that had met for several years to discuss at risk students and their needs. The two teams had several common members.

The task force defined at risk students as those that have certain characteristics that negatively impact their educational goal attainment. The characteristics may be academic, physical, economic, and/or personal. The team defined seven specific criteria to help narrow the definition that included students that scored low on the ACT or ASSET test, were enrolled in developmental courses, had a grade point average below 2.0, or had withdrawn from one-third of their courses.

Meanwhile the ad hoc group decided to undertake a comprehensive study of the college's current student success program. The study had three basic components: a description of all current efforts of student success, a review of literature on student success and retention with a review of an exemplary student success program at another community college, and the development of recommendations to improve the current student success program. The recommendations included the creation of a centrally located Student Success Center that would include all student success services campus-wide, improvements to existing student success programs and developmental courses.

Running concurrently was an Advising Task Force that also reported to the Student Success Team. The task force spent the year reviewing different advising models, and gathering data, including a student survey, to use to develop a comprehensive model for West Shore. An initial implementation for the next year will include a new trial advising for potential graduates.

The college's Supplemental Instruction is run through the Learning and Testing Center, which includes a computer-learning lab and software support for many courses. In addition, various labs are run to promote student success in some of the college's most challenging courses. Meanwhile, the tutoring services are run through the STaRS program. Both peer and professional tutoring are available to students in virtually any course.

A future vision for the campus is to pull the advising, STaRS, Supplemental Instruction, assessment, and Student Services area into a single, comprehensive, student support area.

STUDENT SERVICES

The creation of the new vision and strategic plan, and the focus on student success greatly impacted the college and, in particular, the student services area on the campus. Perhaps the most noticeable impact was the shift on the campus from a more departmentally enclosed college, to one that fostered the need for the campus community to broaden its internal vision to include other areas on the campus. The teams, and the need for increased communication, helped develop a new level of cooperation as departments now needed to work more closely together on campus goals, aims, and tasks. Nearly every department was represented on each of the seven teams. Departments, and in fact, individuals, could now see where the college was headed, and relate their work more closely to the overall vision of the college.

The student service area was no longer viewed as a department that would simply support students and campus programs. Many of the new initiatives and goals were driven by the student services department. There was a greater realization that departments could complement rather than compete with other areas on the campus. There was a need for departments to become aware of other initiatives besides their own and to become a part of the progress made by other areas on the campus.

For the Student Services area, initiatives included new methodologies for the collection of data related to recruitment, retention, and enrollment. The Admissions Office began work on a comprehensive marketing and outreach plan with the director of College Relations. Members of the office served on all seven teams and were members of important task forces such as the Scheduling Task Force, the Advising Task Force, and the At Risk Task Force. The need for new technological advances led to online registration and orientation for students. The Student Services area, working closely with others on the campus, took leading roles in the areas of advising, at risk students, and course scheduling.

Perhaps the most significant impact on the Students Services area is that the offices no longer work in isolation but are now a more vital, vocal partner with others on the campus. The future of the department will be impacted because the college has plans to create a fully integrated student center that will house all of the student support areas: Student Services, STaRS, The Learning and Testing Center, incoming student assessment, and Supplemental Instruction.

RESULTS

While maintaining a steady growth in enrollment, the work done at the college in the area of student success over the past three years produced some remarkable results. The most significant result was the creation of a new vision and strategic plan, which will help lead the college into the future with a clear picture of the organization's future state, and a road map on how to get there. Targeted identifiable goals were created in the strategic plan to address the college's needs, as well as future needs, and to move the college forward. The strategic plan will be updated each year, based on an environmental scan, and will not be a simple plan that, once completed, sits on a shelf.

Another important result is the prominent role that student success now plays at the college. The concept of student success came to the forefront of the institution's planning through the identification of student needs, the work done by the Student Success Team, the need for a student-oriented project for AQIP accreditation, and the confirmation through the institutional climate survey that the campus employees supported a "students first" concept. In essence, a cultural shift occurred on the campus.

The work of the Strategic Planning Team clarified that the college had shortcomings in both data collection and marketing. To address the needs in data collection and marketing the college created two new positions: Director of Institutional Research, and Director of College Relations.

The college has initiated a move to a learner-centered environment to engage faculty and administrators in an effort to shape educational settings that actively engage all students in learning. This is a paradigm shift as the college moves from an institution that provides instruction to an institution that exists to produce learning.

The college has identified several areas that need to be strengthened to assist students in reaching their educational goals; among these are the need for a comprehensive advising model, and the creation of a more student-friendly class schedule. The Women's Resource Center was created to assist at risk students, particularly women. Money was budgeted for the creation of a new developmental math position.

An upgrade in technology provided students with the opportunity to apply for admission and register online. A new Web site will provide students with additional technological opportunities and increased information.

The college adopted a new accreditation model, AQIP, which impacted the creation of the college's strategic planning goals. One goal of the new accreditation model dealt specifically with improving the success of at risk students. The new model also requires more input from the college community, including the board of trustees.

Administrators and faculty from the college have taken a prominent lead role in the MiTQIP project and Gateway to CQI (Continuous Quality Improvement) and will work with five other Michigan colleges as benchmarking partners to develop strategic level quality measurements.

LESSONS LEARNED

There are numerous lessons that have been learned during the creation of the new vision and strategic plan.

* *Changing the culture on a campus is difficult but not impossible.* In the case at WSCC there was strong hidden support for a student success model and putting students first, which helped move the campus culture in a new direction. Naysayers sometimes have strong, loud voices but the silent majority cannot be ignored; in many cases, their voice just needs an outlet.

* *It is great to dream of the future, but hard work is needed to move toward that future.* At WSCC it would have been easy to sit back and see where the new vision and strategic plan would take the college, but it was critical to create teams to push the vision forward. There were missteps, hurt feelings, arguments, and divisional differences. However, there was also a sense of accomplishment, open communication and teamwork.

* *Without support from the top, nothing will happen.* The president and the board of trustees had to embrace the vision and the strategic plan, and believe that student success was a key to the vision for the college. When the board rejected the initial strategic plan, there were hurt feelings and lots of questions. However, through hard work, a vision and strategic plan was created that could be accepted by the board and those on the campus. Once the support of the board and president was secured, it was critical for all on the campus to also accept the plan. Communication was of the utmost importance.

* *Student Services can have a greater role on the campus than just that of a support mechanism.* The personnel from the Student Services area, serving as student advocates, gave voice to many of the ideas and concepts behind the new vision and strategic plan. They serve on each of the seven teams on the campus. They have input into most of the decision-making processes on the campus. Their role in communicating the concept of student success cannot be underestimated. Their role in initiating a cultural change, and creating a vision and strategic plan for West Shore Community College, is one based on leadership and communication.

CONCLUSION

West Shore Community College has taken a tremendous step forward through the creation of a vision and strategic plan that focuses on student success, serving the community, and pursuing greatness. The plan, with its focus on student success, takes into account a new accreditation model, the need for measurable goals, and the need for adaptability.

The creation of the plan illuminated the college's strengths and weaknesses, providing the impetus for change. While many areas have been addressed, there are new challenges for the coming years. Over the next year the strategic planning team members must be trained in such areas as budgets, assessment, and data collection in order to be able to competently revise and update the plan.

The vision and strategic plan changed the culture on the campus, and provided a road map for the future that the faculty and staff can use to move the college forward. The real winners in the process are the students.

5

STRUCTURAL, STRATEGIC, AND TACTICAL INNOVATIONS = SEM AT DEPAUL

DAVID KALSBEEK
AND JANE MCGRATH

DEPAUL DePaul University is the largest and fastest growing Catholic university in the U.S., the seventh-largest private university in the nation and the largest that is not a Research Extensive university by Carnegie classification. Now with over 23,000 students on two primary campuses in Chicago as well as a network of suburban campuses, DePaul has realized 100 years of success in its Vincentian mission of ensuring access for a wide range of Chicago's youth and working professionals to a high quality, values-based higher education. Sustained growth over its 100-year history has accelerated over the past fifteen years and is reflected in the fact that over 30% of its 100,000 alumni have graduated since 1990.

82

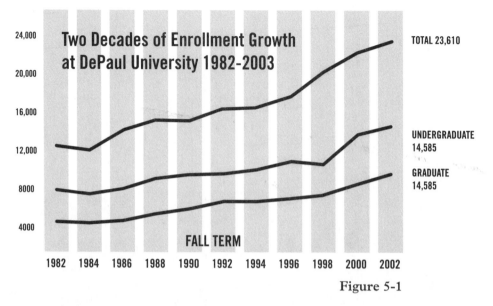

Figure 5-1

DePaul's enrollment growth, particularly in the past fifteen years, has far outpaced that of its peer institutions nationally—by a factor of twelve times the average growth of the nation's ten largest Catholic universities. Enrollment growth at DePaul is not something that has happened to institutions of DePaul's type, but rather is a direct result of a mission-based commitment to building capacity to provide access to as many qualified students as can be effectively served. Originally founded for first-generation, immigrant students in Chicago, DePaul continues to this day a commitment to the education of first-generation college students and those from diverse cultural and ethnic groups in the metropolitan area. This mission is now complemented by a robust array of master's level graduate programs designed to provide a highly reputable, flexible, practical education to working professionals in Chicago and beyond. As the needs for such education have grown in Chicago, DePaul's enrollment growth has been a reflection of a mission achieved. This is manifested most recently in doubling the freshman class since 1997, achieving a 60% increase in full-time undergraduates (building capacity for an increase of over 4,000 students), realizing unprecedented multicultural and socioeconomic diversity in the student body, achieving the largest adult baccalaureate enrollment of all private universities in Illinois, and a rapid growth of graduate students so that DePaul now has the largest masters' level enrollment in Illinois.

Achieving mission by building capacity for growth has been the result most recently of a university-wide commitment to a set of strategic goals and objectives that integrated facilities, financial, academic and enrollment planning. The commitment has paralleled the evolution of an enrollment management model that has attracted national attention as one of the more integrated, innovative approaches in American higher education. This case study offers a brief glimpse into the evolution of strategic enrollment management (SEM) at DePaul University.

The University's recent history is traced in this case study through three distinct periods, commencing with the creation of DePaul's Division of Enrollment Management in 1984 (Phase 1), continuing with a substantial recommitment to enrollment strategy in 1997 (Phase 2), and then concluding with a bold redefinition of EM and a strategic reorganization in 2000 (Phase 3). In each of these three periods or phases, this case study will describe that evolution in three ways: some of the *structural* changes in how DePaul is organized in pursuit of its enrollment goals, some of the *strategic* innovations and initiatives shaping how DePaul pursues its enrollment goals, and finally a sampling of a few of the *tactical* innovations that illustrate new approaches characterizing enrollment management activities. While these structural, strategic, and tactical elements cannot tell the entire story, they do descriptively illustrate some of the fundamental building blocks of the story of DePaul's evolving approach to SEM.

PHASE I OF STRATEGIC ENROLLMENT MANAGEMENT: 1984 – 1996

In his earliest and groundbreaking series of case studies on the emergence of enrollment management in higher education administration, Dr. Donald Hossler (1986) wrote that, "DePaul has developed the most centralized and tightly coupled enrollment management system [of the four institutions examined]. It also represents the only example of transformational change.....What has happened at DePaul is a dramatic success story." Hossler's text is the best description of the early innovations in enrollment management at DePaul.

DePaul indeed was one of the early adopters of an enrollment management model in American higher education. At the outset, enrollment management at DePaul was an institutional response to a sudden decline in enrollment between 1979 and 1983, with new student headcount dropping 30% and creating a severe budget crisis. That crisis created a platform for long-range and strategic planning—leading to a comprehensive review of external, demographic and market trends DePaul faced immediately and in the future. By 1984, DePaul recognized the need to shift from a traditional recruitment approach to an enrollment management model. The campus' response included integrating with admissions and recruitment a variety of new approaches to financial aid, yield management, adult and graduate program promotions, and retention strategies, creating a single administrative division to integrate these processes, and appointing leadership of that division at the vice presidential level, with Ms. Anne Kennedy the first to serve DePaul in that position.

These *structural changes* intended to administratively and organizationally integrate key enrollment-related functions were accompanied by a range of new **strategic** innovations.

* The early enrollment management initiative was quickly tied to a broader strategic move to strengthen DePaul by a three prong strategy of enhancing the curriculum in the College of Liberal Arts & Sciences (the academic anchor), building a more residential campus and expanding out of town recruitment.
* DePaul commenced its "suburban strategy" with the development of campuses in suburban areas designed to expand access to graduate and adult programs.
* Adult enrollment was embraced as a strategic priority, one requiring the same concerted recruitment and promotional activity as that developed for traditional undergraduates; a staff was established to coordinate adult promotions and admissions.
* New academic programs were launched, and some existing programs repositioned for strategic growth. The most notable example was DePaul's decision to remove its computer science department from the College of Liberal Arts and Sciences and create DePaul's School of Computer Science, telecommunications and information systems. Repositioning this academic program was a strategic decision intended to improve market position, increase market prominence, and realize significant growth.

Immediately upon the creation of the EM organization in 1984, not only did the enrollment decline reverse, but enrollment rebounded with a period of substantial growth, increasing from 12,300 in 1984 to 15,700 by 1990. This basic enrollment management organizational structure remained in place for over a decade, with little change in either the structure or the core enrollment strategy until 1997.

PRECIPITATING CONDITIONS, CONTEXT & CONSEQUENCES

By 1997, undergraduate and graduate enrollment had stabilized at DePaul, but annual growth in headcount was occurring at only 1–2% per year. Enrollment in 1997 was 17,800, only 8.5% greater than the 16,400 in 1991. Undergraduate enrollment held steady at about 10,500, and though entering freshmen classes remained constant at 1,200 from 1990–1996, there were several disturbing patterns underlying that stability. Specifically, minority enrollment was in decline, financial aid as a percent of tuition revenue (i.e., the tuition discount) was increasing and reducing the net revenue available to the university, and the applicant pool was not growing. Graduate enrollment likewise was fairly constant at about 7,000. While there was no budget crisis comparable to what triggered the impetus of enrollment management in 1984, the university's leadership was interested in building its capacity for further growth at both the undergraduate and graduate levels. Recognizing the need for new structures and new leadership to take enrollment management to the next level, DePaul took another set of strategic steps.

The second phase of the evolution of SEM at DePaul began with re-establishing the position of vice president of Enrollment Management, after it had been intentionally held vacant for a number of years. Dr. David Kalsbeek was named vice president for Enrollment Management in May of 1997. In making this choice, the university recommitted its resources and energy to an innovative and more strategic enrollment management model.

At the same time, DePaul developed a strategic plan known as *Vision 2006*, which outlined a model of continued enrollment growth from 17,000 to 25,000 students by the year 2006. Vision 2006 was forged around an integrated framework for growth that weaved together financial plans, facilities plans, and plans for faculty expansion and new academic programs—all predicated on and contributing to increasing student enrollment.

The strategic plan outlined two primary goals: *Goal I* was to improve the holistic educational experience for full-time undergraduates. For most of its history, DePaul had served a commuter, part-time undergraduate student body; therefore, forging a strategic goal focusing on full-time undergraduates marked an important turning point for DePaul. Goal I was to be developed by

1. building facilities to support holistic student experience, such as residence halls, recreation centers and a student center;

2. investing in pricing and aid strategies to ensure financial accessibility for a wide range of students;

3. ensuring positive career outcomes partly through expanded experiential learning;

4. developing a new liberal studies core curriculum. At the bottom line, the improvement of the quality of the full-time undergraduate experience would be funded through strategic enrollment growth.

Goal II of DePaul's *Vision 2006* was to become the dominant provider of professional education in the Chicago market—focusing primarily on graduate enrollments in masters-level programs designed for working professionals enrolling part time. This goal was to be pursued primarily through the development of distance learning technologies, expansion of suburban campuses, developing new academic programs, and improved marketing and recruitment—all of which was designed to drive enrollment growth.

So Phase 2 of strategic enrollment management at DePaul paralleled the development of a set of institutional strategic goals and aspirations that both built and built upon enrollment growth. Clearly, business as usual in the Division of Enrollment Management would not be sufficient to achieve these aggressive and ambitious goals.

STRUCTURAL INNOVATIONS

Through the early 1990s, the Office of Financial Aid was aligned organizationally within DePaul's Student Affairs' Division; though it had been part of Enrollment Management in the late 1980s, Financial Aid had been shifted back to Student Affairs as part of an initiative to improve quality services to currently enrolled students. A structural response to the new strategic focus on undergraduate enrollment growth and a renewed commitment to organizational integration for SEM was to realign Financial Aid in 1997 with Undergraduate Admissions in the Division of Enrollment Management, as is fairly typical in private universities. This realignment of Financial Aid and Admissions coincided with an endorsement in the strategic plan of the critical role of Financial Aid in realizing the mission-based enrollment goal of ensuring continued financial accessibility for first-generation and low-income students while pursuing enrollment growth. It also coincided with an institutional commitment to keeping undergraduate financial aid at a below average discount rate while pursuing goals of increased diversity and overall enrollment growth.

The second structural change was to also align the Career Planning and Placement

Center with Enrollment Management. At DePaul, as at most colleges and universities, career services operated on a combination of both a placement and a career development model. In the placement model, staff focus on job placement as a primary outcome; it is an employment service orientation with job searches as the primary activities. This model dominated the career center profession from the 1940s through the 1970s. The career development model on the other hand focuses on career planning as a primary outcome. Career counselors help students identify skills, goals, and career interests; this model dominated the profession in the 1970s to the 1990s. However, the new emerging role focuses on developing career networks, actively developing avenues and processes by which students, employers, alumni, faculty and staff all intersect in career-related activities. Through its realignment with DePaul's Enrollment Management Division, the Career Center affirmed that its primary purpose is not realized when it functions solely as a student service, but rather as a nexus for forging career networks that not only connect students with employment but also connect employers and alumni with the university.

Two related structural innovations were the reassignment of Student Employment from the Human Resources Division to Enrollment Management and the creation of a University Internship Office, both to be integrated within the newly defined Career Center. Under an HR umbrella, Student Employment was seen primarily as a means by which the university met its staffing and workforce needs. This new organizational alignment reflected DePaul's commitment to ensuring that student employment not only become more career-oriented and beneficial for student's career development but also that student employment would be an integral part of a broader strategy to help ensuring financial accessibility of a DePaul education. Aligning University Internships in the Career Center also reaffirmed the division's role in the academic enterprise.

A third example of structural change was the creation of an Enrollment Management Research (EMR) unit in the Division of Enrollment Management. Seven years earlier, the data management function was supported by two staff assistants to the vice president. By 2000, a department of six FTE (full-time equivalent) staff was built to provide information and analysis to fuel enrollment planning and the development of marketing strategy. Largely by reassigning information specialists from functional units (e.g., in the Registrar's Office, in Admissions) to EMR, DePaul created a central function to complement the work of DePaul's Office of Institutional Research in activities such as building the university's information infrastructure, reporting, research and analysis, and information dissemination.

A fourth structural change in Enrollment Management in this phase of SEM was the development of a recruitment manager model to support planned growth in graduate enrollments. This concept evolved from a review of the inefficiencies and ineffectiveness of the inquiry/app/admission/yield processes in college offices, difficulties typically inherent in highly decentralized graduate admissions processes. Four recruitment managers, professionals with mid-level enrollment management experience, were hired to be part of the EM staff, but assigned to help coordinate with the college offices the recruitment and yield activities of each of the major graduate programs targeted for strategic enrollment growth.

STRATEGIC INNOVATIONS

As the Enrollment Management Division was making structural/organizational changes to pursue a strategic vision for building capacity for access and enrollment growth, the university launched several new strategic initiatives in support of its enrollment strategy.

First, the university renewed and expanded its commitment to establishing a network of suburban campuses to provide greater access to graduate and adult programs in rapidly growing suburban regions. An expanded facility in Naperville, a new campus in Rolling Meadows, and a new campus in Lake Forest were added to the existing two suburban campuses. This expanded network of suburban campuses was established to provide access to DePaul for new adult and graduate markets and to increase market share in graduate programs.

A second example of new strategic directions undertaken to support DePaul's enrollment goals was a commitment to developing new facilities at its Lincoln Park campus. A facilities plan focused on how to best provide an enriched, holistic undergraduate learning experience and how to fund it without awaiting a capital fundraising campaign. A new state-of-the-art Recreation Center, a new comprehensive Student Center, a new athletic facility, and new residence halls all represented this strategic commitment to rapidly improving DePaul's primarily residential campus.

Third, DePaul invested in the information infrastructure needed to ensure more integrated and efficient student systems and to build capacity for continued enrollment growth. Selecting PeopleSoft as its enterprise-wide information system, in 1999 DePaul commenced and successfully completed a rapid implementation of this system in eighteen months, not only in Student Systems, but also Financial and Human Resources systems. Immediately after going live with the new system, the Office of

Student Systems and Services was created in Enrollment Management to lead the business process redesign that accompanied the PeopleSoft implementation. Through this new office, Enrollment Management began a comprehensive review and transformation of processes supporting the admission, financial aid, registration, and billing processes that together comprise the enrollment services and transactions required to achieve enrollment goals.

TACTICAL INNOVATIONS

In pursuit of this strategic vision for enrollment growth, Enrollment Management introduced a variety of tactical innovations, changing in fundamental ways its approach to achieving goals and objectives. The several tactical innovations noted below are examples of how the EM Division worked to build its own capacity to support and deliver enrollment growth.

For example, advertising resources were effectively doubled by introducing a "match funding" approach that required that every $1 in advertising spent by Enrollment Management in support of enrollment growth in a particular college had to be matched by $.50 from the college and another $.50 from Academic Affairs budgets. The intent was not only to increase advertising expenditures, but to do so in a way that helped ensure buy-in and collaboration in advertising strategy with the colleges.

The development of DePaul's predictive modeling capacity enabled more targeted freshmen recruitment by statistically qualifying its prospect pool. As is typical of predictive modeling efforts, DePaul's analysis enabled the identification of the 20–30% of the prospect database that eventually accounted for 70–80% of the eventual freshmen enrollment. This tactic allowed for more focused recruitment activities and improved efficiency in recruitment communications.

In a similar innovation, Admissions contracted with outside agencies to manage the bulk of the inquiry processing and fulfillment processes in undergraduate recruitment. Recognizing that rapidly growing interest in DePaul (10% annual increases in freshman applications, for example) would stretch staff to the breaking point in trying to reply to interest and fulfill inquiries, outsourcing this process was a means by which DePaul could build its capacity to manage growth more effectively.

The enrollment strategies introduced in 1997 contributed to significant gains in student diversity, with enrollment of minority students growing at a rate twice as great as that of non-minority students—so that by 2000, students of color represented 30 percent of enrollment. One such strategy was Enrollment Management's reallocation of resources to create in 1998 its Office of Community Outreach, a function intended to identify community programs, agencies and partners working to prepare underprivileged youth for college. Through this community outreach strategy, DePaul developed partnerships and pipelines for highly desirable students and established DePaul as a primary and preferred higher education partner for a targeted number of groups, organizations and institutions serving Chicago's communities of color. The intent was to shift from a traditional recruitment approach for minority students (e.g., direct mail, high school visits, etc.) to a pipeline strategy that elevated DePaul's visibility and attractiveness to students in programs generating large numbers of exceptionally well-prepared prospects.

New staffing positions, job descriptions and staffing configurations were developed as the primary tactical response to all of these new structures and strategies. Twenty percent of the division's current workforce is due to growth. Further, by 2000, over 70% of all professional positions in EM had been formally redefined or redirected in pursuit of new enrollment tactics. For example, a joint position that straddles Admission and Financial Aid was created in order to better manage the process of freshman aid packaging and scholarship awarding. The marketing team created an Internet communications director to work in concert with directors of advertising, recruitment publications, and editorial services in order to integrate Web development with the rest of the marketing communications strategy. Traditional career counselor positions were redirected to cultivate a network of alumni volunteers to assist students in career pursuits.

PHASE III 2000–2004

By 2000, the strategic, structural and tactical innovations were paying off in dramatic fashion, with a total enrollment exceeding 20,000. A tremendous 60% growth in full-time undergraduate enrollment was accompanied by a 30% increase in graduate enrollments, propelling DePaul to have the largest enrollment of masters' level students in all of Illinois, over 30% larger than the flagship University of Illinois-Urbana. But three particular factors triggered another evolutionary stage in DePaul's strategic approach to enrollment management.

The first factor was the way in which DePaul's enrollment grew from 1997–2000. DePaul's overall enrollment growth at both the undergraduate and graduate level, while substantial, was sufficiently imbalanced so that it created increasingly apparent challenges in the net revenue stream. DePaul's graduate-level growth had been particularly spurred by spiraling demand among part-time students in a variety of masters' programs in the university's School of Computer Science, telecommunications, and information systems (CTI), coinciding with the so-called dot-com boom. Since MBA and other professional programs remained fairly stable or declined, much of the enrollment growth in high-margin masters' programs was concentrated in volatile technology fields. Meanwhile, the extraordinary growth among full-time undergraduates was in programs that produced relatively modest marginal tuition revenues. All of this heightened DePaul's sensitivity to the importance of more aggressive and better balanced pursuit of "Goal II" growth (i.e., enrollment in graduate and professional programs) across all colleges.

Second, the board of trustees became increasingly concerned about the perceived lack of university-wide marketing strategy. While recognizing the great success of the marketing strategies in support of student recruitment, the lack of integration of other critical communications vehicles and an insufficient attention to clarifying institutional brand became a topic of concern at the board level. In addition, as DePaul's tuition pricing in certain graduate programs pushed upper limits relative to competitors, it was recognized that enhanced brand marketing would be required to support and sustain such price points. Across the institution, the deans of the schools and colleges were also becoming increasingly insistent upon expanded marketing investments for their individual programs. As the pressure for enrollment growth in high-margin masters' programs increased, so did the pressure from the academic units on Enrollment Management for more marketing research and financial support for growth at the college and program level.

Third, DePaul's leadership had to grapple with the consequences of the resignation of the fifth vice president for Advancement in six years. Fundraising was stalled, alumni participation continued to erode, and various university relations functions were increasingly disconnected from the core elements of institutional growth and success. The university faced an opportunity to develop new structural, organizational alignments for such critical functions as alumni relations and media relations, alignments that would bring different—and hopefully greater—strategic advantage than what is typically found in advancement organizations.

STRUCTURAL INNOVATIONS
With a board-approved decision to center institutional marketing in the Enrollment Management Division, a new era for Enrollment Management commenced, one that

began with a broadened focus on strategic marketing issues and led directly to a wholesale redefinition of Enrollment Management.

The first structural innovation was one that coupled with EM's enrollment-focused marketing functions (e.g. recruitment publications, advertising, Web development) those marketing-related functions previously in University Relations under the Advancement umbrella (e.g., special events, media relations, public relations, alumni communications). The alignment of all of these functions in one division set the stage for a heightened level of strategic integration in the university's external communications with multiple audiences and constituencies.

The second structural innovation was the creation, in the Division of Enrollment Management, of the Office of Marketing Strategy, a leadership unit with a goal of developing integrated marketing strategy across the university. This unit quickly evolved to be a four-person team of marketing professionals with the singular responsibility of assembling and directing market research, coordinating cross-functional planning teams, and documenting marketing strategy in written marketing plans for various institutional partners, including schools and colleges but also including areas such as Athletics.

The third structural innovation in this phase of enrollment management was the alignment of Alumni Relations with Enrollment Management. DePaul recognized that alumni form an influential constituency that should receive the same kind of strategic focus as prospective students in the university's marketing efforts. The traditional organizational alignment of "advancement" treats alumni as "prior students/future donors" and the primary outcome of the university's relationship with alumni is traditionally defined via charitable giving. DePaul's evolving orientation to SEM led to embracing alumni as continuing learners—and lifelong customers whose relationship with the university does not change dramatically upon commencement. In the language of CRM (customer relationship management), it became more important to gain a share of each alum's lifetime education (as well as tuition payments) than just a share of their charitable contributions; the fact that annual tuition revenue from DePaul alumni returning for a graduate degree was ten times greater than the level of alumni giving to the Annual Fund further accentuated the business sensibility of this point.

The fourth, but related, structural innovation was the integration of Alumni Relations and the Career Center under an organizational umbrella of Alumni and Career

Networks. Back in 1997, DePaul recognized that the fundamental function and purpose of the Career Center is the development of a network of connections by which students' career paths can best unfold. By 2000, DePaul also recognized that a base of 100,000 alumni, 80% residing locally in the Chicago area, constituted the foundation of that career network which in turn constituted a part of DePaul's perceived brand value among prospective students. And with so many of DePaul's alumni in entry to mid-manager professional roles (30% of DePaul's 100,000 alumni having graduated in the past ten years), the critical mass of alumni likewise find great value in reconnecting with DePaul around issues of career and professional networks. Aligning these two units both organizationally and physically was a structural innovation that could lead directly to a wide range of new strategic opportunities.

STRATEGIC INNOVATIONS

The first strategic innovation resulting from this structural alignment was the formal redefinition of the mission of the Division of Enrollment Management at DePaul. Statements of the mission of administrative divisions serve an important strategic function of providing clarity and direction for departmental activities, of elevating the importance of some activities over others, and of forging a sense of common purpose and integration between areas that might not otherwise see their connectedness. Clearly, with so many new departments added to this organization ranging from Media Relations to Alumni Networks, traditional connotations and definitions of Enrollment Management were no longer sufficient to build that common purpose. Focusing primarily on enrollment outcomes as the mission of the division was not adequate to take full and strategic advantage of this wider range of functions. What emerged was a redefinition of EM as a process that seeks to define, enhance and improve the institution's market position and prominence. The goal of EM, therefore, became not to achieve the freshman enrollment goal, for example, but rather to elevate and enhance DePaul's position and prominence within the market of high school seniors; what results in the number, diversity, and quality of the freshman class is a function of DePaul's market position as much as it is a result of EM efforts—and that market position is established and reinforced through functions such as media relations, public relations, alumni relations, etc. Defining EM as a strategic process focused on elevating market position and prominence provided a meaningful framework for integrating enrollment-related functions such as admissions and financial aid with functions such as marketing, alumni relations, media relations, etc.

A second strategic innovation characterizing the evolution of this third phase of SEM at DePaul is the recognition of how developing new academic programs is fundamentally a SEM activity. Traditional academic models have new degree programs (new academic products, if you will) developing through a faculty-centered or curriculum-centered process that is often disengaged from market research and enrollment planning. DePaul has long embraced the development of new academic programs as a key to meeting the changing needs of Chicago and as a way of ensuring current and contemporary curricula; in fact, the currency of curricula is a well-documented dimension of DePaul's brand. As a result, about 30% of all graduate degrees granted at DePaul in 2000 were in programs created in the prior ten years. So in a joint venture between EM and Academic Affairs, an integrated, multiphase process for developing new academic programs was defined and developed. This process is intended to achieve optimal levels of connection between faculty developing course content and the curriculum for new degree programs on the one hand and solid market research and enrollment planning on the other hand. That integration ensures that there is clear evidence of market demand, that new programs are developed and priced in a way that can be competitively positioned relative to others in the marketplace, and that enrollment at the outset is as robust as possible through an appropriate ramp up of marketing strategy. New academic programs proposed for future development are more intentionally managed through a "gestation process" designed to bring a necessary and valuable level of marketing discipline to the creative academic process.

A third strategic innovation was the investment in brand research, recognizing that at such a rapidly growing, multi-campus, highly decentralized institution there are many factors that tug against having a clear, cohesive and consistent brand identity in the market. DePaul invested in a multiyear effort to explore, document and test how to optimally leverage its brand identity across multiple colleges and programs, how to build a brand architecture that supports institutional goals while ensuring flexible platforms for specific colleges to position themselves relative to competitors, and how to reconcile any disconnection between the brand as perceived in the market and the institution's strengths and weaknesses. The resulting marketing plans serve as the foundation of future university strategic planning.

A fourth strategic advance in this period was further transformation at DePaul's primary Chicago campuses. The completion of a new Student Center, a new Athletic Center, a new Recreation Center, and a range of new and renovated residence halls completed the university's strategic investment in the facilities at the Lincoln Park campus required to not only enhance the holistic nature of undergraduate life at

DePaul but also to build capacity for further enrollment growth. As the development of the Lincoln Park campus reached completion, DePaul began developing its Loop campus into a residential destination for the first time, with the launch of the University Center of Chicago, a 1,700 student residential development in partnership with nearby Roosevelt University and Columbia College.

DePaul's espoused mission has long been providing access to students, typically first generation and low-income students, who otherwise would not have the opportunity for a quality educational experience. With a freshman class about 33% minority students, 40% first generation, and 30% Pell recipients, DePaul has been able to realize this mission while simultaneously achieving the often-competing goals of increased net revenue, improved academic profile, etc. A new strategic innovation was the integration of two TRIO programs—Special Student Services and McNair Scholars—in the Enrollment Management Division. Organizationally associated with the Career Center and with Financial Aid, these two federally funded programs provide DePaul with opportunities to learn what works best in serving these students at the core of the mission. In particular, the centering of these TRIO programs in EM has served to elevate the institution's sensitivity to and progress toward its espoused goals of access for these populations in innovative, strategic ways.

TACTICAL INNOVATIONS

During this most recent period of rapid change and expansion of Enrollment Management's strategic role at DePaul, a wide range of tactical innovations was developed.

A critical innovation is the refocusing of the enrollment research function. Building off of the EM Division's mission of market position and prominence, the research agenda began to focus more on developing metrics for market position; this includes new approaches to assessing competitive market position in ways beyond simple enrollment overlap or pricing hierarchies, new approaches to mapping market presence and visibility, and new approaches to documenting market performance relative to DePaul's competitive set. This shift in research focus manifests itself in a different array of research methods and techniques than when EM had enrollment and enrollment analysis as its primary focus.

A second tactical shift stemming from this new strategic orientation is the development of alumni networks as the means of engaging alumni in educationally and professionally purposeful ways. Enrollment Management's marketing orientation spawned a range of research that focused on alumni as a market, as a target audience to be understood in its collectivity and via meaningful segments. This was a radical departure from the alumni research focus typical of a development orientation, which focuses on "prospect research"—finding the "n of 1" high potential donor. A market research orientation to alumni results in a clearer understanding of alumni values, wants and needs, in turn spawning entirely new approaches to alumni programs. The focus on alumni networks rather than traditional alumni associations represents a new tactic stemming from the alignment of Alumni Relations with Enrollment Management.

With the redefinition of enrollment management to include a focus on market position and prominence, another tactical innovation was building a process for developing "integrated marketing plans." Beginning with colleges slated for enrollment growth and revenue outcomes, a cross-functional, inter-departmental team of EM professionals was assembled to work with the dean and college staff to develop the annual marketing plan. The team, coordinated by a member of the Marketing Strategy Office, includes professionals representing the core functional areas of recruitment and admissions, advertising and marketing communications, alumni relations, media and public relations, and research. This team meets quarterly with college colleagues to develop written marketing plans that incorporate the roles and responsibilities of the entire array of EM units to further the college's goals and objectives.

Finally, Enrollment Management seized the opportunity to frame a tactical response to the mission-based strategy of financial accessibility, the complexity and scope of which challenges the entire university community. Using data as the foundation, Enrollment Management developed a "Financial Accessibility Workshop Series," intended to identify the interrelated enrollment challenges of ensuring access, affordability and diversity while maximizing enrollment yield, net tuition and market position; this workshop series is designed to effectively stimulate and frame strategic dialogue. The workshop series has had a number of audiences including faculty, deans, student affairs staff, board members, and strategic planning committees. Approximately 100 university leaders and influencers have participated in the Financial Accessibility Workshop Series, and thereby gained a comprehensive understanding of these complex challenges that are at the crux of SEM planning.

Today's Division of Enrollment Management is much different than just seven years ago. The following organizational chart (Figure 5-2) illustrates the complexity and uniqueness of the division.

FIGURE 5-2

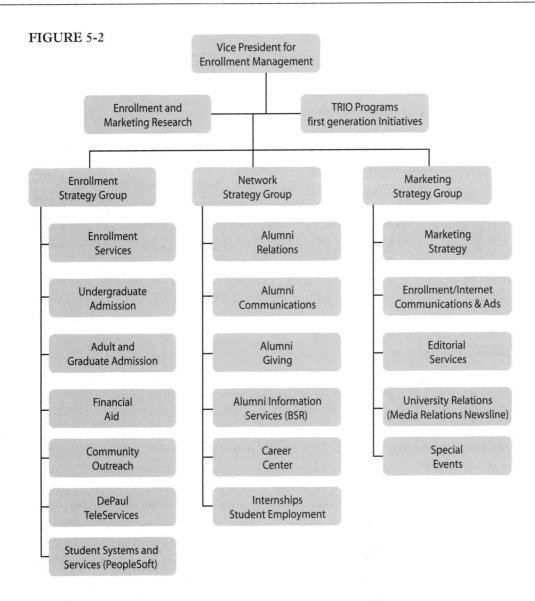

LESSONS LEARNED

In a relatively brief span of time, the scope and focus of Enrollment Management both as a concept and a division at DePaul has evolved significantly. Some of that evolution has been in response to changing external challenges and opportunities. But most of the changing structural, strategic and tactical approaches have resulted from deliberate choices to align under an EM umbrella a wide array of functions often not explicitly linked with enrollment management. At an institution that depends upon tuition for over 85% of its revenue, aligning critical functions such as brand marketing and alumni relations with the university's core business is not only strategic, but common sense. Yet the organizational evolution at DePaul is unique enough that perhaps valuable lessons can be learned from its recent history and success.

One lesson is that a primary obstacle to this type of evolution is the power of firmly entrenched mental models or professional paradigms that resist organizational transformation and realignment—mental models that often function as blinders that screen out new strategic possibilities and opportunities. The deep professional allegiance of Career Center professionals with theories of student development or of Alumni Relations professionals with development are difficult to overcome, despite the benefits of alternative alignments and structures. As Peter Senge has pointed out, organizations are the way they are because of how we think—so beginning to challenge and change complex organizations begins by addressing the prevailing mental models that dictate how we think about the work we do.

A second and related lesson is that organizational structures matter. Many enrollment management organizations work collaboratively across organizational boundaries with their colleagues in marketing or in alumni relations, for example.   But it is only by an organizational, structural integration that these functions can be strategically realigned, redefined, refocused in ways that transform them—and simultaneously transform enrollment management, and in turn transform the strategic futures of the institutions where it is practiced.

A third lesson is the power of information. DePaul's recent enrollment management success is largely the result of its commitment to research and analysis, investments in information systems, data-based planning and metrics-based management. DePaul's approach to everything from marketing strategy to financial aid and accessibility, from alumni giving to yield management, is rooted in a comprehensive commitment to developing competitive intelligence and cultivating a culture of organizational learning.

Finally, a fourth lesson is the need for a flexible organizational structure that is agile and market-responsive. Jim Black wrote in "Defining Enrollment Management: The Structural Frame" that, "David Kalsbeek's (2001) introduction of the concept of 'de-jobbing' to the field of enrollment management suggests a shift from rigid organizational structures and silos they tend to produce, to a more fluid and nimble organization where employee roles and even the structures in which they reside morph to address institutional challenges and opportunities. In this environment, job responsibilities correspond to a particular project or initiative regardless of the individual's organizational affiliation." Clearly, the lessons and perspectives discussed in Kalsbeek's essay on the future workforce of SEM have been at the core of much of DePaul's most recent evolution in SEM.

Combined, these lessons will continue to guide Enrollment Management into the next phase of DePaul's evolution. As this case study goes to press, DePaul is launching a new strategic planning initiative to frame its preferred future for 2012 and is beginning, as well, to search for a new president. Just as in 1984, this 2004 planning process is commencing with a comprehensive review of the structural, strategic and tactical challenges and opportunities facing Enrollment Management. New structural alignments for SEM and new investments in specific EM strategies will be guided by a new set of university enrollment goals and aspirations, goals that will be built on DePaul's prior success, informed by its prior experience, guided by its Vincentian mission, and designed to respond strategically to the array of demographic, economic, political, competitive, financial and organizational challenges and opportunities now facing the university.

REFERENCES

Black, J. (October 2003). Defining Enrollment Management: The Structural Frame [Online]. Available: http://www.aacrao.org/sem13/whitePapers.htm.

Hossler, D. (1986). Creating Effective Enrollment Management Systems. New York: College Entrance Examination Board.

Senge, P. M. (1990). The Fifth Discipline: The Art & Practice of the Learning Organization. New York: Currency Doubleday.

6

WE EAT CHANGE FOR BREAKFAST

KATHRYN H. BAUGHER

BELMONT

University is a private, religiously affiliated, comprehensive university located in Nashville, Tennessee. With an enrollment of approximately 3,600 in the fall of 2003, the university is in the midst of an aggressive growth phase encompassing headcount growth, facilities growth and improvement, endowment growth, program evaluation and enhancement.

Belmont was one of the early innovators among educational institutions to examine and put into practice the principles of Continuous Quality Improvement or Total Quality Management. This period of study, adoption and implementation brought significant changes and improvements to the university throughout the 1990s. The basis for most of the initiatives in the area of strategic enrollment management grew out of this early commitment.

THE CONTEXT

In January 1993, Belmont brought on board a new dean of Admissions with the expressed directive to bring together the various enrollment offices under a common structure and to bring about change with the administrative database. Additionally, the university administration desired to shift the overall enrollment pattern of the university toward more traditional 18–22 year-old students while maintaining and enhancing programs for adult and graduate students.

Throughout its history, Belmont University has been fortunate to have upward growth in its enrollment. In the 1980s, this trend continued without much planning and improvement due primarily to the hard work of dedicated Admissions counselors. Belmont Admissions focused on the students that came to them. Sporadic purchasing of names and a few attempts in various marketing venues yielded few results. There was no deliberate plan for marketing.

As Belmont moved into an era of continuous improvement in the late '80s and early '90s, the Admissions staff began to examine their processes. With new leadership in 1993, a definite plan began to emerge for developing geographic territories, building the prospect base for entering freshmen, and shoring up data for enrollment prediction and reporting.

The situation in 1993–94 was troubling. The prospect pool, a mere 4,000, was expected to yield nearly 1,000 enrolling students annually. The contacting series of letters and phone calling was antiquated and out of touch with current students' interests. The recruiting literature was one-dimensional, lacking the ability to accurately portray the university. Admissions processing of all types from requests for information to applications was convoluted and unimaginably complex. A great deal of change was required—quickly.

The period between 1994 and 1996 was a time of critical development for the enrollment services offices at Belmont; in 1994–95, a study was completed to recommend an integrated database system for the university. With the selection of SCT Banner, a new way of doing business was about to emerge. Concurrently with this study came the completion of the initial Student Services Streamlining report. This report was commissioned to identify student needs and demand and shape a plan for streamlining and improving student services. A three-phase action plan was designed which included what could be done immediately, what could be done in the near-term and what would be coming down the road with advancements in technology. This report was the genesis for Belmont Central (the university's one-stop student service center) in 1995–96: the creation of Student Financial Services, and the foundation work for the entire Division of Enrollment Services and the current Web-based services

THE STORY

What follows from this point is a collection of actions and decisions in sequential order. One can begin to see how these actions and decisions build on and influence one another. The steps taken at Belmont to move forward in enrollment management may not be necessary in other organizations.

THE DECISION TO PURCHASE SCT BANNER
—A DECISION TO DRIVE THE UNIVERSITY FORWARD

The Belmont team that studied and recommended the purchase of the SCT Banner system, as well as the administrative group that agreed and purchased the system, did so with several points of deliberation:

1. the team did not want a system that would be modified to mirror the way it currently did its work; it wanted one that drove us toward improvement;
2. the team was not willing to purchase a huge mainframe system but instead, was looking for a client/server model;
3. the team was not going to add staff to implement nor was it going to outsource the implementation;
4. the team intended to install a comprehensive system that was exceptionally capable in all areas, exactly as it was designed to work with essentially no revision that would drive up costs or cause later problems; and
5. the team would move as quickly as prudent to design each upgrade of the system purchased to make full use of the investment and to avoid lags in services of some modules.

Since its original purchase, Belmont has successfully installed almost all modules available in the current system, including Web features and imaging technology. It has done so by utilizing existing staff to manage and actually "do" the implementation; therefore, Belmont knows its system and knows how to troubleshoot the problems or issues encountered. The team's ability to innovate and be efficient has been enhanced by this approach to implementation. Particularly in the areas of enrollment services, this technology has been pushed to its capacity and the division has been pushed by the technology toward better services for students.

THE STUDENT SERVICES STREAMLINING REPORT

During the spring of 1994, the dean of Admissions, the registrar and the director of Financial Aid met numerous times to discuss the possibility of combining certain internal functions of each operation. The goal of these discussions was to examine the possibility of reducing duplicate functions as they related to enrollment services. Additionally, during the summer of 1994, the vice president for Quality came in contact with a student services center on the campus of Northwest Missouri State University that she felt held some promise for ways the offices of the division could work together. In August of 1994, the president commissioned a team of front-line employees led by the director of Financial Aid to study and recommend ways to streamline student services. The report from this team reflected three phases of implementation—those to begin immediately, near term solutions, and long-range solutions. This report served as the springboard for the creation of Belmont Central and for numerous improvements in the years to follow. This original thinking drove an ongoing sense of improvement and change.

THE CREATION OF BELMONT CENTRAL
—ENDING THE RUN-AROUND AND DOING MORE WITH LESS

Belmont Central was created in 1995 from the Student Services Streamlining report. The campus knew it would be several years before the ideal computer system was in place at Belmont, and also that it had to affect a human solution to the problems students were facing with administrative run-around. Belmont Central became that solution. Part of the Registrar's Office was taken and converted for this space, and four employees were transferred from the "home offices" of Admissions, Financial Aid, Student Accounts, and Records to create the first group of Belmont Central coordinators. No new personnel were added. The way work was done was literally reconfigured. Students were thrilled with the ability to go to one office to transact nearly every administrative process with the university—check on financial aid awards, pay the bill, drop/add classes, etc.

Since that time Belmont Central's work has changed dramatically. Many of the processes that had to be transacted in person can now be done on-line. But especially at a private university like Belmont, people want to talk with people, especially when they have questions or concerns about their registration, housing, or bill. Belmont Central continues to be the face of administrative processes and the voice on the other end of the phone to explain a bill to a parent, to answer a question about graduation require-ments, or to help a student through the registration process. The work of Belmont Central continues to be evaluated as well. In 2002, an additional employee was needed in the Registrar's Office due to new work recently added there. Belmont Central's work had changed so dramatically due to technology, one of those employees moved into the necessary position in the Registrar's Office—leaving three employees in Belmont Central. Efficiency and effectiveness in processes and staffing continue to be sought.

THE CREATION OF STUDENT FINANCIAL SERVICES —MANAGING PROCESSES BY ANSWERING QUESTIONS

As the enrollment division continued to examine processes and look for ways to streamline forms and work to better serve students, they stumbled upon a way of managing this kind of change that has served them well. They ask questions. They uncover the questions students and families ask as they are moving through campus processes and try to design the processes to answer these questions. Obviously, the entire division answers the question, "How do I enroll at Belmont?", but, more specifically, students and families have specific questions like "How do I register for classes?", "How do I get a room and a meal plan?", or "How do I pay my bill?" By uncovering these questions, one can begin to see where this same question is asked in multiple offices and look for ways to combine and streamline those services into one location. Such is the case with Student Financial Services.

In 1995, the offices of Financial Aid and Student Accounts were separate from one another—just as most colleges and universities did at the time. But both of these offices answer the question—"How do I pay my bill?" And in most colleges and universities, they bounce a student back and forth between the two offices until the student can determine the answer. Belmont's solution was to combine the functions of these offices into one area and train the counselors in that area to know the process from beginning to end. One person can sit down with the student, review the charges on her account for accuracy, review her financial aid award, make sure all paperwork is completed, tell her about payment plans, etc. The counselor shares all the options for managing financial obligations.

Of course there are restrictions on how the accounting area is managed in order to comply with standard accounting principles, but that has been done easily. A shared leadership model in that area with a different look to the reporting structure is present. The director of Student Financial Services has a background in both financial aid and student accounts. She directly manages the student account functions of the office. The associate director of Student Financial Services is the director of Financial Aid. She manages the day-to-day operations of the office and all of the usual financial aid functions. But what it really takes for this to work well is a commitment to student service—understanding that this is the best way to deliver services to students and working on how to work together to accomplish that. And the financial bottom line has benefited from this structure as well. Complexity and outstanding debt to the university continues to decline while the overall revenues continue to soar due to growth.

THE CREATION OF THE ENROLLMENT SERVICES COUNCIL AND THE ENROLLMENT DIVISION—MANAGING THE SPACE IN-BETWEEN

In the midst of these changes, it became apparent that a new division was emerging and that new ways of managing would be needed. In 1996, the Division of Enrollment Services was created and the Enrollment Services Council (ESC) was formed to provide leadership. This council meets bi-weekly for two hours. Key to that early formation was the development of partnership agreements to manage shared processes. While it is true that various offices within the division manage various tasks, it is also true that they own "front" and "rear" parts of each other's processes. For example, the Admissions Office inputs all data from an application into the software system. These data eventually become the foundation for the student record owned by the Registrar's Office. If Admissions does not get it right, the Registrar's Office begins with faulty data in the system. It became evident that "the space in-between" should be managed better.

To undertake this task, a process and associated paperwork called partnership agreements were formed. The offices worked together to identify areas that shared processes and to locate where the processes needed improvement. Then the partners sat down together and described the "ideal end state" from both points of view. They identified key requirements and ways to measure progress. Then regular reports on these key measures were made.

What a difference the partnership agreements made. Instead of improving individual offices, they were working together to improve the whole process. They measured and improved and then normalized some processes so that measurements were no longer needed. They made partnership agreements with other areas of the university that affected the work they do, such as Data and Information Systems, and Finance and Accounting. They added new processes and measured those. They learned to focus on the overall process and not just their small corner of the world. Every two weeks at the ESC meeting they talked about what was working and not working—without pointing fingers or placing blame on other offices because they learned that they all had a stake in the success or failure. It is possible to have the very best office of admissions, and financial aid, and registrar, etc. in the country and not have the best enrollment division because these groups do not know how to manage the hand-offs or the "spaces in-between."

STRATEGIC PLANS—THE VALUE
OF PLANNING FOR AND GAUGING YOUR SUCCESS

In 1992–93, Belmont undertook a strategic planning initiative to map out a direction for the next ten years. Actually having achieved most of those goals within five years, another strategic plan was put forth in 1999. Both of these plans included significant sections related to enrollment in both traditional and nontraditional programs, such as growing the traditional-aged undergraduate population, adding health science graduate programs, and examining and updating offerings for nontraditional learners. After the adoption of the 1993 plan and with the employment of the new dean, a strategic enrollment marketing/management plan was written for the first time. Throughout the 1990s, Belmont focused on enrollment management to build a stronger traditional undergraduate program, a solid adult education component and strong graduate schools. The focus was more on FTE enrollment growth of undergraduates than on headcount. After the adoption of the 1999 plan and with the coming of a new president, a one-year study of enrollment growth was conducted and in 2001, a strategic enrollment growth plan was written which has guided work since that time.

Every year since 1993, enrollment goals of all kinds have been outlined and progress toward these goals has been noted. These range from overall headcount growth in various programs to the implementation of document imaging in admissions to estab-lishment of a Minority Recruitment Task Force and so on. This type of road map is critical in planning. It is also extremely useful for tracking accomplishments and for sharing your story with new employees to help them gain perspective and direction.

NEW PRESIDENT AND NEW INITIATIVES
—THE ENERGIZING FORCE OF CHANGE

Dr. Robert Fisher joined the Belmont community in 2000 as president of the university. One of the charges given to him by the board of trustees at the time of his hiring was to grow the university from a headcount enrollment of 3,000 to 4,000. Dr. Fisher's charge to the university was to embrace this challenge and the other growth opportunities facing Belmont, such as endowment growth and facilities expansion. While there is always some fear and angst in the midst of such challenges, the university community began gearing up to take on this charge.

The creation of the Enrollment Growth Plan, the creation of the Enrollment Services Council (ESCX), the "Good to Great" discussion and the development of the Flywheel team are all strategies employed to tackle the latest challenge. In the midst of these strategies, headcount enrollment has surged from 3,026 in 1999 to 3,629 in Fall 2003. Over 400 residential spaces have been added; a 5,000-seat arena and new student life center have been completed; a parking structure was built and plans are underway for additional classroom spaces, a theatre and additional residence space.

THE ENROLLMENT GROWTH PLAN—THE FIRST STEP IN THE JOURNEY

Once the growth challenge had been issued, a study was conducted and a five-year enrollment growth plan was developed. The study included data from national sources about majors of choice for college-going students, how the university's population measured against expected enrollments, strengths and weaknesses of its programs, etc. From this the division determined possible areas for enrollment growth and were able to adopt strategies to assist it. Stepped goals for every type of student enrollments were established including initial enrollment goals, retention goals and graduation rates. For example, freshman headcount enrollment was 426 in 1999; subsequent annual goals have been 460, 500, 540, 575, 600, 630 and 650 in Fall 2006. Actual enrollments have been 426 in 1999, 469, 491, 525, and 603 in Fall 2003. Obviously from this, Belmont realizes that enrollment does not grow in nice, clean steps but rather in fits and spurts, but it is helpful to see where the campus is as it moves toward its ultimate goal of 4,000 total headcount in 2006.

Nine areas were addressed in the enrollment growth plan with specific strategies identified in each area. These nine included:
1. increase freshman class size,
2. improve recruiter effectiveness,
3. develop prospects,
4. increase size and limit volatility of traditional transfer population,
5. maintain and enhance University College enrollment,
6. reverse downward trend in graduate program enrollment,
7. target academic programs in recruitment,
8. centralize direction of all recruitment efforts and personnel, and
9. strategically employ scholarship funds.

In addition to the initial intake activities, action plans were also developed for retention. Six areas were identified in this venue, again with strategic plans deployed for each area. The six areas included: provide exceptional customer service, foster engagement with the local community, expand and enhance residence life, foster engaging campus life, promote academic life, and improve attention to at risk students.

The growth plan is monitored on an ongoing basis and is formally updated each year and distributed widely. Two groups play key roles in the persistent focus provided to the enrollment growth plan—the Provost's Council and the Enrollment Leadership Team. The Enrollment Leadership Team manages the enrollment growth plan at the strategic level while the Provost's Council works with the enrollment growth initiatives as part of its normal work. The Enrollment Leadership Team meets on a bi-monthly basis to consider the enrollment growth plan and other enrollment services issues. This group comprises the dean of Enrollment Services, provost, president, and senior associate to the president and director of Special Initiatives. This group considers on-going indicators, manages strategic initiatives, plans for changes and budgets for initiatives. The Provost's Council is a work group composed of all the academic deans, the dean of Enrollment Services, the dean of Students, director of Institutional Research, provost and associate provost. This group meets weekly for two hours to manage all aspects of student life and enrollment, including academic life. Part of the work done by the Provost's Council is to manage the initiatives of the enrollment growth plan. The resource allocation study to be discussed later in this chapter is also a function of this group. This constant management and review of the enrollment growth plan makes it a living document that informs decision-making and action throughout the university. Belmont is clear about its goals and its progress and can plan accordingly.

THE CREATION OF THE EXPANDED ENROLLMENT SERVICES COUNCIL (ESCX)—LINKAGE AND ALIGNMENT WITH ACADEMIC PROGRAMS

Over the course of five to six years, the Enrollment Services Division and the Enrollment Services Council had become extremely functional and normalized. Work with the academic programs was sporadic, however, due to turnover in administrative functions on the academic side and a lack of ability to dedicate personnel specifically to student-based administrative functions. A few of the colleges added "Student Services liaisons" or "directors of Student Services" to coordinate these functions, but there was no common structure to accomplish goals. In 2001, with the complete support of the academic program, the dean of Enrollment Services solicited appointments from the deans for representatives to join an Expanded Enrollment Services Council (ESCX). This group meets bi-weekly, alternately with the Enrollment Services Council. Information is exchanged and projects can be undertaken with easy access for input from these personnel. Graduate programs, undergraduate programs, adult and continuing education, Data and Information Services, and all Enrollment Services offices are represented here. This group has developed a common graduate application and data entry process, common information packets for admitted and deposited students, and is currently working on a Web site for advisors to access all administrative information. Spreading out the information and the responsibility for the work of student enrollment issues has made partners of folks in the academic areas.

THE GOOD TO GREAT DISCUSSION—SHAPING NEW CONVERSATIONS

Jim Collins' recent book *Good to Great* has laid the foundation for recent discussion at Belmont and has helped to shape the way the campus talks and thinks about its work. The goal is to continue to refine the vision and mission, to continue to discover those things about which it is passionate and about which it can become the best in the world. The concepts laid out in Collins' book have been helpful in this regard. Two concepts particularly, the hedgehog concept and the flywheel, have helped to shape these conversations and provide a common language for strategic thinking. They have spent more than a year discussing the three questions of the hedgehog: "What are you passionate about? What can you be the best at the world at doing? What drives your economic engine?" Literally hundreds of conversations and discussions have spun around these questions, and solid answers to these for Belmont have surfaced. Obviously, once these questions have been answered, there is a strong foundation for decision-making on all other fronts.

THE FLYWHEEL TEAM—DEVELOPING STRATEGIC MARKETING

Jim Collins' concept of the flywheel described in his book, *Good to Great*, was adopted by the university marketing team as its driving force and subsequently its name. The concept of the flywheel is that of the smaller wheel that takes great effort to start and which starts slowly, but over time begins spinning faster and faster and ultimately turns all the other wheels of an engine or machine. For Belmont, aligning all the marketing efforts of the university and coordinating its efforts was seen as crucial to the overall effort at the university. Getting the wheel of effective marketing spinning faster and more effectively could drive the other wheels forward.

Members of the Flywheel Team represent all areas of the university that participate in extensive marketing. Additionally a larger group has formed of all those people at the university that do any type of marketing or advertising. This larger group meets semi-annually to receive updates and information from the flywheel team relative to respective marketing directions. Members of the Flywheel Team include representatives from Athletics, academic programs, Enrollment Services, adult degree programs, Student Affairs, Development, Church Relations, and University Marketing and Communications staff. Sharing information across areas this diverse is a key purpose of this group. Projects undertaken by or coordinated through the Flywheel Team have included a total revamp of the university Web site and creation of an intranet site for non-marketing needs of the university, confirmation of the university "brand promise," update of the university logo and athletic logo, revision of admissions recruiting literature, development of advertising campaign for "brand" marketing, development of a tracking system for all advertising, and development of a budget system to track all advertising expenditures.

THE RESOURCE ALLOCATION STUDY—PUTTING OUR MOUTH AND MONEY WHERE OUR ENERGY AND PASSION ARE

During the Fall 2002 semester, Belmont began a complete review of the university academic program, particularly focused on alignment with the vision and mission; alignment with the hedgehog concept; measurable data related to outcomes, revenue generation, quality indicators, demand and demographics, etc. The purpose of the review is to bring resources in alignment with purposes—that support is increased for programs of great quality in order to grow and bring revenue to the university and those that can add value to students' lives. In effect, some programs are sustained, and some are revamped or closed.

LESSONS LEARNED

With so much change and limited resources, what are the lessons Belmont has learned that could be helpful to others?

WITH MATURITY OF SYSTEMS
COMES THE ABILITY TO INNOVATE AND BE FLEXIBLE

Because a Continuous Improvement initiative was begun in 1990 and most of these changes have been natural progressions of that initiative, Belmont has been at this for a long time. And real change takes time. Development of strong systems takes time. Once strong systems have been developed, you can see how to tweak and turn your systems to make them more flexible. You can see the next step in your journey of progress. When you are starting out, you frequently are stepping by faith, but you will get to a point of real progress if you stay the course over time.

GET THE RIGHT PEOPLE FOR THE JOB—NO MATTER WHAT IT TAKES

Many changes have been made at Belmont in the past ten years, and lots of good people have been active in them. Most of the best employees have stayed around—to a large extent because we all thrive on doing good, challenging work. Take the time to hire the right people. Do not settle for someone just to fill a vacancy, no matter how difficult it is to manage with that vacancy. Develop a sound job description and tailor the interview to those specific points. Through questions, ask people to provide specific examples of similar work and decision-making in the past. It is amazing what people will tell you in a job interview if you ask the right questions. Good people make good decisions, and they build good systems. Find the good ones.

CREATE SYSTEMS THAT TREAT EVERYONE LIKE THEY ARE THE PRESIDENT'S BEST FRIEND

Mistakes seem to congregate around certain people. It seems that once someone has had some type of bad experience—others seem to follow. And these tend to be just the people you really do not want this to happen to—a faculty member's child, a friend of the president, etc. And what Belmont has discovered is that this is often created by good intentions. We frequently pull these people out of our normal flow of events to give them special treatment, and by doing so, they miss the next regularly scheduled letter or phone call or whatever—then it just spirals downward from there. So, Belmont has decided that it wants all its prospects to receive the kind of treatment they would earn if they were the president's best friends. If a system is designed in this way, it can focus on improving the system because it will ensure that students and their families receive the very best treatment possible.

WHEN SYSTEMS WORK WELL, YOU HAVE TIME TO FOCUS ON THE EXCEPTION

And once you have built systems to treat everyone exceptionally, you do have time to deal with the truly unusual situation. Belmont's best example of this is in Student Financial Services. The better it gets at awarding students and notifying them, the more time it has to deal with the special circumstances and appeals that are an inevitable part of the process. Ten years ago, from February to September was spent in making manual awards. Now awards can be made generally within twenty-four hours of receipt of information. This gives Belmont most of the summer months to give individual attention to those students who have difficult circumstances. And those students who do not are delighted to have their awards quickly and move on to other things.

IT IS ALL ABOUT MANAGING THE SPACES IN-BETWEEN

The most dangerous parts of any system are the functions between two offices—after a student is admitted and Financial Aid needs their information for awarding, or after a student is registered and the student needs a bill. Managing the spaces in-between, the hand-offs of information, the places not clearly owned by one office, is the measure of how well your division is really running. At Belmont, people are just about tired of my restaurant analogy, but here it is: When I go to a restaurant, I want good food and good service and generally, I want to be left alone. The last thing I want to hear from my server is that my food will be late, or it is not delivered correctly because somebody in the kitchen made a mistake. It's all O'Charley's to me. They are all one organization. I do not see the server as separate from the kitchen. And you can bet it is the server that will not get a tip. The students just see Belmont. They do not want to hear what those people in some other office did. It is all Belmont to them.

YOU CAN DO MORE WITH LESS—MOST OF THE TIME

Along the way in its journey, Belmont was encouraged and at many points required to do more with less—to find more efficient and effective ways to do things. The creation of Belmont Central is a striking example of this. No new people, no new resources—create a new office within the division. Using technology to improve services is another clear example. Do not let limited resources stifle your creativity—find ways to let that energize you to find new ways to do your work. And when improvement comes, there are sometimes resources that follow.

MANAGE PROCESSES BY ASKING QUESTIONS

Learn to ask the question that each office, each process, each person is answering for your student. Find those broad questions and structure your work and your organization around those questions. This is one of the fastest ways to break down barriers between offices in an organization—because you have now found common ground. Obviously, this is not always easy or painless. But it is generally efficient and effective.

MAKE PARTNERS

When you share processes with other offices, you have to work together toward improvement. You cannot just grouse about bad data or bad service and then pass that along to your students. To truly make improvements in your own processes, you have to work with others who supply information and things to you. Using a formal process like partnership agreements can help to open up the conversation. To have a genuine dialogue about what you both need and what you can both contribute to get where you need to go is the only means to improvement.

PUT YOUR MOUTH AND MONEY WHERE YOUR ENERGY AND PASSION ARE

Be clear about your mission. Discover what drives your campus—what really lights the fire of the faculty, staff and trustees. Then put your mouth and money and energy there. Do not waste time and energy and resources on things that do not ultimately make a real difference. When there is clarity of purpose and vision and when it is supported with time and budget, people get serious, and they get excited. And this clarity of purpose must go throughout. It cannot be one thing for the academic side of the house and something different for other divisions. You are one institution, and you have one purpose. Find it, align with it, and support it in every possible way.

CLOSING THOUGHTS

The Belmont story is one of diligence to stay the course and to embrace change as it comes—of finding a purpose and a passion and driving that forward with great intensity. Belmont truly has learned to "eat change for breakfast." If your institution is one that finds itself in the midst of such circumstances (and most of us do), learn to embrace the challenges and thrive on the energy created by change.

7

A NEW UNIVERSITY EMBRACES ENROLLMENT MANAGEMENT

FGCU In its young six-year history, Florida Gulf Coast University (FGCU) has achieved significant success in increasing enrollment, student diversity, and quality. Current and prospective students say the technology, small classes, affordable cost, new facilities, and the positive pioneering spirit shared by faculty, staff and students impress them.

However, the university must meet one of the unique challenges of this era: consumers are becoming much more discriminating in selecting an educational provider. While academic reputation, cost and the traditional campus experience will continue to draw many students to FGCU, for a growing number of others, convenience and personalization have become benefits for which they are willing to pay.

INTRODUCTION

In its young six-year history, Florida Gulf Coast University (FGCU) has achieved significant success in increasing enrollment, student diversity, and quality. Current and prospective students say the technology, small classes, affordable cost, new facilities, and the positive pioneering spirit shared by faculty, staff and students impress them.

However, the university must meet one of the unique challenges of this era: consumers are becoming much more discriminating in selecting an educational provider. While academic reputation, cost and the traditional campus experience will continue to draw many students to FGCU, for a growing number of others, convenience and personalization have become benefits for which they are willing to pay. Students expect courses to be offered at convenient times and delivered in instructional modes that mirror their learning style.

To meet student expectations for immediate service, FGCU has embraced the concept of enrollment management in order to effectively optimize technology and integrate student processes that do not directly impact the overall educational experience. The enrollment management organization of the future needs to incorporate self-services, automated and timely responses, interactive databases, and targeted communication and personalization. FGCU has worked strategically and systemically to build a university that is a highly market-responsive organization. Increasingly, customized approaches to marketing and recruitment provide the most relevant information to carefully targeted prospective students. Interactions with students are thoughtfully choreographed from first contact through graduation, and strong bonds are fostered between the student and the institution. This process was developed by the creation of a university "story"; a carefully constructed public image; the development of name recognition in local, state, and national markets; the creation of a strategic enrollment management plan; and the examination of results and development of future goals.

THE FGCU STORY

Visionary citizens began the initiative to bring a new state university to Southwest Florida, and with the support of the Florida Board of Regents and the full Florida Legislature, Florida's tenth state university was conceived in 1991. The Board chose the location between Bonita Springs and Fort Myers from among twenty gift sites offered by private landowners. Dr. Roy McTarnaghan was named founding president in April 1993, and the university's academic and campus planning committees began the effort to address emerging higher education needs for the 21st century in Southwest Florida. According to Susan Evans, special assistant to the president, several small and large decisions were made to develop a new university culture that was similar to that of the corporate world, including the use of technology in the learning/teaching process, multiyear contracts as an alternative to faculty tenure, and no preference given to faculty for parking. The first FGCU student was admitted in January 1997; and the university officially opened on August 25, 1997. FGCU's second and current president, Dr. William Merwin, started in June 1999 and immediately initiated a highly participatory strategic planning process for students, faculty, and staff to chart the next chapter of FGCU.

Over its six-year history, the university has marked a rapid progression through stages of accreditation and expansion. The institution received Southern Association of Colleges and Schools accreditation in two years—one of the fastest review processes in the country—and the NCAA probation period was cut from the typical four years to two. An average of four campus buildings per year have been built over the last six years, and housing numbers have expanded from 500 students to over 1,300. Starting with four professional colleges, there are now five distinct areas of the university: Arts and Sciences, Business, Education, Health Professions, and Professional Studies. There are currently thirty-four undergraduate programs and eighteen graduate programs, including highly touted programs such as business administration, who received international accreditation in record time by the Association to Advance Collegiate Schools of Business (AACSB); marine biology, with exceptional laboratory facilities on the Gulf of Mexico; and hotel and resort management to meet the burgeoning tourist needs of the local area. The Foundation Board raised over $30 million dollars in two years from 2001–2003, promoting the university as an innovative and fast track institution that continually impacts positively on the ever-growing community of Southwest Florida.

UNIVERSITY IMAGE

Although FGCU was still a relatively young and emerging university, its unofficial tag as "Florida's Newest University" was becoming less relevant in the fall of 2000, as it did not reflect the long-term institutional image that FGCU sought to establish and since other universities had opened in Florida. The focus on newness did not create the competitive advantage critical in providing the sustained enrollment growth needed over the next five to ten years. A comprehensive marketing strategy with appeals to multiple student markets has been essential for FGCU to compete with the other four-year public institutions in the state, which all have well-established histories and program offerings, and loyal alumni bases.

In an effort to develop an institutional brand image, an analysis of institutional strengths, challenges, and demographics was undertaken.

INSTITUTIONAL STRENGTHS

Florida Gulf Coast University has several clear advantages over other institutions of higher learning, particularly in the areas of location, size, technological prowess, and faculty.

FGCU has a superb location. Fort Myers and Southwest Florida have been cited by business leaders in the state as one of Florida's fastest growing areas—and one of the most livable communities. The university offers a safe and beautiful campus within a short distance of the premier urban centers of Tampa, Fort Lauderdale, West Palm Beach, and Miami.

The university commenced in the fall of 1997 with approximately 2,500 students. Today, nearly 6,000 compose the student body with 4,000 undergraduate students. This "small" size is a very appealing feature for prospective students and their families who seek a more intimate university setting that allows greater personal interactions with faculty and staff.

The university is designed to integrate technology into every aspect of the educational experience. Multimedia capabilities in most classrooms through interactive podiums allow for computer presentations, Internet displays, and video broadcasting. In Spring 2003, distance learning accounted for 45% of all graduate enrollment and 14% of undergraduate. Although a limited set of degree programs are offered exclusively online, a growing percentage of FGCU students take a mixture of traditional and online courses throughout their academic careers.

Faculty often cite their own desire to be part of developing the culture of a university as the primary reason for their selection of FGCU. The current faculty has already earned the university substantial research grants from various organizations, including the National Science Foundation, the Corporation for Public Broadcasting, and the National Fish and Wildlife Service.

INSTITUTIONAL CHALLENGES

One present disadvantage of the campus is FGCU's limited number of residential halls. Current housing construction will bring the total number of available spaces to 1,500 by 2005, meeting the projected need by 25%. Another challenge is that of enhancing community appreciation for the role and contribution of the university, in an area that has for many decades seen the community college as the focal point of local higher education.

FGCU also is moving to distinguish itself from the well-established and well-respected Edison Community College (ECC), a prominent player in the same postsecondary education market, and emphasize how each institution can complement the other. The task becomes not only to market FGCU as an institution of choice for high school graduates, but also to foster a community mindset that supports the concept of a seamless transition from the community college to baccalaureate completion at FGCU.

These issues emphasize the urgent need for a comprehensive marketing strategy. FGCU is attempting to market its identity, as a comprehensive and versatile public university responsive to the higher education needs and market forces of the rapidly growing Southwest Florida population. It is identifying and building a set of strong program offerings such as biotechnology, resort and hospitality management, and golf management that highlight its unique features and strengths built upon local needs and attributes. A newly developed Alumni Relations Office will attempt to highlight the presence of FGCU's graduates that total approximately 3,300 of whom most live and work in the local area.

DEMOGRAPHIC TRENDS
The designated service area of FGCU encompasses Lee, Charlotte, Collier, Glades, and Hendry counties that make up the Southwest region of Florida. FGCU also draws significantly from Sarasota, Desoto, Broward, Miami-Dade, and Palm Beach counties that border its five-county local service area. While the percentage yields of high school graduates for the FGCU primary service area have steadily increased over the past five years, the Florida Board of Education's Division of Colleges and Universities projects that by 2017 the number of eighteen-year-olds will increase by a combined 30%.

The Florida Board of Education also notes higher than expected numbers of public high school graduates throughout the state with a 27% increase through 2007–08. It projects the upward trend will peak in the year 2008–09 and the numbers will remain relatively stable through 2014. As a result of this process of defining the image, FGCU was positioned to develop name recognition.

BUILDING NAME RECOGNITION
In 1997, a marketing study was conducted internally to identify and prioritize marketing directions and efforts. The Marketing Task Force recommended a number of measures, including to:
* Define and establish a clear image and identity for the institution.

* Establish a systematic review process for marketing and advertising activities.
* Use market research and segmentation methods to get the most out of marketing efforts.
* Emphasize that institutional marketing at FGCU is everyone's responsibility.
* Ensure that internal communications encourage consistent and effective marketing across all academic and operational units.

In 1998, the university established an internal group known as the Marketing Advisory Council, whose goal was to discuss institutional marketing issues and make recommendations for the implementation of promotional ideas.

Just prior to the Fall 1999 academic term, senior FGCU administrators prepared a review and update of the university marketing efforts for incoming President Merwin. This update showed that, in the absence of a clear institution-wide plan and corresponding budget, the approach to marketing tended to be reactionary and piecemeal rather than a proactive, coordinated, and integrated effort. Therefore, it was recommended that the administration budget funds and resources yearly; that they establish a pattern of activities, events and publications for the full academic year and manage a fixed budget rather than submit "emergency" requests for funds. It was noted that annual evaluation could help determine what works, what does not, what priorities must be set, and what is a realistic budget for each priority.

In Spring 2000, President Merwin requested that MGT of America, Inc. conduct a marketing review study. The national management research and consulting firm identified this primary set of objectives:
* Structure and implement a university-wide marketing strategy.
* Develop a mechanism for annual budget planning, resource allocation, and benchmarking.
* Coordinate marketing with institutional mission, strategic planning, and enrollment efforts.
* Determine desired institutional image and identity based on competitive advantages.
* Implement and evaluate tailored marketing activities and prioritize markets.
* Create a family of quality publications and collateral visual display materials.
* Make FGCU the "school of choice."

In Spring 2001, the university selected the services of STAMATS Communications,

Inc. to develop a cohesive series of promotional publications with emphasis on identity recognition. The plan (STAMATS Communications, Inc., 2001) unified all FGCU's publications into an integrated copy and design family alongside an integrated marketing campaign. Key messages about features, quality and benefits were identified through a series of focus groups and surveys. The end result of these marketing production efforts was the unveiling in Fall 2001 of an undergraduate viewbook, graduate viewbook, and six yield brochures—financial aid, parents, deciding student, diversity issues, international students, and transfers. Such promotional materials were central to the development of a strategic enrollment management plan.

ENROLLMENT MANAGEMENT PLAN

FGCU has embraced the concept of enrollment management, a strategy designed to enable an educational institution to achieve and maintain optimal enrollment from recruitment through graduation (Dolence, 1996). Enrollment management is concerned with a number of critical student aspects, including college choice, transition to college, student retention, student satisfaction, course scheduling, student outcomes, and demographic changes. The institution's enrollment success is predicated on its ability to optimally and systemically engage in four critical areas: student recruitment, student retention, integrated marketing, and service.

INTEGRATED MARKETING

Marketing, recruiting, and enrollment management go hand-in-hand, yet they are not one and the same. An integrated marketing plan works in tandem with a strategic enrollment management plan.

Using image-assessment data in combination with an internal strengths and weaknesses assessment and environmental scan information, FGCU has begun to construct an enrollment data-driven integrated marketing plan. The university is gradually achieving a consistent look in most publications, Web pages, stationery, and business cards, as well as in promotional materials at both college and departmental levels. The Community Relations and Marketing Office is in the process of identifying the graphic elements that are to tie together all publications, print and digital.

Florida Gulf Coast University fully launched its first integrated marketing campaign in August 2001. Emphasizing its central message through a strong branding effort, the campaign covers the University's five-county service area and the Miami--Dade area. After extensive research involving focus groups, knowledge of the university by way of the new marketing campaign was communicated through the use of a consistent message, "Vision. Value. You."

1. Formula for Success

The marketing campaign, developed in conjunction with STAMATS Communications, Inc., raises the audience's awareness of FGCU and helps establish its identity as a public state university committed to providing a high quality educational experience at affordable prices.

The Office of Community Relations and Marketing released the following explanation of the formula for success (The FGCU Formula. [n.d.]. Retrieved April 15, 2003, from http://www.fgcu.edu/info/formula.asp):

Florida Gulf Coast University: V2 (u) + ☼ = FGCU.
Vision times Value plus the Florida sun.

The first V is Vision.
* We stick to a Vision for undergraduate education that stresses the classic skills of analysis, reasoning, and problem solving.
* We educate students in small classes, in which top-flight professors know and guide each student individually.
* We use the most sophisticated teaching and research technologies while making sure that every student is comfortable with computers and the Internet.

The second V is Value.
* A first-rate education at an exceptional price: small classes, options for distance learning, one-on-one relationships with professors, and one of the most modern, well-equipped campuses in the nation—all for public university tuition.
* FGCU is part of Florida's acclaimed public university system. That's why FGCU can offer the things that you associate with a private university education (top professors, small classes, and plenty of high-tech tools) at a public university price tag.

The U is You.
* Your ideas and your energy are the reasons that FGCU remains innovative.
* Your openness and sense of service are the reasons that FGCU brings students of such diversity together for common purposes.
* You complete the formula.

Then add the sun, which lights and heats and energizes the formula. That's brilliant!

This marketing message has been delivered through a rich mix of media to maximize awareness of FGCU throughout its service area and the rest of South Florida. According to Ms. Audrea Anderson, associate vice president for Community Relations and Marketing, a few examples of marketing campaign coverage that have been generated through her office include: theater ads appearing in Fort Myers, Naples, Port Charlotte; a billboard ad running in Miami-Dade county; television ads presented on network local affiliates and Comcast Cable channels (Lifetime and MTV); newspaper ads in the Ft. Myers' *Daily News-Press* and *The Naples News*, as well as in the *Miami-Herald* and *Charlotte Sun-Times*; magazine ads in national, regional, and service districts; community publications preference in high school newspapers and yearbooks; as well as local souvenir booklets. A current initiative is underway to define appropriate outlets in prime regional and out-of-state student markets.

2. Internet Presence

The On-line/Technology Committee of the Marketing Advisory Council worked with campus leaders to revamp the FGCU Web site in an ongoing effort. They aimed to provide technical improvements as well as updating the design. Once implementation was achieved in Spring 2002, a survey instrument was created to assess the new Web site's look, functionality and navigation features. Results are still being tabulated.

In sum, with consistent messages targeted through geodemography, FGCU is beginning to invest in strategies that aggressively recruit academically talented and diverse students, retain a higher percentage of them to graduation, and consequently shape its institutional image.

STUDENT RECRUITMENT

Employing the enrollment management model, the Division of Enrollment Services has revitalized and coordinated recruitment efforts, focusing on personalized, timely communication with prospects, a solid campus visitation program, and a belief in the value of a diverse and talented student body. What follows is an overview of recruitment outreach initiatives currently being implemented or enhanced by enrollment services personnel through an emerging strategic enrollment management plan.

1. Financial Aid and Admissions Linkages

Staff members within Admissions and Financial Aid offices are engaging in cross-training activities to strengthen mutual understanding and effective communications. The management of academic and endowed scholarships is currently a time-consuming and arduous task. FGCU is looking at an automatic computer-generated process to consider and review scholarship applicants.

2. Telecounseling and Campus Visitation

FGCU's inaugural telecounseling program utilizes the telephone to develop a one-on-one relationship with prospective and enrolling students and their parents. Empowering a corps of dedicated and energetic student and faculty volunteers, these targeted phone outreach efforts are proving effective in assessing levels of interest, encouraging campus visits and attendance at information sessions, and converting applicants to matriculants.

The university, recognizing the special importance of campus visits, eagerly looks forward to the completion of the new Sugden Welcome Center currently being built near the main campus entrance slated for completion in Summer 2004. The new Welcome Center will serve as the gateway to Florida Gulf Coast University and its community, reflecting the friendliness and courtesy of the campus, providing visitors with accessible information and referral services. Through the Center, FGCU will:

(1) provide a state-of-the-art facility with informational kiosks and interactive podiums to welcome prospective students, their families, and other visitors to campus;

(2) offer publications, orientations, and tours that are designed to meet the diverse needs of students, alumni, tourists, international visitors, faculty, staff, and dignitaries, by focusing on the history and traditions of the university; and

(3) seek to attract the most academically talented and diverse student body to the campus through hospitality, visual media and informative publications, advising, campus tours, volunteerism, and nurturing and effective communications.

3. E-Recruiting

FGCU emphasizes incorporating electronic mail into the front-end of the admissions cycle, with timely e-mail communication to inquiring and undecided students. Through targeted and timed messages to prospects and applicants during the recruitment cycle, this has contributed to improving communication and interaction between current and prospective students as well as with faculty and staff involved in various admission conversations.

4. Prospect Management

The university has installed ApplyYourself computing software, a stand-alone, front-end admissions prospect management system designed to capture crucial recruitment data. FGCU admissions professionals are now able to more effectively identify high-interest candidates at any point in the admissions funnel, as well as provide personal interactions with, and targeted messages to, prospects. They also work at offering personalized interaction with interested students throughout the recruitment process.

5. Geodemographic Analysis

Geodemography, a combination of geography and demographics, allows for the identification of geographic markets with the highest recruitment potential. In the fall of 2001, Carnegie Communications, Inc., under the direction and guidance of Dr. Jeffrey Papa, senior educational consultant, provided an in-depth analysis and assessment of FGCU's 1999–2001 inquirers, applicants, and enrolled students. These groups were profiled across forty geodemographic clusters. The resulting information has assisted in the creation of "target groups" that form the core of FGCU's student recruitment communication efforts with personalized messages and tailored promotional materials.

6. Admissions Technology

SCT Banner's Web for Admission was implemented in late Summer 2003, and integrates the online application with the Banner student information system, thus eliminating a good deal of mundane manual data entry and freeing up application processors to perform other critical office tasks. Additionally, the engagement in Electronic Data Interchange (EDI), regarding student record data, will be an efficient and effective means by which transcript information can be transmitted between institutions electronically. The advantages include: automatic computer transfer of information, thus ensuring reliable and consistent interpretation of student records; faster transfer of student records; and better service to students in timing and delivery of relevant portions of their academic records.

7. Territory Management Model

A new territory management model initiative will soon assign each undergraduate admissions officer to a geographic recruitment territory and give the counselor personal responsibility for tailoring recruitment plans appropriate to that area. Staff members will strive to meet application and enrollment targets and assume responsibility for monitoring these goals throughout the admissions cycle. Such territories will include the metropolitan areas of Fort Lauderdale, Jacksonville, Tampa, Orlando, and Miami.

8. Recent Alumni Support

The Admissions Office is working closely with the new Office of Alumni Relations to invite recent graduates to assist with the institution's enrollment efforts, especially in securing alumni admission representatives to serve as university ambassadors in key primary, secondary, and tertiary student markets in Florida and select out-of-state regions. These representatives will attend select college fairs/nights and sponsor new student receptions in key cities such as Sarasota, Fort Lauderdale, Tampa, and Miami.

9. Parent-to-Parent Program

Parents of current students play an important volunteer role in communicating with parents of prospective students, through a number of initiative programs, including a revised parents' Web page and a proposed parent-to-parent Web chat and virtual open houses.

10. Community Outreach

FGCU encourages high school and community college counselors, as well as community leaders, to visit the campus. The university makes its campus available as a meeting location for conferences and other community needs. A "Speakers Bureau" Web site details presentations and sessions offered by FGCU faculty and staff. In addition, all guidance counselors and transfer coordinators in FGCU's primary and secondary markets are kept up-to-date via personalized correspondence.

STUDENT RETENTION

Under the direction of the dean of Enrollment Management, the Retention Management Council (RMC) was established in Spring 2001. Composed of members from a variety of departments and programs on campus, the RMC is actively engaged in developing and recommending strategies for student retention and success, identifying literature and research-based strategies, analyzing and collecting retention data, promoting appropriate activities, formulating a model for campus-wide retention, and evaluating retention strategies, activities, and processes. According to Dr. Alice Brunner, director of First-Year advising and orientation activities, among the First-Year initiatives and retention practices currently in place at FGCU include:

* **The Learning Academy,** a residential learning community supported by interaction with professors. Positive retention outcomes were reported from the pilot program initiated in the fall of 2001.

* **Eagle View Orientation,** a mandatory two-day freshman orientation and parents' program.

* **Styles and Ways of Learning,** a required class that provides orientation to first semester freshmen.

* **Supplemental Instruction,** which focuses on courses with a history of high attrition. Trained student SI leaders assist students with out-of-class learning and skill building.

* **First-Year Advising,** where master's level counselors and peer advisors work with freshmen throughout the year on academic planning.

* **Academic Retention Program,** which provides encouragement, guidance and support for students on academic warning or probation. Staff assists students with goal setting, study skills, tutoring, motivation, time management and stress management.

* **The Writing Center,** facilitated by FGCU faculty, provides guidance and critique for students seeking assistance with developing writing skills.

* **FastTrack,** a Web-based system that allows for a quick response and intervention when academic problems arise in the classroom.

SERVICE

Enrollment Services' staff members have demonstrated great levels of commitment to their positions and to the university itself in terms of time and willingness to introduce and implement new ideas. This entrepreneurial spirit cannot be underestimated in terms of its effect on customer service and continuous quality improvement.

1. Customer Service

Developing and adhering to a customer service perspective is essential in assuring the overall success of the university. In Fall 2000, Carnegie Communications, Inc., under the auspices of Dr. Papa, conducted two energizing and motivating one-day customer service seminars for faculty and staff, including identifying customer needs, energizing staff, resolving conflict, and managing feedback. Periodic customer service reviews and refresher courses are planned as part of a concerted continuous quality improvement effort.

Currently, due to state budgetary crises, administrative staff members are overworked and simply not able to fully meet the administrative demands of the university. At least eight additional Enrollment Services' staff positions have been identified, with appropriate justifications and funding needs in order to address critical divisional needs. With anticipated enrollment growth monies from the state in the upcoming fiscal year, the hope is that a portion of these new position lines will be funded to help rectify the already stressful staffing infrastructure. In the meantime, the current staff often stay late, come in early, and help each other in an effort to keep up with student customer needs.

2. Continuous Quality Improvement

In May 2002, the dean of Enrollment Management at FGCU contacted the Florida Institute of Government to develop a process through which the Division of Enrollment Services could concentrate on continuous improvement. The dean desired that several outcomes be addressed, including: an enhanced collegial environment; greater willingness to collaborate within Enrollment Services; strategies for problem solving and conflict resolution; and increased focus on accountability to performance standards. The end result was a compilation of data, observations and recommendations gathered by the external consulting firm of Schroeder Management Consultants, during the seven active months in which the project was conducted. Initial indications are that the exercise has proved useful in addressing the original concerns. Recommendations included more regular staff meetings, central communication outlets, professional development opportunities, and divisional social gatherings.

THE RESULTS

Enrollment management has enabled FGCU to strive for optimum enrollment, encompassing recruitment, retention and graduation rates. This institution-wide process has begun to permeate virtually every aspect of each university function and culture, enabling us to meet and exceed desired percentage goals.

For the 2002–03 academic year, the university met and exceeded its targeted annual student Full-Time Equivalency (FTE) goal by 9%. Headcount for Fall 2002 was approximately 5,260, an increase of 24% over the previous year. Since 2001, student applications from secondary markets, including Broward, Dade, Palm, and Sarasota counties, have increased by 31%. Overall applicant quality from these Florida counties has remained consistent with average SAT test scores that have increased by fifteen points.

A personalized outreach approach utilizing the ApplyYourself prospect management system, geodemographic research data, and an effective out-of-state student tuition waiver program enabled the Division of Enrollment Services to attract and recruit additional students from the northeast and Midwest regions of the country. There is an enrollment yield projection for these areas of 48% increase.

Even without a coordinator of multicultural student outreach in 2002–03, there has been a collaborative and synergistic campus-wide outreach effort to increase enrollment of students of color. This included hosting special receptions and visitation programs for academically talented minority students, sending out targeted direct mailings, offering special on-campus visitation programs, and increasing scholarship and financial assistance opportunities. Overall, this led to a preliminary 7% increase in Summer and Fall 2003 over 2002 in new first-time-in-college minority students.

In terms of student retention, the freshman-to-sophomore persistence rate is maintaining currently at approximately 70%; a seven percent increase over the last year. The university hopes the labors of the Retention Management Council will pay off in the years ahead, with a goal of 75%–80% freshman retention rate in the next three-to-five years. The Retention Management Council now has the tools to identify the set of characteristics that indicate a student's likelihood of re-enrollment. And, faculty and staff are on the lookout for "at risk" students in order that the university may take effective intervention measures.

LESSONS LEARNED

Ernest Boyer once said, "Asking a college to quickly change its approach is akin to asking an ocean liner to make a quick right in the middle of the Atlantic Ocean" (Dennis, 1998).

The keys to building an enrollment management culture are asking the right questions, building productive relationships, engaging in internal marketing, and taking appropriate and systemic action. Important questions in FGCU's adoption of strategic

Enrollment Management have included:

* How can enrollment management improve the institution—short-term and long-term?
* Does the campus have the infrastructure for this approach?
* What role do faculty and staff play in enrollment management?
* How does enrollment management drive or impact university-wide strategic planning?

In building relationships, the dean of Enrollment Management has found it important to increase confidence levels throughout the Enrollment Services' staff by allowing people the freedom to take risks; to ask questions and share ideas; to articulate proposed changes clearly; to create a sense of shared ownership and staff empowerment; to identify mutual strategic goals and concerns; and to connect the strategic enrollment management effort to the institution's overall strategic directives.

Engaging in internal marketing has proved an invaluable public relations tool. Shared information has generated a sense of shared ownership and buy-in from staff and faculty. A keen sense of collaboration and synergy has led to timely addressing of challenging enrollment issues. Change has been introduced, as best as possible, incrementally and systemically, minimizing confusion and overreaction on the ever-changing higher education marketing terrain.

Led by the dean of Enrollment Management, key stakeholders have been engaged collectively, collaboratively, and regularly, so that enrollment management design can be matched with institutional culture. A series of scheduled meetings are held each semester with leadership teams from each of the five colleges and non-academic units (e.g., Student Affairs, Instructional Technology) to maintain awareness of enrollment management challenges and accomplishments as well as to secure ongoing support.

The next planned steps in the continual development of enrollment management includes integrating financial aid packaging and other retention schemes, providing additional staff development, and communicating proposed changes to all concerned in various forums, including e-mail, committee meetings, e-newsletters, and Web postings.

CONCLUSION

In its brief six-year history, Florida Gulf Coast University has taken a number of significant steps to embrace enrollment management. These have included embracing geodemography to identify and target successful recruits; developing an innovative and effective campus visitation program; effectively qualifying and grading inquiries to build the applicant pool; moving towards implementation of a territory management model to offer a more proactive, individualized approach to student recruitment; and improving financial aid programs and planning for students and parents.

FGCU has a history of investing in improving its educational product. While this is a worthy strategy, basic marketing principles suggest there must be a balance between product development and promotion. With adequate resources, the Enrollment Services and Community Relations and Marketing branches can significantly impact institutional image, student satisfaction, retention, and ultimately enrollments.

If Florida Gulf Coast University is to achieve its vision of becoming the "University of Choice" in Southwest Florida, the entire institution must work together to effectively manage those "moments of truth" staff and faculty experience everyday with students both future and current. FGCU must continue to strengthen shared service values, improve communications, collaborate for solutions, expand service opportunities, integrate enrollment processes, and most importantly, regularly assess and enhance strategic enrollment management and integrated marketing game plans leading to ultimate student success.

REFERENCES

Anderson, A. (2002, October). Florida Gulf Coast University. Personal Communication.

Brunner, A. (2002, November). Florida Gulf Coast University. Personal Communication.

Dennis, M.J. (1998). A Practical Guide to Enrollment and Retention Management in Higher Education. Westport, CT: Bergin & Garvey.

Dolence, M.G. (1996). Strategic Enrollment Management: A Primer for Campus Administrators. Washington, DC: American Association of Collegiate Registrars and Admissions Officers.

The FGCU Formula, {n.d.]. Retrieved April 15, 2003 from http://www.fgcu.edu/info/formula.asp.

132 Evans, S. (2003, April). Florida Gulf Coast University. Personal Communication.

MGT of America, Inc. (2000, July). Presentation at Florida Gulf Coast University: Marketing Study and Strategic Recommendations. Fort Myers, FL.

Papa, J. (2001, October). Presentation at Florida Gulf Coast University: Geodemographic Research: Strategic Marketing and Recruitment. Fort Myers, FL.

Schroeder Management Consultants (2003, August). Presentation at Florida Gulf Coast University: Enrollment Services continuous improvement project. Fort Myers, FL.

STAMATS Communications, Inc. (2001, January). Presentation at Florida Gulf Coast University: Research, marketing, and publication proposal for Florida Gulf Coast University. Fort Myers, FL.

8

USING INCREMENTAL STEPS TO STRATEGIC ENROLLMENT MANAGEMENT PLANNING

CHRISTINE KERLIN

EvCC Everett Community College (EvCC) enjoys a long-standing place in the history of two-year colleges in the State of Washington and in its local community. Founded in 1941, it has evolved from a small local junior college serving a university transfer function to one of 34 public comprehensive colleges providing academic, technical, personal enrichment, adult basic education, and industry training programs to approximately 9,500 students each quarter. Its location thirty miles above Seattle comprises growing urban and suburban areas, decreasing rural spaces, a Navy base, Boeing industrial sites, a rapidly expanding health industry, and spectacular views of the Puget Sound and Cascade Mountain range.

INTRODUCTION

In professional circles and in the literature, extensive discussion focuses on the actual operation and outcomes of strategic enrollment management. This chapter, however, will provide a case study of operations and events that led up to the establishment of enrollment management planning at a mid-size community college. This case study illustrates that middle management at an institution that is not actively involved in enrollment management can find ways to "set the table" for more deliberative enrollment management strategies at a later time in the future. The purpose of this approach is to offer encouragement to colleagues who may wish to get a start on achieving the outcomes offered through SEM but happen to be in an environment where the comprehensive approach often seen at "best practices" colleges is not yet within their reach. This is a story of an incremental approach to strategic enrollment management.

In attempting to create a chronology that the reader can easily follow, it is difficult to be both parsimonious and precise. Ideas, decisions, and actions interact with each other over variable periods of time, and implementations often span weeks and months. Furthermore, the perspective of the author—who was one of the players described below—must be constantly analyzed and scrubbed to assure maximum objectivity. With these challenges in mind, this case study is written to conform as faithfully as possible to the actual chain of events.

BACKGROUND

Everett Community College (EvCC) enjoys a long-standing place in the history of two-year colleges in the State of Washington and in its local community. Founded in 1941, it has evolved from a small local junior college serving a university transfer function to one of 34 public comprehensive colleges providing academic, technical, personal enrichment, adult basic education, and industry training programs to approximately 9,500 students each quarter. Its location thirty miles above Seattle comprises growing urban and suburban areas, decreasing rural spaces, a Navy base, Boeing industrial sites, a rapidly expanding health industry, and spectacular views of the Puget Sound and Cascade Mountain range.

Like many community colleges, enrollment went along fairly well in its first several decades, with a successful "build it and they will come" outlook. Events, though, caught up with EvCC in the 1980s and 1990s. Increased competition, fluctuating economic and demographic trends, and repeated organizational change challenged the college's ability to meet its enrollment targets. In the 1980s, failure to meet state enrollment targets forced a significant reduction in the budget, which compromised the college's ability to offer adequate classes and triggered an erratic enrollment pattern.

In 1988, a "Program and Enrollment Plan" was developed by the Administrative Council with campus-wide input. It outlined the challenges and opportunities facing EvCC at the time and recommended numerous steps toward change. The plan was a strong one, and, even in retrospect, an intelligent map for the future. Its strength was its assessment of the educational programs and facilities needed to provide updated educational opportunities and access to local students. Several of the recommendations were implemented with positive effects. About the same time, a separate plan focused on co-locating student services and a single Entry Services Center was built by a group christened the Portland Committee. Their goal was to improve the entry and retention services to students, thereby strengthening enrollment and student success. Parts of their planning resulted in improved services, and others failed to come to fruition. Despite such efforts, though, in the mid-1990s the college was coping with a declining enrollment and mired in a deep financial hole as a result. New solutions were actively sought as a matter of survival.

Several executive leaders—and others—were engaged in efforts to both stabilize and build enrollment, but a consolidated approach was lacking. The 1988 Plan appeared to have lost its vibrancy and was revealing its weaknesses: it did not address the methodology for attracting students to its educational programs; it did not support continued assessment and revitalization of the planning and implementation processes; it did not tie its efforts to targets and resources. In other words, other than an expressed desire to enroll more students in new educational programs, there was little institution-wide infrastructure and planning to support it. Finally, in 1996, a group of mid-managers, some relatively new and without the history of the 1988 Plan and the Portland Committee, began to examine the situation with a holistic "enrollment management" perspective. Though a comprehensive institutional plan to improve the enrollment picture did not seem feasible at the moment, some incremental steps seemed possible.

GETTING STARTED

Several positive factors were in place in 1996–97. A new director of College Relations whose portfolio included marketing, public relations and publications, had joined the college in 1995. A new director of Enrollment Services with a background in enrollment management was hired in 1996. The dean of Students and the vice president for Instruction and Student Services were supportive of new initiatives to kick-start enrollment. The vice president for Administrative Services wanted to participate in plans that linked enrollment with budget planning. The campus community, by and large, seemed motivated to change some ways of doing business in order to turn the enrollment picture around.

Though some key players were in place and the motivation was evident, the support needed for the initiation of a comprehensive enrollment management plan, with or without bells and whistles, was not present. The current president was engaged in other issues and the strategic planning process was stagnant. The organizational structure and politics of the institution were not conducive to any restructuring that would lead to the creation of an enrollment management leader or division.

Within this climate, several mid-managers found themselves sharing tangible ideas for improving enrollment without a formal vehicle to link them together under a college-wide vision, with goals, strategies and performance indicators. They proceeded anyway.

The new director of Enrollment Services built a picture of the current situation—a modified SWOT (strengths, weaknesses, opportunities and threats) analysis. On the positive side the college offered a reasonable array of both university transfer and technical programs, with some notably strong areas and faculty, and had a full family of curriculum guides for each certificate and degree program. There was an existing and extensive information system, using a data system developed for and shared by all thirty-four community and technical colleges. Though bulky and somewhat disjointed, a significant amount of data was available. The college also had a touchtone information and registration system supported by the statewide system office. Additionally, current staff in the Admissions, Counseling, Multicultural Services and other student services offices had strong skills and were motivated to reach out to prospective and new students. Furthermore, the college had a significant, albeit unorganized, alumni base due to its relatively long history, a reasonably positive local image, and name recognition.

The challenges were many, though. There was no outreach or marketing plan and no methodical response and follow-up system for inquiries and applications. Though state system mandates assured frequent reports of enrollment in a wide variety of categories, the information was not easily accessible or disseminated on campus. Publications were fragmented around campus, and material to attract prospective students was sketchy. Advertising was not integrated into any larger plan of image enhancement. Instructional offerings were not related to the outreach and marketing activities that periodically happened. Staff resources focused on recruiting were slim, though retention services were somewhat stronger. Nearby community colleges provided competition, both perceived and real. And, due to the slide in enrollment, fiscal resources were scant.

In collaboration with the director of College Relations and using the existing High School Relations Committee as a forum, the director of Enrollment Services developed a lengthy list of ideas regarding enrollment. This list was circulated to the larger campus community in January 1997. The cover memo indicated that the college should undertake a strategic enrollment management initiative to forge links among instructional planning, budgeting, enrollment planning, marketing and services, but that in the meantime several immediate efforts should proceed—a list of which was attached. There was no executive response to the request for a comprehensive enrollment management initiative, but the responses to the more specific list of possibilities were generally positive and ideas continued to flow.

Continued discussions between the director of College Relations, the director of Enrollment Services, and several other mid-managers had two positive effects. First, a shared sense of the situation and possible solutions was created. Second, an ad-hoc plan entitled "Building Image / Building Enrollment" (BI/BE) was generated in June 1997 by the director of College Relations and the director of Enrollment Services. This plan represented the first blueprint for public relations, marketing and recruitment within recent memory. The plan identified goals and activities that both directors believed could quickly impact the enrollment picture. Straightforward activities, such as developing a mailing series with appropriate publications, following up inquiries, creating a high school visitation schedule and on-campus events, and placing ads in key publications in the region, were listed, along with the responsible person or office, and the support needed to implement the activity.

At the time of its development the document really represented nothing more than a best guess, by two directors, about what the college should do on a variety of fronts to strengthen its position. Little data existed that informed the college of its markets, so intuition and experience—and limited budgets—guided their vision. Some of the activities listed were assessed as basic and essential to any educational enterprise that seeks students, such as responding to inquiries. Other activities were seen as follow-up, once the essentials were in place. Other activities fell into the latter category where the moral or financial support was not available immediately but might be eventually. The importance of this document, though, was that it drew a big picture of what was desirable for the college to propel its enrollment trend-line upward. In the absence of a formal strategic enrollment management thrust, "Building Image / Building Enrollment" represented a grassroots effort to integrate some key enrollment management techniques into the college's operations. This document was circulated to the department and division heads in student services and instruction, and served as the springboard for specific proposals that soon followed.

FOLLOWING THE BLUEPRINT SYSTEMS

"Building Image / Building Enrollment" provided a very brief summary of the current college and local environment, and extensively outlined the themes, messages, activities and program elements that could be undertaken for the coming year and beyond. As an incremental step toward the wished-for enrollment management plan, this blueprint spawned activities that made a large impact. Those activities are described below.

Compared to its neighboring colleges, EvCC had neither a consistent nor constant public image. This situation was not solely due to college indifference; it was compounded by a jumbled marketplace of competing media and the lack of a significant budget to buy into each media segment. The decision was made by the two directors to emphasize local print media, and use radio and TV sparingly. In consultation with others, the director of College Relations organized a thematically and stylistically coordinated advertising campaign. The director of Enrollment Services contributed a weekly calendar of advertising topics and the advertising requests of other departments were orchestrated as well in order to create a constant visual presence in local newspapers. The director of College Relations also reviewed other sources of public information in the region and placed EvCC information and news in those markets as well. Underlying this campaign were efforts to have a consistent visual image, an enlarged photo library, weekly news releases, and other elements.

Marketing campaigns require more than just copy and designs for ads. A key element is the ability to respond intelligently to the anticipated increased public interest. This notion provides a small but clear example of the need for linkages and collaboration in order to achieve enrollment goals. As a result of the coordination between College Relations and Enrollment Services on the marketing issues, it was decided that almost every ad, listing, or news release would contain a single phone number in the

Enrollment Services Office. This went a long way toward assuring an informed response as well as the uniform capture of the data about the inquiry. Implementing the fulfillment structure, though, required some work.

The marketing campaign, as well as other outreach efforts described below, required a formal support structure not only in the College Relations Office, but in the Enrollment Services Office as well. The need to envision an admissions funnel was clear. This concept is a particular challenge to community colleges, where selectivity is rare, commitment fees such as application and admission deposit fees are low or nonexistent, entry points are multitudinous, and the school is often chosen only because of pure convenience and low cost. Nonetheless, the philosophy of the admissions funnel can be strategically employed in such a way to strengthen the position of the community college in attracting students and attaining a position as an institution of choice, with measurable inputs. Specifically, EvCC needed to think in terms of an admissions funnel in order to attract and cater to "suspects," "prospects," "applicants," "admitted," and "enrolled" students.

In the case of EvCC in 1996–97, an inquiry system did not exist. Inquiries received across the college—in the instructional departments, in the Counseling Center, in the Admissions Office, etc.—were sent the requested items, and the inquiry information was then immediately discarded. Fortunately, the computerized information system contained a pre-built module for inquiries, but the college had not been using it. First, the inquiry module was activated and protocols were established for entering inquiry data. Second, a common approach to mailing requested information was adopted. Third, the college community was asked to forward all inquiry data to the Admissions Office. Though other offices were encouraged to respond to inquiries directed at them with any specialized information they had, they were assured that all inquiries forwarded to the Admissions Office would receive a common packet and follow-up. Within a year the inquiry database contained thousands of contacts.

Using the admissions funnel model, the college needed to develop materials for prospective and admitted students. At the time, the college did not have any explicit marketing pieces so they needed to be invented quickly. A model of a four-color "viewfolder" was developed along with a series of follow-up postcards. The viewfolder contained very general text about the college and could be used at visitations, fairs, and in mailings. The first inquiry would receive a viewfolder, a general form letter of welcome, and any special inserts representing a specific request. This would be followed up two weeks later with a postcard reiterating the college's interest in assisting the prospective student. A subsequent application for admission would be followed with a formal letter of admission and other entry material, and then followed again by a different postcard featuring a welcoming message from the president. Additional publications included April and August newsletters to prospective fall students, a poster, and fliers for special programs such as Study Abroad, Athletics, etc. Eventually, the college's Web site became another focal point for attracting and informing prospective students.

At the time, the college did not have an active outreach program. High school visits had been made in response to a request from the high school. Local fairs, too, were a matter of accepting an invitation. "Building Image / Building Enrollment" called for an aggressive schedule of outreach contacts and on-campus events. As a result, new events such as Parents' Night, Career Tracks, and High School Counselor Breakfasts were created, and all local high schools were canvassed to set up a quarterly visitation calendar. Outreach options to special populations, such as the Navy, ethnic groups, career-changers, etc. were identified. These efforts were designed to attract new prospective students and maintain contact with them. The inquiry and admission databases, as well as an enlarged number of publications were the cornerstone of an ability to do so. Active outreach programs are another challenge for community colleges. Unlike baccalaureate institutions, community colleges rarely employ admissions professionals. Often the outreach function is delegated to the Counseling Center or to a coordinator who also wears office management hats, and efforts other than periodic high school and fair visits are not envisioned.

"Building Image / Building Enrollment" included the goal of building a year-long class schedule instead of producing only a quarterly schedule. Collaborative efforts among Instruction, College Relations and Enrollment Services led to an agreement to produce the class schedule on a quarterly basis, with additional sections for a "sneak preview" of classes offered in future quarters. For example, the fall class schedule would include listings for winter and spring. This was no small achievement since it required extra work in each department during each schedule producing period. However, it was broadly agreed that such an annual class schedule would attract new students, assist continuing students, strengthen advising, and provide a competitive edge.

All of these efforts required a re-direction of funds and a request for additional funds. Herein lies a significant challenge for incremental mid-management efforts in enrollment management. Without the support of a comprehensive college-wide plan, each effort starts from scratch in its pitch for implementation, and runs the risk of appearing fragmented and unrelated to other goals and tasks that already have budget and human resources attached to them. The efforts described above, and others, were successful for several reasons. First, the situation was fairly desperate and motivation was high to look outside the box for solutions. Second, at least two of the key players were new to the college and enjoyed the benefits of their honeymoon period. Third, the leaders in Instruction, Student Services, and Budget were supportive and had the wherewithal to support incremental financial initiatives without requiring an executive plan. Fourth, the financial investment was as slim as possible; each proposal was an austere form of the ideal. And finally, the existence of the "Building Image / Building Enrollment" plan—as narrow as it was—provided a thematic and operational framework that fostered the power of shared vision and collaboration. No one else had an active plan, so this one looked good.

Following several presentations, reports, and cost projections, additional funds were provided for advertising and a new family of recruitment publications. These funds initially came from cracks and corners in budgets from several divisions. This approach is not unlike the situation where one requests a grant to fund a proposal. If successful, the money is there, but it's soft. Though this can be aggravating to a department manager who sees the need for ongoing and permanent funding in order to build a program, it may be the only way to start. In the scenario described above, several different funds were provided at different times, with no promise of continuation. Fortunately, the eventual success of the implementations convinced the budget leadership to make the allocations permanent several years later.

Funds also came from internal re-allocations. For example, when the director of Enrollment Services reviewed her budgets through the lens of enrollment management, it appeared that several current expenditures could be re-directed toward the critical task at hand. Elimination of some practices and streamlining of others brought savings in some line items that then could be used to support new efforts. In this case this effort did not require an exhaustive re-engineering design with committees and deadlines, though this might prove fruitful as a strategy in other settings.

FOLLOWING THE BLUEPRINT STAFF RESTRUCTURING

The activities described above were carried out within current staff levels. Staffing, though, was seen as a critical element to assure success and quality, and changes in human resources were needed. The Portland Committee's earlier dreams of an Entry Services Center, and key elements in the "Building Image / Building Enrollment" plan recognized the need for restructuring the entry services of the college. In early 1997, a proposal was made to combine the separate Admissions and Registration offices into a single Enrollment Services Office. This required money for a remodeling effort, so once again, a rationale had to be developed.

Fortunately, the Portland Committee's plan was still driving interest in the co-location of all student services, though the committee itself was disbanded. The scope of that plan had been large, and its prospects for implementation were weighted down by the politics of turf and the lack of sufficient capital funds for such an expansive remodeling effort. The 1997 proposal was to simply combine two offices, where the chief work consisted of tearing down the wall that separated them and creating a shared lobby and service desk. This proposal, though extremely significant in the ability to incrementally implement several aspects of the "Building Image / Building Enrollment" plan, was not large enough to thwart itself. Again, the support of several at the dean and vice presidential levels carried the day. Within five months the two separate offices opened their doors as a single operation and service center called Enrollment Services. This office provided such services as recruitment, admissions, registration, records, data reporting, international student services, Running Start (a high school dual enrollment program), advising, and credential and graduation evaluation.

During the remodeling period, the staffing structure of the new office was designed. Functions that had been duplicated by each office could now be combined, and the flow of students (from inquiry to graduation) could be coordinated more efficiently. This was achieved in several ways. First, as a result of ongoing training, all staff were expected to share a common set of skills and knowledge and to be cross-functional in several areas. Second, though a single individual might retain chief responsibility for a specific area (such as transcripts), one or more additional staff were expected to be skilled in that area also in order to act as backup. Third, a front line of four service desks were aligned and staffed with persons who were trained to respond to all sorts of requests (from inquiry to graduation) and perform the essential transactions for those requests. This significantly reduced student runaround and duplication of services. It also shielded some specialists from continuous interruptions so that they were more productive. Fourth, due to some savings in staff time, the new enhancements related to inquiry and application processes were assigned to specific staff, with a work area designed to accommodate the new processing demands.

The most important achievement, though, was that the synergy of the new group was able to provide a better overall college response to prospective, new and continuing students in terms of enrollment services. One key outcome of the group was that it was able to see that the whole (a newly combined team) exceeded the sum of the parts (a small staff in two separate offices).

The remodeling plan did not end the staff restructuring efforts, however. As stated above, staffing was seen as a critical element to assure success and quality. It seemed neither wise nor effective to work hard at attracting more students if staff could not provide an adequate response to their needs. On the one hand, the expansion of a responsive database, better written publications, and smoother customer service in Enrollment Services were seen as major "infrastructure" requirements to meet increased volume of interest in the college. On the other hand, the quality of the outreach and enrollment service needed to be addressed in order to appropriately enroll and retain students. As a result, the need for entry advising became the focus.

The issue of advising was not a new one for EvCC—and is a complex issue at many community colleges. Advising was (and is) theoretically the responsibility of the faculty as well as the staff of the Counseling Center. Though there are positive dimensions to that kind of model, gaps remain, particularly in the evenings and during term-breaks, when both of those resources are typically not available. Furthermore, on the EvCC campus, faculty involvement and interest in advising was spotty at best. The Portland Committee had addressed several advising dilemmas and the discussion was still alive. One approach had been to create several advising days throughout the summer, staffed by faculty under a special budget and payment arrangement. Though helpful, this approach did not address the underlying problems and certainly did not address the staffing needs required for a beefed-up outreach program.

The "Building Image / Building Enrollment" plan listed several items related to outreach and entry advising. Several activities were devised and assigned to current staff, but more human resources were needed. A proposal was made to add two new staff to the Enrollment Services area to act as both outreach workers as well as campus advisors. Because they would have staff status rather than faculty status, they would be available in the evenings and during breaks; the college would gain eighty hours per week throughout the year to enhance the recruiting and new student advising efforts. The fiscal demands of this proposal exceeded previous budgetary requests of all the earlier proposals and were, thus, a more difficult proposition to carry. The Advising

Committee was used as a forum, and presentations were made to deans and vice presidents. Clearly, this required the consensus of the instructional side of the house as well as student services in order to gain any strength within the budget planning. In 1998, the proposal was approved. Funding, though, was found in part by reducing the summer faculty advising budget. Shortly thereafter, Enrollment Services added two full-time coordinators of Outreach and Advising whose duties reflected the cross-functionality expected of other staff members and who were able to implement several aspects of the "Building Image / Building Enrollment" plan.

There is one more staffing adjustment worth describing because of its relationship to enrollment management. This part of the story neatly illustrates the serendipity of an incremental approach to strategic enrollment management and the value of snatching incremental opportunities. This part of the story focuses on the value of data in enrollment management. Though the college's data has been mentioned several times up to this point, the situation was far from perfect. Building and using databases, retrieving data to support proposals, and using data to make decisions was limited by three factors:

1. the statewide database was not very flexible and often mysterious in its workings;
2. there was no staff time to substantively restructure the approach to data collection;
3. there were no resources to analyze the data the college did have. A part-time institutional researcher employed with grant funds had departed in 1996 and the position had not been re-filled. All of the steps taken above were taken with minimal data, a risky approach.

Fortunately, the state legislature at that time demanded new and comprehensive reporting of college outcomes and performance; failure to do so would result in financial penalties. EvCC was overwhelmed with the project and it became very clear that a full-time institutional researcher was needed to develop the required data. Though late in the scheme to implement incremental steps toward enrollment management, the hiring of an institutional researcher in 1998 was one of the best things to happen that could possibly position the college for future steps toward comprehensive enrollment management.

TURNING POINT
Image and enrollment were building. The public was responding to the enhanced

marketing campaign. The enrollment of students direct from high school was increasing. To be honest, these results were probably the happy confluence of local demographics and a fluctuating economy, as well as the results of the "Building Image / Building Enrollment" efforts. It is not false to say, though, that the steps taken were having positive effects for the college. The simple fact is that the creation of an infrastructure enabled the college to respond to and grow the increased interest. EvCC was positioned for success.

At this time, 1999, the president of the college departed and a new president came on board with a new agenda. Other leadership changes occurred, and it seemed like a new era. Michael Dolence, a well-known consultant in strategic planning and enrollment management, was invited for a day of presentations and meetings. The new president fired up a strategic planning initiative. Within the first few formative meetings the now associate dean for Enrollment Services proposed and accepted the task of creating an environmental scan to support strategic planning. The production of the environmental scan, with the support of the new Institutional Research coordinator, marked another important incremental step toward enrollment management. The environmental scan wove together key quantitative and qualitative information that illuminated the college's position in the marketplace, its enrollment history and prospects and regional demographics.

The college's interest in avoiding enrollment roller coasters, the strategic planning process, and the sparks generated by the environmental scan converged in the consensus that a specific initiative toward enrollment growth needed to be one of the major initiatives of the strategic plan. And, as the strategic planning process progressed, and as the executive focus on the college's future sharpened, a challenge emerged that finally brought the college to strategic enrollment management.

So far the college's various efforts in building enrollment reflected a number of traditional elements of enrollment management: SWOT, data analysis, marketing and recruitment plan, enhancement of the infrastructure to respond to increased interest in the college, an environmental scan, inclusion in the college's strategic plan, and the fortuitous addition of an institutional researcher. However, these efforts were only loosely connected and still not linked to instructional and budget planning. In fact, the college seemed stuck in thinking of enrollment planning as a series of marketing and recruiting strategies that would culminate in the college's ability to "make its enrollment target." While a certain amount of pragmatic attention was paid to offering an attractive class schedule and a strong slate of certificates and degrees, the efforts of recruitment and instruction often did not connect. As expressed by the associate dean for Enrollment Services, "I know we want more students, but what types and how many?" In that situation, the institution was vulnerable to recruitment plans based on the biases of the enrollment staff. But that was about to change.

By 2000, the college's enrollment was strong. In several areas, enrollment was overflowing. The college was successfully addressing its most pressing financial problems. From this position of relative strength, the college began to analyze its growth potential and its need to both respond to the higher enrollment demand and build capacity for even larger enrollment growth in the next ten to fifteen years. This translated into a need for more seats, more classrooms, and more buildings. In the State of Washington, as in some other states, public institutions must make proposals for capital improvements, seek approval, and get into the queue for future funding. The college was at the proposal stage, the deadline was looming, and data and a plan to support the proposals was needed. Specifically, the college needed to project specific enrollment targets, areas of growth, and types of facilities needed to support that scenario. Future directions needed to be identified and, thus, provide the rationale for capital requests. Put simply, EvCC had a sudden need for a comprehensive enrollment plan.

From the point of view of the associate dean for Enrollment Services, the moment was perfect to propose that a strategic enrollment management planning process could be useful. The supporting tools of strategic enrollment management (SEM)—data, and an environmental scan—were already in place. The chief barrier to such a process, though, remained the same one that had dampened earlier efforts: lack of an institutional commitment and structure to assure a comprehensive process. Nonetheless, the need was great, and the proposal to devise a speedy preliminary strategic enrollment management plan was accepted. A small SEM committee formed in March 2000.

The president, three vice presidents, one instructional dean, and the associate dean for Enrollment Services met intensively for about six weeks. They churned out a report that framed the college's current position, described enrollment directions, and tentative targets for enrollment in various categories, such as university transfer, vocational and technical, distance, adult basic education, etc. The document sketched the scenario of the college's enrollment future and shaped and complemented the capital proposals. Mission accomplished.

The process was far from ideal. Analysis was quick and dirty, campus-wide consultation was not strong, and the hastily comprised committee structure did not spread accountability for some of the decisions implied in the plan. But again, viewed from the "incrementalist" point of view, it was a positive step. It was clear that a more thorough plan would help the college at a number of levels, and the executive leadership saw that.

In fact, during the six-week process two important issues had emerged. First, there were serious flaws in the college's data. The ability to determine enrollment trends in various programs was undermined by incorrect course coding and lack of consistency in categorizing courses and types of students. Facts no longer appeared to be reliable facts. Second, the financial implications of decisions about growth and no-growth areas were unclear, and an acceptable method of assessing those implications was not at hand. In other words, the college was still severely challenged in creating a comprehensive plan that linked enrollment targets with instructional and financial resources. The SEM goal of optimization was not yet within reach.

The president, though, was interested in expanding the SEM process. By the end of 2000, a larger committee was appointed and charged to develop a deeper and more comprehensive vision for enrollment growth for the next five years. Though mostly representative of several campus interest groups, the committee focused most clearly on designing a plan that identified the desired enrollment plans of the various instructional divisions, all leading to a carefully orchestrated 15% enrollment growth at the end of five years. The environmental scan was used to project probable demand and need. New strategies in distance education and continuing education were folded in. Recognition of the college's current limited physical capacity shaped some of the decisions. As deans saw their areas being affected they were either more or less active in the committee. Student services were not central to the discussion since the focus was so strongly on instructional enrollment patterns.

At this point, the college's position provided a good example of the value of comprehensive enrollment management during fat times. Enrollment was strong, and there were signs that enrollment would steadily increase. Moreover, the enrollment of full-time students was burgeoning. Ironically, this very abundance was threatening the college's fiscal stability. At the risk of being simplistic, the reasons were two-fold. One, enrollment was exceeding the state-funded enrollment target, so there were no additional dollars to support the over-enrollment. Two, due to the tuition rate scale, full-time students did not net as much tuition income as part-time students. This situation was threatening the college's reserves.

Finally, the issue of enrollment was no longer seen solely through the marketing lens but through the financial lens. Enrollment planning, while fundamentally tied to vision, mission and the instructional "product," had to be managed with respect to income and expenses. This was a breakthrough perspective, and consequently the vice president for Administrative Services began playing a crucial role in terms of analyzing financial strategies. Perhaps the most helpful tool was a spreadsheet that analyzed all college programs in terms of expenses and income, based on current enrollment.

The financial data generated new perspectives on planning the growth of the instructional offerings. Familiar desires, such as expanding technical program seats were moderated by a hard look at the loss column of those programs. Growth in self-support programs was envisioned as a way to offset income limitations from programs funded by state dollars. Social science and humanities classes were revealed as low cost opportunities to grow capacity and perhaps shelter programs of higher cost. While these perspectives seem intuitive, the discussion can become more realistic when the dollars can be calculated in plain sight for each proposal for growth, retrenchment, or change.

While advances in financial impact models were being made, the committee was still struggling with the basic data. With each new question asked, both the financial and enrollment historical data revealed weaknesses. In some cases, the data simply was not amenable to being crunched the way it was desired. In most cases, though, the detective work was plagued by continual findings that the interplay of incorrect coding and intricacies of the data storage system yielded contradictory, unreliable, and sometimes senseless numbers. Without going into gruesome detail, it should suffice to say that correcting the problems was frustrating in the short run, and rewarding in the long run (SEE FIGURE 8-1). The team learned a great deal about the system and corrected bad coding and data collection habits. It is highly probable that this situation is not unique to EvCC.

Marrying the newly improved financial and enrollment data finally led to a solid SEM report to the president twelve months later—a report that outlined desired growth patterns over the next five years in various instructional divisions and employed a number of strategies in both state-funded and self-supported programs.

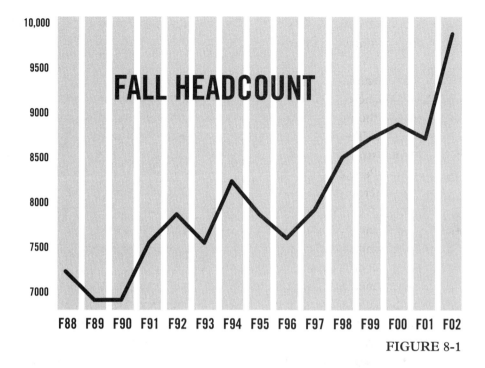

FIGURE 8-1

The year and a half spent on the preliminary fast-track SEM plan and the subsequent more detailed and solid plan supported by data, combined with the fruition of the overall strategic planning process, fulfilled many of the promises touted by SEM leaders. The college knew its ground, had a plan, and maintained an improved data system to monitor performance. The college even easily weathered a one-quarter downturn due to a turnover in funded workforce enrollment. Compared to its predicament five years before, the turnaround was impressive. In fact, things were impressive enough that eighteen months into the plan, Fall 2002, the college had already reached most of the five-year enrollment goals and was progressively restoring its desired financial reserve levels.

The SEM process also paved the way for some continued incremental improvements. As noted above, the formal SEM process focused largely on the relationships among enrollment, costs, and instructional programming, with less time spent on marketing, student services, and academic support. Because of the enhanced understanding about building an infrastructure that supports outreach, enrollment and retention, new processes in Web site design, transfer credit practices, and learning assistance were implemented by those units responsible for such work.

Few things are perfect though, and there were several weaknesses in the six years of incremental steps, eventual SEM process and the current SEM plan that are instructive.

LESSONS LEARNED

It is first important to acknowledge that there was little reason for the college to fail in growing its enrollment over the past several years. Unemployment was hitting new highs, massive tuition assistance programs were sending numerous unemployed and low-income folks to college, and the college district's population had jumped 36% between the 1990 and 2000 Census. The college would probably have grown without much help. But that is not really the point. Unmanaged or mismanaged growth presents difficult problems for an organization. Quality, efficiency, fiscal management, and the ability to achieve desired missions are thwarted in the absence of substantive planning—a lesson the college had learned the hard way during both lean and fat times. With that said, let us look at what can be learned.

The importance of good data cannot be overemphasized. With all the best intentions in the world, the leaders behind the 1988 plan, the Portland Committee, and "Building Image / Building Enrollment" plan did not pay enough attention to the data. The visible data appeared to be "enough" and it was easy to rationalize that by saying that EvCC lacked adequate resources to fully analyze what was available. However, hindsight indicates that if earlier efforts had really drilled into the data, its flaws (and opportunities) would have been more quickly revealed. Solid data may have enabled mid-managers to make a stronger case earlier for SEM planning. Better data may have saved the frustrating confusion when the preliminary and detailed SEM plans were being formulated. Colleagues who may feel that they are in the same position should consider posing some previously unasked research questions—especially questions that link enrollment and financial data—and carrying out some non-routine quality control tests as a way of seeing how responsive and accurate their underlying data are. It is when we move beyond the normal everyday use of our data that we find out how robust or elusive that data are.

The committee approach to SEM planning has some flaws. Michael Dolence (1993), Bob Bontrager (2002), and other authors (1996) describe the various models used by institutions to accomplish strategic enrollment management planning. The broad-based committee structure, which is the model employed by EvCC during its SEM planning, appears to be an attractive option for a mid-size community college, where the creation of a specific position or a unique department or division may seem like overkill. The strength of the committee structure is that it answers the need for SEM planning to be comprehensive and inclusive, and it allows the opportunity for diverse views to be heard and for arcane but necessary types of information to surface. The pitfalls, as experienced at EvCC, were

1. that representation often meant the appointment of people by virtue of their position rather than their interest;
2. that the committee work was on top of their regular duties; and
3. that once a committee's work appeared to be done, it was difficult to convene them for the continuous monitoring and renovation of the plan.

These tendencies can be mitigated by vigilant leadership at the top, and/or by the appointment of a highly placed authority as committee chair, but it is still a challenge. Colleagues who are pondering the best structure for SEM planning at their institution should first seek to assure the long-term commitment of the president and vice presidents. Then, when considering the structure, also seek and build interest in the stakeholders through individual meetings and data presentations. Early and continuous groundwork, of which EvCC did not do enough, will help a committee structure be a success.

Campus communication is a continuous challenge. Visible and aggressive enrollment planning is perceived as a threat (or a bother) by many on campus; Perhaps that is why the off-the-radar-screen incremental approach worked so well at EvCC as a prelude to formal SEM planning. At EvCC, the formal SEM process was carried out concurrent with the re-energized strategic planning process for the whole college. This served as something of a veil that prevented SEM from being "front page news" at the college. The chair of the SEM Committee sought to counteract that by offering open campus forums on SEM, sharing draft schemes, and actively seeking the feedback of some campus opinion-leaders. In retrospect these were good and necessary steps, but they were not enough to combat a simple perception that SEM planning would result in more students and, thus, larger unwanted and uncompensated loads on faculty. On the other hand, because SEM planning was occurring while the campus was suffering from over-enrollment, there was not a sense of urgency to plan for enrollment—after all, why does a college need to plan enrollment when there is already enough? Combating complacency and making the case for SEM as a tool to help an institution optimize its resources and stabilize its financial planning is an obscure proposition at best, and challenges the communication strategy of the SEM leaders.

The incremental approach may be just as valuable for a college as a formal SEM planning process. This lesson is perhaps the moral of this story. Many of us hear colleagues bemoaning the lack of executive-led enrollment planning at their college. Many of us work in colleges where there is a need for enrollment management but no single vehicle to design that process. Perhaps this case study can inspire enrollment professionals—and management at the dean and director levels—to address those matters over which they do have control: Web site design, electronic and print communication methods with prospective students, retention strategies, data collection and analysis, and instructional programming, to name a few. From the EvCC point of view, our ability to focus on the critical relationships among enrollment and financial data and instructional programming was strengthened because much of the spadework on developing an infrastructure to support marketing and enrollment had been done through the earlier deliberate incremental improvements. The key may be to recognize and employ an incremental approach as a way to set the table for a full-bodied SEM approach at some later date.

FINAL NOTES

EvCC is in the process of reviewing its SEM plan and process. The difficulty of maintaining the interest and involvement of a large committee, a new direction by the president to involve the board in evaluating desirable program mix of the college, a structural reorganization at the executive level to emphasize institutional advancement, and the continued rush of enrollment have challenged a by-the-book approach to SEM. On the other hand, this is simply another example of how enrollment management needs to fit within unique educational environments and changing cultures.

Since SEM did not start at EvCC "by-the-book" it would be surprising if it followed any predictable trajectory. This case study may be instructive to most of the colleges and universities in the U.S., which are also subject to internal and external strengths, weaknesses, and change. As this case study demonstrates, there is no single route to strategic enrollment management.

REFERENCES

Bontrager, B. (2002, November). Strategic Enrollment Management: An Introduction to Core Concepts and Strategies. Monograph prepared for the annual Strategic Enrollment Management Conference of the American Association of Collegiate Registrars and Admissions Officers, San Diego, CA.

Dolence, M.G. (1993). <u>Strategic Enrollment Management: A Primer for Campus Administrators.</u> Washington DC: American Association of Collegiate Registrars and Admissions Officers.

Dolence, M.G. (1996). <u>Strategic Enrollment Management: Cases From the Field.</u> Washington DC: American Association of Collegiate Registrars and Admissions Officers.

9

DEVELOPING AN ENROLLMENT MANAGEMENT ORGANIZATION

BOB BONTRAGER

OSU Oregon State University's enrollment history has been a dynamic one in the recent past. In a span of twenty years, university enrollment:

* reached its highest point ever,
* dropped to its lowest point in thirty years, then
* rebounded in a five-year span to a new record enrollment.

The resurgence was prompted by the adoption of an enrollment management organizational structure. In many ways, the experience at Oregon State parallels the history of the profession, thus offering a useful case study in the application of enrollment management concepts and strategies.

INTRODUCTION

Oregon State University's enrollment history has been a dynamic one in the recent past. In a span of twenty years, university enrollment:

* reached its highest point ever,
* dropped to its lowest point in thirty years, then
* rebounded in a five-year span to a new record enrollment.

TABLE 9-1

	ENROLLMENT TREND	INSTITUTIONAL MESSAGES	INSTITUTIONAL ACTION
STAGE 1 Denial	Down	The enrollment downturn is temporary; we don't have to worry. It's just (pick one) demographics/ the economy/our competitor(s)'s strategy. We are subject to forces beyond our control.	Form a committee. Talk
STAGE 2 Nominal	Down	We need to do something. We need a "silver bullet" recruiting/ marketing strategy.	Fund ad hoc, short-term strategies lacking enrollment management (EM) expertise.
STAGE 3 Structural	Up for a year or two, then down again	This isn't as easy as we thought.	Limited restructuring. Continue to employ short-term strategies based on minimal EM expertise.
STAGE 4 Tactical	Building to optimum enrollment	To achieve optimum enrollment will require fundamental changes.	Substantive restructuring. Strategic planning based on reliable data and strong EM expertise. Targeted funding.
STAGE 5 Strategic	Achieving optimum enrollment	We control our enrollment outcomes.	Stable EM structure and funding. Top-level EM leadership. Consistent planning and assessment cycle.

The resurgence was prompted by the adoption of an enrollment management organizational structure. In many ways, the experience at Oregon State parallels the history of the profession, thus offering a useful case study in the application of enrollment management concepts and strategies.

AN ENROLLMENT MANAGEMENT TRANSITION MODEL

The transition to becoming an enrollment management organization is not an easy one. To do so requires a fundamental shift in both administrative structure and institutional behavior. Such transitions tend to proceed in a series of stages, and Oregon State was a textbook example, at least among moderately selective institutions with excess capacity. A typical model for implementing enrollment management at these types of institutions is illustrated in Table 9-1 (adapted from Dolence, 1997).

In the *Institutional Action* column, "cosmetic restructuring" is defined as realigning existing core departments—e.g., Admissions, Registrar's Office, Financial Aid—into a new enrollment services/management structure. Often this includes promoting an existing director from one of these departments to oversee the new combined unit, rather than creating a new position to be filled by an individual with specific expertise in enrollment management. By contrast, "substantive restructuring" refers to realigning a larger number of departments around a more comprehensive enrollment management perspective, creating a new position to provide leadership, and hiring an individual with specific enrollment management experience and expertise.

Within the transition model, two additional points warrant highlighting. The first is the shift in institutional message from the reactive "subject to forces beyond our control" to the proactive "we control our enrollment destiny." Institutions that are not actively managing their enrollments are, in fact, subject to forces beyond their control, whether those forces are demographic, economic, or competitive. Enrollment management concepts and strategies allow institutions to control their enrollment destiny by accounting for the many prevailing forces at work, implementing strategies that compensate for them, and, wherever possible, exploiting them.

The second highlight is the concept of optimum enrollment. "Optimum" as used here is a comprehensive concept, with the desired outcome defined not as one enrollment goal, but many (Dolence, 1993; Bontrager, 2002). Depending on institutional mission, there are many optimum enrollments, based on a wide range of variables. These include:

* academic ability;
* academic program interest;
* special skills (fine arts, leadership, athletics);
* ethnicity;
* undergraduate/graduate status;
* financial status;
* resident/non-resident status; and
* program and facility capacities.

Managing enrollments requires attention to each of these variables, rather than just the aggregate numbers that tend to receive more emphasis.

DESCRIPTION OF OREGON STATE UNIVERSITY

Oregon State University is Oregon's land, sea, and space grant university, one of only fifteen institutions nationally to hold these joint designations. OSU held the Research I classification under the former Carnegie taxonomy, and is a Doctoral-Extensive institution currently. OSU enrolls 19,000 students, including 15,500 undergraduate and 3,500 graduate students. Among OSU undergraduates, eighty-four percent are Oregon residents, fifteen percent are from other U.S. states, and one percent are international students. Students of color comprise 12.1 % of the student body, the highest of any Oregon public university outside of the Portland metropolitan area, where the vast majority of the state's students of color reside. OSU offers seventy-nine undergraduate majors and ninety-five minors and concentrations, as well as ninety-seven master's and doctoral programs. OSU's largest colleges in terms of undergraduate enrollment are Engineering, Liberal Arts, and Science.

OSU's graduate enrollments have been stable. Thus, the focus of this case study will be the effort to effectively manage undergraduate enrollments.

THE COMPELLING CASE FOR CHANGE

Oregon State was established with other land grant universities in the late 1800s and grew steadily through the 20th century. Fueled in the 1950s, 1960s, and 1970s by the GI Bill, the Civil Rights Movement, and the vast numbers of the baby boom generation, OSU achieved a high enrollment of nearly 17,700 students in 1980. From 1980 through 1996, the university continued to mirror national demographics. The exception was 1991 to 1995, when increased spending on recruiting activities enabled OSU to enroll more freshmen. Those gains proved to be short-lived, however, as failure

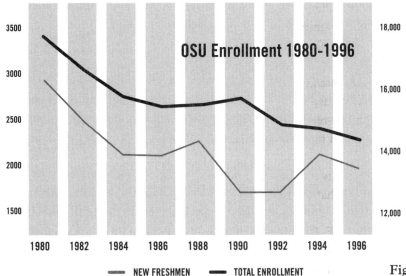

Figure 9-1

to address retention issues led to a drop in retention, and a continued downward enrollment spiral as illustrated by Chart 9-1.

OSU's enrollment history parallels the emergence of enrollment management as a profession. Like many flagship public universities, OSU was slow to respond to eroding demographics and declining enrollment in the early 1980s. The prevailing thinking was that the high levels of name recognition and legacy predisposition would shield the university from continued enrollment declines. After a fourteen percent drop in enrollment from 1980 to 1985, concerns were calmed briefly by an upturn in both demographics and enrollment from 1986 to 1990. When enrollment entered another free-fall in the early 1990s, however, it was clear to all involved that significant action was needed to address the "enrollment problem."

Additional motivation to address enrollment issues came in the form of dwindling financial resources throughout this period. Enhancing net revenue has always been a goal of enrollment management. The drop in both federal and state support to higher education over the past two decades has added another important financial considera-tion: efficiency. At Oregon State, as elsewhere, it is no longer good enough to bring more students and revenue to the university. We now are asked to do so in the least expensive, most cost-effective way possible.

INSTITUTIONAL STORY: ESTABLISHING AN ENROLLMENT MANAGEMENT PERSPECTIVE AT OREGON STATE

From the mid-1980s to early 1990s, Oregon State went through stages 1 and 2 of its transition to enrollment management, with the attendant early denial and later efforts to address the university's enrollment issues. As enrollments began to decline, the university relied far too heavily on its land grant status and dominant market position among Oregon students. The prevailing wisdom on the campus at that time was that the historical inertia of name recognition and attraction of in-state students would ultimately prevail and overcome forces perceived to be beyond the university's ability to counteract, most prominently the decrease in high school graduates. By 1990, the combined effects of enrollment and state funding declines were so severe that campus leaders were forced to take notice. In the early 1990s, they took the tentative steps of forming committees and devoting much conversation to the enrollment problem. Money was allocated to fund ad hoc recruitment strategies designed to attract more students. These activities were poorly conceived, lacked coordination, and achieved virtually no success.

The heart of the Oregon State enrollment management story commences in 1993 with the beginning of Stage 3, when the university made these structural changes:

* Three departments—Admissions, the Registrar's Office, and New Student Programs (open house programs, orientation)—were combined into a new enrollment services unit.
* The registrar was promoted to the new position, director of Enrollment Services. This change was limited in three respects. The registrar retained her registrar responsibilities; she was initially offered only a minimal salary increase to take on the enrollment services role; and, by remaining at the "director" level, she had two other "directors" reporting to her.
* Additional funds were allocated to boost salaries of Admissions staff, for additional out-of-state recruiting, and for new recruiting activities (e.g., evening receptions for admitted students in targeted recruiting areas).

These changes did prompt an increase in new freshmen. However, as is inherent to Stage 3, the changes proved to be too limited in addressing the full range of enrollment issues. Increases in new students failed to stem the decrease in overall enrollment. Conceptually, the university failed to grasp the full implications of enrollment management and continued to think in terms of ad hoc, short-term strategies delivered

TRANSITIONING FROM STAGE 3
TO STAGE 4: FROM STRUCTURAL TO TACTICAL

The director of Enrollment Services was astute in observing these shortcomings and in 1994 sought to boost Oregon State's enrollment management expertise by adding an experienced enrollment manager to her staff. In doing so, she propelled Oregon State through the latter stages of Stage 3 and into the beginning of the Stage 4 enrollment management transition.

The transition from Stage 3 to 4 is perhaps the most challenging point in creating an enrollment management organization. Prevailing assumptions are challenged, higher expectations are established, and staff members are held more accountable to measurable results. Most significantly, departmental responsibilities and alignments are viewed from a different perspective, one that focuses on achieving optimum enrollments rather than building institutional structures based on historical precedence. This typically results in new reporting lines, restructured departments, and revised position descriptions. In short, this transition involves a series of fundamental changes enacted over an extended period of time. Often this is the time of greatest challenge.

True to form, OSU's experience at this point in the transition has not been easy and is still in process. In the first two years there were multiple attempts to restructure operations in order to achieve desired outcomes. Ultimately, the Enrollment Services unit was disbanded and a new unit named Admission and Orientation was created under the leadership of the newly hired enrollment manager. This essentially "cleared the decks," enabling the new unit to begin building a true enrollment management organization. Establishing strong enrollment management concepts in the front-end processes of admission and orientation led additional and more comprehensive restructuring as OSU entered the tactical stage.

One of the biggest temptations to overcome in addressing enrollment issues is the tendency to begin by implementing new strategies without paying adequate attention to infrastructure. At Oregon State, this phenomenon manifested itself in the implementation of new recruiting activities, even as the core business practices in Admission and Orientation continued to operate at a sub-par level. In the context of rolling admissions, students with complete admission files waited more than a month for a decision.

Requests for information could take weeks for a response. It was clear that the infrastructure was not in good shape. Thus, entering the tactical stage of the enrollment management transition required building an infrastructure to support enrollment goals.

Enabling initiative. People want to excel at their work. Given that basic premise, it is remarkable how frequently institutional structures create barriers to staff productivity and satisfaction. Enrollment decline itself poses one of the greatest threats to staff initiative and morale. Few factors affect an institution's sense of well-being as much as whether enrollment is up or down in a given year.

Oregon State's protracted enrollment struggles from 1980 to 1996 had a debilitating effect on staff's sense of pride, purpose, and initiative. There was a resignation to disappointing enrollment results and quick excuse-making when things did not go as planned. Most significantly, staff did not enjoy working in Admissions. Thus the first goal was to tap into the Admission and Orientation staff's inherent desire to excel and create new license for them to take initiative in their work. A new mission statement for the office was developed with broad staff input (see Appendix 3). While revised to reflect special emphases desired by the OSU staff, the statement borrowed heavily from a mission statement developed by Wayne Sigler for the Admissions Office at the University of Minnesota (Sigler, 1996).

Building morale. The creation of the mission statement itself boosted morale, as staff members were given freedom to take additional initiative and, in that process, saw that their expertise was respected. Additionally, opportunities were sought to build morale through enhanced working relationships and opened channels of communication. Each functional subunit within the office was recast a team, which began to meet regularly to establish goals, review outcomes, and share information. Monthly all-staff meetings were created to discuss an office-wide agenda. Upper-level university administrators—including the president, provost, and deans—were invited to share their perspectives on the work of the Admission and Orientation Office and answer questions about the broader university agenda. The message to the staff was that their work was important to the university, and their individual perspectives mattered.

In addition to these changes in office practices, special effort was made to create non-work settings for staff to interact and communicate on a more personal level. These social events were held both during and after business hours and were planned by volunteers from all levels of the office structure, providing another opportunity for cross-functional collaboration.

Creating the capacity to excel. Enabling initiative and building morale are required components, but to fully develop the capacity to excel requires the addition of measurable goals. At Oregon State, because of significant infrastructure issues, it started at a basic level. A number of procedural measures were set, beginning with simple metrics such as:

* Decision on a completed admission application: two weeks;
* Response to inquiries: one week (peak time), two days (non-peak);
* Number of admission files processed daily by evaluators; and
* Number of personal contacts daily by admission counselors to prospective students.

Initial reaction by the staff to these measurable goals was negative. They resisted counting their actions, based on the fear that failure to produce adequate numbers would result in negative performance evaluations. The key was clarifying that the intent of tracking output was not punitive, but rather a means to identify areas there were opportunities to improve.

Business practice reengineering. Like many offices, the Oregon State Admission and Orientation Office had evolved over time, resulting in a jerry-rigged structure, with duties and responsibilities added periodically to meet transient needs. This was in contrast to the well-oiled machine sought, an operation characterized by equal parts effectiveness and efficiency.

The office engaged in a reengineering process designed to streamline operations, realign staff positions, and improve productivity. Each function and staff position in the office was reevaluated for efficiency and alignment. Results were dramatic. The time required to process a completed application dropped from two months to one week. Response to inquiries from prospective students decreased from one month to two days. Along with the increased productivity, staff satisfaction increased dramatically.

Implementing new strategies. With a revitalized infrastructure in place, the office began to implement new strategies designed to increase the number of new students enrolling at Oregon State. These included:

* A comprehensive marketing plan, carefully coordinated with recruiting activities.
* Market segmentation, utilizing geodemographic research.
* Financial aid leveraging.

* Implementation of comprehensive fall orientation and First-Year Experience programs.
* Online services.

Each of these initiatives could warrant their own chapter to fully explain. The key point here is that attention to core infrastructure issues created a context in which the office could be successful in implementing new strategies. Had it not first attended to those foundational issues, the strategic initiatives would not have been nearly as successful. Having taken the more deliberate, long-term approach, the office achieved dramatic enrollment increases, as will be detailed later in this case study.

PROCEEDING THROUGH STAGE 4: ESTABLISHING A TACTICAL ORGANIZATION

For many institutions, the story would stop there. Reversing an enrollment decline would often be construed as having "fixed" an enrollment problem. However, enrollment management is not defined solely as increasing the number of new students, no matter how dramatically. Similarly, to implement enrollment management has implications far beyond admission and orientation functions. For all the attention given to enrollment matters when numbers are down, it is at least as important—and possibly more so—to aggressively address enrollment issues when the numbers are good. Indeed, one of the greatest pitfalls with regard to managing enrollment is complacency.

At Oregon State, in spite of success in increasing enrollment, in reality it had only scratched the surface in terms of becoming a true enrollment management enterprise. Though the number of new students was up significantly, retention rates were flat. While the office had improved collaboration among campus departments, core enrollment service areas such as admissions, orientation, registration, and financial aid continued to be structured in silo fashion under the vice provost for Academic Affairs. The vice provost role itself was a conglomeration of disjointed functions and departments, as illustrated in **Table 9-2.**

Further complicating this picture was a history of filling the vice provost position with the head of an OSU academic department. The position regularly turned over in five-year cycles. Thus, key enrollment-related units were repeatedly reporting to an individual with no background in central university administration or enrollment management, and were working within a structure that itself did not support an enrollment management agenda. For all those reasons, in the context of record enrollment, Oregon State sought to make

Table 9-2

further changes and step fully into the tactical stage of an enrollment management transition.

A window of opportunity emerged with the resignation of the vice provost for Academic Affairs. A series of discussions on potential restructuring ensued around these goals:

* Bringing key enrollment departments and functions together under the leadership of an enrollment management professional.
* Eliminating the turnover of leadership inherent to the vice provost role.
* Raising enrollment expertise to a higher level in the university structure.

An executive summary of the proposal to establish an enrollment management structure is provided as Appendix 4.

Organizational Structure Before Enrollment Management

Vice Provost Academic Affairs

* Admission and Orientation
* Curriculum Processing
* Financial Aid
* Institutional Research
* Faculty Promotion and Tenure
* Registrar's Office
* ROTC
* Summer Session and Pre-College Programs
* Undergraduate Academic Programs
    - Academic Support Programs
    - Freshman orientation course
    - First-Year Experience

As could be expected, reaction to the proposal was mixed. Before the proposal was submitted, directors of the departments to be included in the new enrollment management division were consulted to determine their level of support. With minimal discussion, they saw the merits of the proposed restructuring and became advocates. Convincing the rest of the campus was more difficult. The outgoing vice provost for Academic Affairs was adamantly opposed to the proposal, viewing it as a negative reflection on his leadership of the enrollment-related departments and being reluctant to add an administrative position. The latter concern had merit, as establishing a new enrollment management structure and leadership role would add a layer of administration, something generally to be avoided. Perhaps less valid was the knee-jerk negative reaction to "adding an administrator." Whatever its merits, this argument carried a great deal of weight among the academic deans, who had a prominent voice in the decision.

However, the proposal had an important ally—the president. While acknowledging the concerns of many, he noted that the importance of enrollment to the university warranted extraordinary measures. Indeed, the president had long since identified enrollment as the university's top priority. With his support, the proposal carried the day and in March

2001, OSU's Enrollment Management Division was established (see Table 9-3).

In addition to creating the Enrollment Management Division, a key component of this model was the intentional alignment of Enrollment Management with the Academic Programs Division. The functions of Academic Programs were closely tied to Enrollment Management and the new organization structure was intended to make explicit the need for those units and functions to work collaboratively. Beyond the organizational structure, the assistant provost offices were moved to the same location on campus to further reinforce the collaborative nature of their roles.

While having support among department directors, other staff members were far less familiar with the concept of enrollment management. They were at various places on a continuum ranging from curiosity to outright skepticism. Open forums were held with staff at all levels from each of the Enrollment Management departments. Under the direction of an outside facilitator, staff members were encouraged to say whatever was on their minds and ask questions. The first such meetings were not easy. Displaying classic behavior in the face of change, some staff reacted quite negatively, expressing concern about becoming affiliated with this unknown "enrollment management" entity. As a result of this initial session, new lines of communication were established with the input of all involved. Six months later when the second such forum was held, the tone had taken a 180-degree turn. Staff members had adequate time to learn more about the concepts of enrollment management and see the advantages, particularly in terms of procedures and programs that were made easier by the new level of collaboration that existed among departments. They had become advocates of the new structure and, more importantly, the enrollment management perspective. Out of these conversations, a mission and purpose statement was developed, and is provided as Appendix 5.

Even though staff within enrollment management units quickly became "sold" on the new structure, convincing the rest of the campus is still very much in process. Within six months of the establishment of the Enrollment Management Division, Oregon State found itself in a major financial crisis, with an unexpected budget shortfall of $19 million. This forced the university into crisis management mode and led to a reversion to prior understandings and behavior. Part of this was renewed scrutiny and questioning of new initiatives, including enrollment management.

In spite of continued record enrollment and demonstrated increases in net revenue, support for enrollment management again became more difficult to obtain. This challenge was exacerbated by the departure of the supportive president. In the wake of

Table 9-3

his departure, the assistant provost for Enrollment Management was removed from the President's Cabinet, along with other "non-academic" administrators including the dean of Students, director of Marketing, and director of Multicultural Affairs. In addition, the Enrollment Management Division was moved from Academic Affairs to Student Affairs, reflecting the view that Enrollment Management departments were providers of student services, rather than direct supporters of the university's academic mission.

While regrettable, these developments are understandable and give us a clear mandate for the future. They are understandable when viewed from the perspective of the still-developing status of enrollment management as a concept and function in higher education, especially in the public sector. Even after nearly thirty years since it first came on the scene in private institutions, enrollment management still is not widely viewed as a required structural component in higher education. Thus, its presence on a given campus is often subject to the individual perspective of persons who are making the decisions at a given point in time.

Organizational Structure After Enrollment Management

Vice Provost Academic Affairs
* Institutional Research
* Faculty Promotion and Tenure
* ROTC

Assistant Provost Enrollment Management
* Admissions
* Pre-College Programs
* Financial Aid & Scholarships
* Registrar's Office
* Student Orientation & Retention
  - Programs
  - Freshman orientation course
  - First-Year Experience

Assistant Provost Academic Programs
* Academic Support Programs
* Curriculum Processing
* Summer Session

This fact demands that enrollment professionals be active educators regarding the concepts of enrollment management and the benefits to the institution. This is not a one-time or short-term event, but an ongoing task. It is more than making a point in a neutral context. It requires extraordinary effort to overcome prevailing perceptions and misconceptions, which have strong historical precedence.

At Oregon State, a great deal of work remains to be done in this regard. The campus is roughly three-fourths of the way through Stage 4 of its enrollment management transition. A viable organizational structure is in place, with considerable and growing enrollment management expertise among the staff. A Strategic Enrollment Planning Group has been established to set targets for optimum enrollment, prioritize among competing enrollment goals, and maximize net revenue. This new committee is co-chaired by two academic deans and has regular points of review and approval with the university's top decision-making groups, as described in Appendix 6. As these recent changes take hold, Oregon State has the opportunity to evolve into Stage 5 of the Enrollment Management Transition Model, characterized by strategic implementation of enrollment management concepts, achievement of optimum enrollments, and stable funding.

RESULTS

Oregon State has been fortunate enough to achieve many of its enrollment goals through careful planning, strategic investment, and delivery of top-quality services. From the recent low of 13,684 students in 1996, by Fall 2000, enrollment had grown to 18,034, an increase of thirty-one percent. Over this period, the number of new freshmen grew from 1,854 to 3,200, an increase of seventy-two percent. Quality measures of incoming students and retention rates have remained steady. Enrollment of students of color has increased to the highest numbers ever, though percentages have dropped slightly in the face of such large overall increases. The cost of enrolling a new student has dropped from $650 to $575, addressing the efficiency issues that are of growing importance.

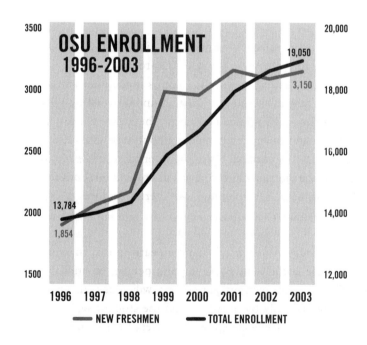

Casual observers attributed these gains to more favorable demographics, noting that many institutions around the country have achieved enrollment gains in recent years. However, the number of high school graduates in Oregon, from which OSU gets more than eighty percent of its students, increased by only fifteen percent during this period. To put it simply, a move into the latter stages of transition to enrollment management resulted in gaining control of enrollment outcomes. The dramatic jump in enrollment has put Oregon State into a completely different posture with regard to enrollment management. It has gone from enrolling as many qualified students as possible to facing the full range of capacity issues. These include the physical and program capacity of the campus as well as the composition of the student body based on residency, ethnicity, student level, and other characteristics. In short, OSU is now in a position to truly manage enrollment, rather than just seeking to increase aggregate numbers. Perhaps most importantly, campus decision-makers are increasingly looking past outmoded assumptions to a more realistic understanding of what it means to manage enrollment in the present context.

LESSONS LEARNED

There are many lessons on the road to enrollment management. Oregon State's experience suggests three that bear highlighting.

Results are necessary, but not sufficient. Oregon State imagined that its positive enrollment results would allow it to make the transition to enrollment management more quickly. In reality, while early successes allowed the campus to open certain conversations, it did not find the going as easy as imagined. Colleges and universities are venerable institutions with long histories and engrained cultures. The higher education arena is rife with conventional wisdom and outright mythology about what it takes to effectively recruit and retain students. In this context, even strong enrollment results sometimes cannot hold the line against the inertia, which draws persons and institutions toward historical, more familiar perspectives. Overcoming this inertia requires a continual education process backed by hard data.

Enrollment results need to be personalized. As noted early in this chapter, colleges and universities have multiple enrollment goals, each important to one or more institutional constituencies. While many campus supporters will focus on aggregate enrollment, others will be persuaded only by results within the student segments with which they have the most interest. Indeed, the glow of an overall enrollment increase can quickly be extinguished when talking to an individual or group whose target segment of the student population experienced a decline. Building support for enrollment management requires the development of enrollment targets and reports tailored to an institution's many constituencies, ranging from internal colleges and departments, to communities of color, to legislators.

Celebrate progress. The enrollment management literature generally refers to a period of three to five years for establishing an effective enrollment management organization. However, it will typically take longer to establish a lasting enrollment management perspective and structure on a campus. At Oregon State, it took ten years to establish a viable enrollment management structure. After three years with the structure in place, the campus continues to work toward achieving broad understanding of enrollment management concepts institution-wide.

CONCLUSION

To borrow a common saying, enrollment management is a journey, not a destination. This certainly is the case for Oregon State. It has come a long way, with still much to be accomplished as it strives to become a viable and stable enrollment management organization.

REFERENCES

Bontrager, B. (2002). Strategic Enrollment Management: An Introduction to Core Concepts and Strategies. Washington, DC: American Association of Collegiate Registrars and Admissions Officers.

Dolence, M.G. (1993). Strategic Enrollment Management: A Primer for Campus Administrators. Washington, DC: American Association of Collegiate Registrars and Admissions Officers.

Dolence, M.G. (1997). SEM and the 21st Century. Paper presented at the American Association of Collegiate Registrars and Admissions Officers' Strategic Enrollment Management Conference, Orlando, FL.

Sigler, W. (1996). On the Road to Enrollment Management at the University of Minnesota. In M.G. Dolence (Ed.) Strategic enrollment management: Cases from the field. Washington, DC: American Association of Collegiate Registrars and Admissions Officers.

10

ENROLLMENT MANAGEMENT ARCHITECTURE

JIM BLACK

UNCG The University of North Carolina at Greensboro (UNCG), one of sixteen public institutions in the University of North Carolina system, enrolls 14,500 students in on- and off-campus bachelor's, master's, and Ph.D. programs. The institution has a long history with enrollment management. More than twenty years ago, the university created an enrollment management organizational structure and hired its first chief enrollment officer. Evolving through the years, the current structure includes Undergraduate Admissions, Financial Aid, University Registrar's Office, Student Success Center, Student Academic Services, and Evening University.

THE ENROLLMENT MANAGEMENT CONTEXT

The University of North Carolina at Greensboro (UNCG), one of sixteen public institutions in the University of North Carolina system, enrolls 14,500 students in on- and off-campus bachelor's, master's, and Ph.D. programs. The institution has a long history with enrollment management. More than twenty years ago, the university created an enrollment management organizational structure and hired its first chief enrollment officer. Evolving through the years, the current structure includes Undergraduate Admissions, Financial Aid, University Registrar's Office, Student Success Center, Student Academic Services, and Evening University. Other evidence of the institution's acceptance of enrollment management as a legitimate discipline is manifested in the university's nationally ranked School of Education. In 1986, UNCG became one of the first (if not the first) institutions in the country to offer an enrollment management course in its higher education graduate program. Dr. Bert Goldman, who created the course, still teaches it today.

Despite a long-term understanding of and commitment to the discipline of enrollment management, the university had not institutionalized strategic planning, integrated processes, developed the necessary infrastructure, and dedicated the resources found in a mature enrollment management organization. Until seven years ago, there had never been an enrollment management plan or adequate resources to support basic operations such as postage, printing, and telephone services. Processes were anything but seamless and were extremely manual. Departmental silos were dense, usually by design, and virtually impenetrable—making interoffice communication and coordination nonexistent. Literally, department heads within the same division did not speak to one another.

Before 1996, enrollment goals were based primarily on the need to meet certain revenue targets rather than the likelihood that the goals could be achieved. Consequently, for many years the university did not realize enrollment goals and thus, revenue projections. When this occurs, the standard institutional response is to search for blame. Typical of most institutions, UNCG found a convenient scapegoat in the Undergraduate Admissions. Unfortunately, the Admissions staff had never been consulted about enrollment goals nor had they been given an opportunity to share admissions strategies with key decision-makers. Hence, inferences were made in a vacuum, and the Admissions staff quickly became victims. Morale was understandably low, and any motivation to improve the recruitment effort was driven by a survival imperative rather than thoughtful, data-driven decisions.

One such institutional panic-driven decision was to lower admission standards. In 1995, the acceptance rate was 88%—effectively open admissions. Though the size of the entering class increased with the lowering of standards raising total enrollment, the effect was short-lived. The first-year retention rate for the 1995 cohort was the lowest in more than a decade, at seventy-one percent. While difficult to measure, another negative outcome of lower admissions standards was that of tarnishing the institution's image. Once damaged, institutional image is difficult to repair.

About the same time, UNCG hired a new chancellor, Patricia A. Sullivan, who quickly established a "student-centered" vision for the university. Sophomore and senior satisfaction surveys administered throughout the University of North Carolina system revealed that UNCG was not perceived as "student-centered," ranking lower than all of its top five competitors within the system on eleven of twenty-two survey items.

BUILDING A COMPELLING CASE
In the fall of 1996, Jim Black became the associate provost for Enrollment Services at The University of North Carolina at Greensboro. Prior to his arrival on campus, he began to develop a situational analysis for the university, designed to raise awareness of the complex dynamics impacting enrollment and to create a sense of urgency. Such dynamics included demographic trends, college-going rates, transfer practices, market share, competitor comparisons, academic program trends, pricing trends, financial aid patterns, institutional image data, cost/benefit comparisons for existing recruitment strategies, retention and graduation rate comparisons with similar institutions, student expectation data, as well as student services usage and satisfaction rates. By understanding the multitude of factors influencing enrollments, members of the campus community could consider their own role in achieving institutional goals.

Combined with awareness, a sense of urgency became a powerful force. As a state-supported institution with a long history and healthy endowment, UNCG had a sense of urgency that was not one of survival. However, faculty and staff clearly wanted the institution to improve its position in the higher education marketplace. Low admissions standards, low satisfaction ratings, abysmal retention and graduation rates, and a poor or "plain vanilla" image were seen as an embarrassment by some and a threat by others. Many also viewed enrollment growth opportunities as a way to garner operating resources and faculty or staff positions.

Coinciding with the situational analysis presentations was the development of the university's first comprehensive enrollment management plan, which called for one million dollars beyond the existing Enrollment Services' budget. Approximately one-third of this amount was needed to strengthen existing operations while the remaining dollars were needed for new initiatives, staff positions, and infrastructure. Because seventy-five percent of the university's budget is in Academic Affairs, the necessary funds could be found in only one place—the academic units.

Over a period of nine months, the associate provost shared information with the academic deans at least once a month. Information was presented in sound bytes, each building on the next and flowing from the original situational analysis. The purpose was to tell a story so compelling that the deans would sacrifice their resources for the common good. Obviously, they must see the potential of a return on their investment, but they also must trust the message as well as the messenger. Building relationships was fundamental to fostering that trust. Every professional interaction with them was designed to present an institutional problem that impacted them directly and to demonstrate with supporting data and thoughtfully engineered strategies that Enrollment Services had the answer.

By the end of the nine-month period, the academic deans were presented with the enrollment management plan and a price tag. Following an awkward pause and a few loud gasps, the deans unanimously agreed to support the plan. Intellectually, they had reached the point where they fervently believed that without the full implementation of the enrollment management plan they would not achieve the ambitions they had for their school.

A year later, Associate Provost Black presented data demonstrating that enrollment growth had generated nine million in additional revenue. Among other things, the increase included with it forty-four new faculty positions. The deans were pleased with the nine to one return on their initial investment and offered additional financial support.

Through the leadership of the provost, Edward A. Uprichard, and the academic deans enrollment efforts became an institutional priority. Budget allocations were based largely on enrollment growth and decline. Consequently, faculty and department heads had a strong incentive to engage in recruitment and retention efforts. Enrollment became one of five strategic directions in the university's long-range plan. This had implications for funding, but more importantly, it meant that every administrative and academic unit had to think about recruitment and retention in the departmental planning process. Departmental strategies, collaboration with Enrollment Services and the Graduate School, evaluation of enrollment efforts, and annual reports that served as a system of accountability were all byproducts of the planning process.

The alignment of the university's vision, institutional planning, resource allocations, incentives, the skill development of the staff, and a sound action plan proved to be a powerful force for changing the culture. Faculty and staff became more marketing-savvy and learner-focused. Discussions about departmental marketing or student retention became commonplace. Even the lexicon on campus was influenced by enrollment management concepts.

All of this, however, is not intended to suggest that the culture has evolved without struggle and conflict. To the contrary, the campus has had significant dissonance over issues such as defining what it means to "be a leading student-centered university," raising admissions standards versus expanding access, managing capacity while seeking funding for enrollment growth, and valuing advising in the tenure and promotion process. Though it may seem counterintuitive, this conflict has been the secret to our success. Opposing viewpoints challenge the status quo and keep an organization on the "bleeding edge." Such fragileness compels an institution to change. Absent of widespread change, no enrollment organization can significantly affect and sustain desired outcomes.

THE ENROLLMENT MANAGEMENT PLAN

The planning process was as inclusive as possible but practical matters limited the degree to which broad-based involvement actually occurred. The associate provost developed the framework for the plan along with a road map for the planning process. Both were shared with academic deans, Faculty Enrollment Management Committee, Administrative Planning Group, and the Enrollment Services staff. As each component of the plan was completed, it was disseminated to the groups referenced above for comment. Much of the feedback received was incorporated into the planning document.

Based on the data collected for the situational analysis and the goals of the university, the entire Enrollment Services staff crafted a shared vision statement. This process lasted three months with multiple revisions. There have been minor revisions throughout the years to reflect changes in aspirations. The most recent version of the vision statement follows:

The Enrollment Services staff at The University of North Carolina at Greensboro works creatively and diligently to attain market prominence, achieve optimal enrollments, support the academic mission of the university, and enhance student success. We fervently believe that there is no sustainable competitive advantage or secure enrollment position without a focus on staff performance. Hence, team learning and knowledge management are central to our enterprise. Through shared learning and a commitment to teamwork, we will become a national model for quality enrollment services.

While the vision statement was being drafted, peripheral components of the plan were under development. These components included an introduction to the plan as well as the enrollment management concept, an organizational chart, core values, and a narrative to accompany the situational analysis expanding upon the original interpretation of the data. Regarding the latter, linkages between research findings and other components of the plan were established in this section of the plan.

Once the vision statement was complete, it became a driver for the core components of the plan. For example, the following eight key performance indicators (KPIs) were identified, each with measurable objectives:

1. enrollment headcount,
2. student quality,
3. student diversity,
4. retention rates,
5. graduation rates,
6. student satisfaction,
7. staff satisfaction and professional growth
8. institutional image.

Staff satisfaction and professional growth, for instance, is measured by a staff satisfaction survey conducted every two years, 360-degree evaluations of directors and associate directors, annual staff turnover rates, participation in professional development activities, and the like. Objectives are tracked on an annual basis and shared with the staff. Progress on objectives reveals areas of strength along with areas that need improvement. Frequently, information for the progress reports guides planning and decision-making.

Other core components of the plan consist of marketing, recruitment, retention, service, student relationship management, staff learning, and infrastructure. The marketing component describes marketing messages identified through an extensive competitor analysis, constituent focus groups, and the Admitted Student Questionnaire administered by The College Board on behalf of UNCG. Essentially, the messages represent institutional strengths that position UNCG against primary competitors. The marketing messages are not unique outside of the campus' immediate competitor set, yet in head-to-head competition with the five institutions with which UNCG has the most application overlap, they effectively distinguish the university from the others. They focus on student benefits and outcomes, rather than mere facts. Among the messages, there is one primary message, "Where students come first," that permeates everything UNCG does (e.g., publications, Web pages, presentations, business cards, signage) and four secondary messages that are incorporated where appropriate. Consistency and frequency of use have been essential to shaping image.

Also included in the marketing section is an overview of UNCG's marketing mix. UNCG has implemented a multi-channel approach to communicating with prospective and current students. The mix includes advertising primarily for local adults, transfers, and evening students (newspaper, radio, billboards, trade publications); e-mail; Web-mail; Web pages; Flash presentations; PowerPoint presentations, CD-ROMs, videos, direct mail pieces, digital publications, phone contacts, college fairs, community college programs, private visits, and other face-to-face encounters. Admissions staff, faculty, UNCG students, parents of current students, alumni, the chancellor, and many others are the authors of these various communications. Whenever possible, the UNCG person is sought who will have the most influence on the student or those who influence the student (e.g., their parents, friends, teachers, guidance counselors).

Some aspect of the multi-channel approach works with every market segment. By segmenting the prospective student pool, the communication becomes more relevant and thus, more effective. Segments in the UNCG Enrollment Management Plan include high school juniors, prospective freshmen, transfers, adult students, evening students, local students, out-of-state students, international students, potential scholars, minority students, first generation students, returning students, and students who were initially denied admission. Each population selects a college for different reasons. The plan attempts to identify the motivators and barriers for enrolling associated with each segment, and then describes a communications plan designed to remove enrollment barriers while capitalizing on enrollment motivators. Through Web portals, personalized e-mails and Web-mails, telecounseling calls, digital publications, and other such mediums, communications can be tailored to a single individual—often referred to as vertical marketing.

The marketing component of the plan looks at issues beyond promotion, namely place, price, and product. A detailed plan for marketing research is also integrated into this section of the plan. In order to continuously improve and maximize return on investment, UNCG must know what works. Hence, it regularly evaluates the effectiveness of its marketing efforts. To be more precise, every marketing initiative has a written objective that explains the purpose, the intended audience, and the method of evaluation. Principally, the campus wants to know if the objective was achieved and if it met the needs of the intended audience.

The recruitment component flows naturally from the marketing function. This section consists of the dates, assigned tasks, and planning elements of special recruitment events held throughout the year. To illustrate, this year's recruitment events include three programs for prospective students in the fall, nine area receptions, seven information sessions for adults and transfers, two admitted student open houses in the spring, a minority student visitation program, and an open house for high school juniors. Each event is designed for a different audience with different objectives.

Admissions representatives are assigned geographic territories or, in the case of the adult/transfer staff, a feeder community college to cultivate. Territories are managed differently depending upon the manager and the population being served. Promotion and individualized communication, for example, are unique to each territory manager. However, there are several common elements: twenty-four hour response to e-mail requests, evaluation of admissions cases, calls to request missing information or to describe the next step in the enrollment process, and recruitment visits to schools in the designated territory.

Another major recruitment thrust is telecounseling. From mid-September until April, twenty paid student telecounselors call prospective students based on a qualification rating system that allows them to target prospects who are most likely to be influenced by a call. Each call has a distinct purpose and "call to action," an action step such as applying for admission, completing the financial aid process, reserving housing, or registering for orientation. Student telecounselors are trained and given a script to use as a guide. Similarly, faculty callers participate in a training session prior to calling admitted students who have indicated an interest in the faculty members' academic program. The purpose of these calls is to sell the student on the academic program but more importantly, to establish a relationship between the admitted student and the faculty member. Albeit a bit idealistic, the goal is for the student to end the call longing to take a class with the faculty member with whom they spoke.

One edition of the plan provided direction on the conversion of parts of the communication flow from paper to electronic methods. This conversion took a team of dedicated people a year to complete. Now, UNCG has electronic newsletters and brochures, VIP Web pages generated dynamically around the student's self-identified interests, online applications and reservation forms, Web-enabled CD-ROMs, customized Web-mail, real-time Web chat, and much more. Though partially prompted by a need to reduce costs, the result of shifting to electronic communications has been instantaneous gratification for students requesting information, increased opportunities for customization, and processing efficiencies.

Finally, operational issues were included in the recruitment section of the plan. Fulfillment, inquiry processing, and application processing are critical functions in the recruitment effort. Process mapping and then streamlining existing processes improved turnaround time significantly. The UNCG processing mantra is "first in the mailbox." For an institution such as UNCG, being first to respond to an inquiry, deliver a transfer evaluation, notify a student of admission, award financial aid, issue an I-20, and so on, gives the university a competitive advantage.

In the retention component, a three-pronged approach was employed. The first prong focused on improving retention on the front-end, namely through the admissions process. For five of the last seven years, admissions standards were increased, resulting in modest gains in retention and graduation rates. Admissions is primarily driven by a formula that predicts first-year grade point averages. The formula uses weighted scores for verbal SAT, math SAT, and high school grade point average, with the heaviest weight on the latter. Approximately three years ago, UNCG contracted with The College Board to do an analysis of every variable UNCG had in its database plus any it had on applicants to determine if there was a better way to predict success. In the final analysis, UNCG's existing formula proved to be the best predictor of success. Among the variables considered, high school grades were by far the best predictor of success.

Since then, UNCG has analyzed performance data on entering freshmen to identify common characteristics of students who experience academic difficulty and are eventually suspended as well as those who are academically successful and leave voluntarily. Most of the data are inconclusive or reveal characteristics that UNCG has elected not to factor into the admissions process. For example, UNCG knows that males, out-of-state students, and those who decide to live off-campus the first semester are less likely to persist voluntarily or otherwise.

Along the same line, UNCG has had a high percentage of enrolling students for whom it was not their first choice institution. From 1995 to 2000, the percentage of first choice students increased from seventy percent to eighty-two percent. Though there is still work to be done in this area, UNCG has convinced senior management that reducing the number of entering students who are predisposed to leave should be an institutional priority. Conversely, increasing the number of first choice students has become one of ten university goals in the UNCG 2008 Profile.

The second prong relates to retention strategies implemented by Enrollment Services. For instance, Enrollment Services administers the Student Success Center that encompasses both a federally funded TRIO program and an institutionally funded learning assistance program. Both programs offer essentially the same services (tutoring, academic counseling, skills workshops, learning style assessments) but to different populations. The federal program is restricted to serving students who meet one or more of the following criteria: low socioeconomic status, first generation, a documented disability, or minority status. The learning assistance program is open to all students.

Enrollment Services also directs the university's new student transition course, UNS 101, and a required course for students on probation their first semester, SAS 100. The former uses a textbook developed in-house that focuses on success strategies such as time management, test-taking, note-taking, decoding professors along with an introduction to campus resources such as the Library, Computing Services, Health Services, and Counseling Services. In addition to practical strategies and resources, the course provides opportunities to discuss relevant issues such as multiculturalism, substance abuse, and values clarification. The SAS 100 course has some of the same elements but is tailored to the individual. Students on probation must meet with a member of Enrollment Services staff for an individual diagnostic and to sign an agreement. Based on the diagnostic, students are placed in a course section with others who have similar issues (e.g., academic problems, balancing work and school, emotional difficulties). The course begins the second week of classes and meets once a week for eight weeks thereafter. Attendance is mandatory and includes outside of class individual meetings with the instructor. One unexcused absence results in automatic suspension. Of over three hundred participants last spring, only five were suspended for absences. At the conclusion of any given semester, approximately sixty percent of the participants continue in good academic standing.

Other retention programs managed by Enrollment Services include a peer mentoring program, where peer mentors team teach the UNS 101 course with faculty, and Supplemental Instruction, which at this point is only a modest pilot program. Like the other retention strategies housed in Enrollment Services, these tend to focus on high-risk experiences rather than high-risk students. UNCG considers every student to be at risk to some degree, so it has elected to target high-risk experiences such as 100 and 200 level gateway courses with high rates of Ds, Fs, and Ws. Supplemental Instruction is UNCG's solution to this particular high-risk experience. Similarly, peer mentoring is designed to proactively make student-to-student connections. Like most new students, those at UNCG are particularly vulnerable the first semester. Making friends and getting involved are difficult for some, and UNCG wants to help them make connections early in their life with the university.

The third and final prong relates to the coordination of campus-wide retention initiatives. Enrollment Services has been instrumental, for example, in improving the advising process. Enrollment Services sponsors the Advising Council who meet biweekly to coordinate advising issues such as consistency and accuracy of advising information, the migration to new general education requirements, the study and eventual reduction of degree substitutions and waivers, as well as training. Regarding training, Enrollment Services supported the formation of a Master Advisors Program hosted by the Advising Council. Support included hosting planning retreats, assisting with the development and presentation of the program proposal, acquiring financial resources to support implementation, and designing a qualitative, online advising evaluation, so that advisors could incorporate student data in their promotion and tenure portfolio. Currently, Enrollment Services is working in concert with the Advising Council to develop a virtual advising module that provides students with accurate information; related business transactions like degree audits, change of major simulations, a scheduling tool built around the students' preferences for course times, days, type, and availability; electronic advisor approval; an online advisor appointment system; registration; and payment.

Service is another major component of the enrollment management plan, which consists of service standards shared by the associate provost with every new employee during the first two weeks of employment, a plan for regularly reviewing all policies and procedures, a review of mission critical processes to ensure they are student-focused and streamlined, a glossary of enrollment-related terms, and a description of the student services model. The UNCG model of student services blends high touch, high tech, and what Disney calls "high show" service delivery.

Students may receive services through intuitively designed Web pages, Campus Pipeline (the students' customized portal), Web chats that are available from 8:00 in the morning until 11:00 at night during the week as well as select hours on the weekend, e-mail, phone, fax, and face-to-face. Online services, forms, and business transactions are available in one place—at the Virtual Information Station (http://infostation.uncg.edu/). For students who prefer interacting with a person face-to-face, they can visit the one-stop shop Information Station. Generalists who have been cross-trained in twenty-three different areas operate both Information Station and the live Web chat. They are capable of answering roughly eighty percent of the questions they are asked. When in doubt, however, they refer the student to a specialist. In fact, parameters have been established to indicate which questions the generalist should not attempt to answer. For example, in the area of financial aid, the generalists provide information about deadlines, process steps, forms, and the basic types of financial aid. They do not engage in interpretation of policy such as determining independent status.

The student relationship management portion of the plan weaves together the marketing, recruitment, retention, and service components. Student relationship management centers around cultivating relationships with students from the first point of contact a student has with the university as a prospect through her life as an alumnus, often called the "cradle to endowment" model. Like most institutions, UNCG has been diligent about cultivating relationships with prospective students and potential donors. However, when students are enrolled in the university, a time when they are closest to the institution, UNCG has been less intentional about nurturing relationships. Obviously, relationships form between faculty, staff, and peers everyday but usually through serendipity rather than a thoughtful communications plan or strategic initiatives.

Just over two years ago, Enrollment Services created a position, manager of Internal and External Communications, a marketing professional who has been instrumental in orchestrating communications with prospective and, more importantly, current students through the student portal, direct mail campaigns, publications, Web sites, Web-mail, and visual images. Specific examples include signs welcoming students to campus, electronic birthday cards, a series of messages pushed to students during their first year that provide success strategies, and recognition of student accomplishments such as dean's and chancellor's list certificates.

Another ingredient to managing relationships with students is managing their expectations. When an institution claims to be student-centered, as UNCG has done in its vision statement, it must clearly define what student-centered means or every negative response to a student request or enforcement of a policy will result in a student complaint. Frankly, this is not something the campus has done particularly well; hence, the term "student-centered" often becomes a two-edged sword. It does, however, serve as a compass for making consistent decisions about policies, processes, and daily practices. An example is that staff is taught that their role is that of institutional trust agent. Without trust, no basis for a relationship exists. Staff is also taught that every encounter with a student is an institutional moment of truth, and how well they manage that moment of truth influences the student's image of the individual, their office, and ultimately the university.

For staff to successfully manage moments of truth, they must have the right attitude as well as the right tools; hence the impetus for including staff learning as a centerpiece of the enrollment management plan. As the Enrollment Services vision statement implies, the division believes that staff and their intellectual capital represent the capacity to produce results.

Like new students, new employees are searching for their place in the university. UNCG wants to help them develop a sense of belonging, find their niche, and bond with the school. By frontloading orientation and acculturation experiences, the university enhances employee satisfaction and retention. Experienced, satisfied employees are committed contributors to organizational goals and directly influence student satisfaction. Strategies for new employees include:

- ◆ A one-on-one meeting with the associate provost to introduce:
    - ∗ the university's mission and vision statements
    - ∗ Enrollment Services' vision statement
    - ∗ Enrollment Services' expectations and service standards
    - ∗ the organizational structure of the division

◆ A campus tour with a student ambassador

◆ Access to ShareNet, our student services intranet, that consists of:
  * a calendar of events
  * important deadlines
  * a campus locator with detailed maps
  * frequently asked questions and related answers
  * a glossary of student services terms
  * departmental, divisional, and institutional mission statements
  * a directory of student service providers with direct phone extensions and e-mail addresses
  * process maps of steps to completing student enrollment processes
  * a listing of learning opportunities along with an online registration form
  * a description of the learning rewards program
  * access to the password protected staff learning transcript
  * access to the student information system, Banner
  * access to Campus Pipeline
  * access to the Web chat generalists

◆ A subscription to the Enrollment Services' listserv that provides a venue for:
  * regular updates from the associate provost
  * monthly departmental updates
  * business announcements
  * a forum for discussion of relevant issues
  * informal staff surveys

◆ Monthly Enrollment Services team meetings

◆ Assignment to a staff mentor who is responsible for coordinating:
  * individual conferences with the mentor (as needed)
  * a tour of each Enrollment Services office along with staff introductions (coordinated by departmental mentors)
  * a luncheon with departmental mentors to discuss "The Real Story" (e.g., timesheets, benefits, office culture, workload, Banner)

Enrollment Services has found employee evaluations are completely ineffective if staff are unaware of expectations. Futile attempts to hit some unknown, moving target can be frustrating and demoralizing for staff. In Enrollment Services, it is the goal for all employees to know clearly what the performance and behavioral targets are in order to position employees for success.

Employee performance is measured against communicated expectations. Those who exceed expectations are rewarded through merit increases as funds are available, promotion to appropriate positions within the department or Division of Enrollment Services, opportunities for additional professional development, and other perks as determined by the department and the associate provost (e.g., tuition waivers, travel dollars, notes of thanks copied to the supervisor, public praise and recognition, gift certificates, massages from a licensed therapist).

Every functional area has related performance expectations associated with it. Staff assessments are administered to identify gaps between skills and knowledge and relevant expectations. Resources are invested as necessary to provide individualized learning experiences to address performance deficits as well as behavioral issues. Supervisors mentor employees as they engage in individual learning plans offering encouragement and just-in-time feedback. Individual learning plans typically include learning opportunities in three domains: (1) area of functional responsibility (e.g., data processing, reporting, compliance, counseling, advising, retention), (2) the field of employment (e.g., financial aid, admissions, registration, student academic services), and (3) the broader environment (e.g., enrollment management, UNCG, higher education). Learning across the domains fosters skill development in one's job while increasing understanding of how one's work relates to the larger whole.

Options for staff learning include but are not limited to the following:
* attendance at conferences or workshops
* participation in a UNCG conference jointly hosted by Enrollment Services and other divisions within the university
* topical salons facilitated by Enrollment Services staff
* book clubs hosted by Enrollment Services staff
* attendance at the guest lecturer series sponsored by Enrollment Services
* site visits to other institutions
* functional area training and documentation review (departmental-based)

* cross-training with other functional areas
* Banner training and documentation review
* Campus Pipeline training
* software training
* involvement with professional organizations
* leadership development offered internally, through the Center for Creative Leadership, or a professional organization like AACRAO
* utilization of learning resources posted on the Enrollment Services Web site and offered through the Staff Learning Center (e.g., books, journal articles, training videos, audio tapes).
* monthly Enrollment Services team meetings
* enrollment in classes

In addition, twice a year Enrollment Services hosts a one-day immersion experience for faculty and staff. Participants select one of twenty student scenarios to follow. Intentionally, these scenarios are designed to present participants with challenges and obstacles faced by students engaging in our enrollment processes. Participants apply for admission, take a campus tour, apply for financial aid, receive a financial aid award letter, meet with an advisor, are given an advising code, register for classes, receive a bill, are canceled for non-payment, and re-register.

The purpose of this exercise is threefold. First, it introduces staff to the enrollment processes of the university. Second, it allows staff to see enrollment processes through the eyes of a student. UNCG wants staff to understand and be empathetic to the student experience. Third, it provides a feedback loop for all student processes.

Arguably the most vital component of the enrollment management plan is infrastructure. Without the necessary infrastructure, execution of the plan is sporadic and quality suffers. Fundamental pieces of the UNCG infrastructure include organizational structure, staff skills, financial resources, space utilization, technology, information management, a system of accountability, incentives, and internal communications. Since most of these are not applicable to other institutions, this is the extent of the description of infrastructure other than to say that no enrollment organization can do everything. Nor can an enrollment organization outperform its infrastructure. Therefore, it is imperative that strategies are complemented with the necessary infrastructure.

THE RESULTS

Over the last seven years, the total student enrollment has increased by more than 2,500 students with a corresponding increase in student credit hour production. In North Carolina, enrollment funding for public universities is linked to student credit hours. The funding level for credit hours varies based on the classification of the program (bachelor's, master's, or doctorate) and the cost to offer the program (low, medium, or high). The credit hour increases experienced at UNCG over this period generated approximately thirty-six million dollars in enrollment growth funding.

The freshman class experienced the most dramatic growth since 1996 at thirty-four percent. Transfers increased by twelve percent; graduate students by nineteen percent; and the retention rate of first-year students by five percentage points. Similarly, four-year graduation rates increased by seven percentage points.

Quality indicators for entering freshmen increased as well. The average SAT score improved by thirty-seven points, and the mean high school grade point average rose from 3.1 to 3.5 on a 4.0 scale. During the same period, the minimum predicted grade point average (PGPA) for automatic admission increased from 1.5 to 2.2 on a 4.0 scale. Applicants with a PGPA of 2.00 to 2.19 are reviewed on a case-by-case basis to consider academic trends, course difficulty, high school difficulty, and the impact of any extenuating circumstances. As PGPA requirements increased, applicant acceptance rates dropped from eighty-eight percent to seventy percent.

While increasing enrollment numbers and quality, UNCG was also able to enhance diversity. The percentage of minority freshmen increased from twenty-three percent to twenty-eight percent with similar increases in overall minority representation. These increases positioned UNCG as the most ethnically diverse institution of the historically white universities in the UNC system. Furthermore, the number of degree-seeking international students doubled at about the same time.

In comparing UNC student satisfaction data, UNCG improved its relative position among the other fifteen campuses in the system. Nonetheless, UNCG did not improve student satisfaction in all categories. The most significant improvements were in satisfaction with registration and financial aid services. Both areas boost robust Web-based services that were largely not available to students in 1996.

Staff satisfaction has gradually improved with each administration of the staff survey.

The highest ratings are related to the leadership style of the associate provost, support from their director, and Enrollment Services being a good place to work. The lowest ranked items include communications within their respective offices as well as communication between Enrollment Services offices. Improvements in staff satisfaction combined with a declining local economy have contributed to a forty-four percent reduction in annual staff turnover.

Institutional image, as tracked by The College Board's Admitted Student Questionnaire, has improved dramatically as well. Win rates have increased with every competitor. Likewise, factors important to the students' college decision-making process such as cost, value for price, surroundings, academic reputation, and personal attention are more frequently associated with UNCG than with competitors. Finally, UNCG is frequently being described more positively than it was during the 1995 administration of the Admitted Student Questionnaire. An internal survey of current students supports these findings and suggests that student perception closely mirrors the reality of the student experience.

LESSONS LEARNED

First and foremost, UNCG has learned that there are few quick fixes. Enrollment management is a journey with a dynamically changing terrain. It requires careful surveying of environmental factors—looking outward and forward—reacting proactively to the current reality as well as to predictions of the future. Indeed, the savvy enrollment manager must be grounded in reality while constantly conveying a vision to which people in the organization can aspire. By regularly assessing the current reality and comparing it to the vision, the enrollment manager can create a healthy tension around the gap that exists between the two. This tension is what propels an enrollment organization to excel.

Secondly, UNCG has learned that execution is everything. There is no inherent or sustainable competitive advantage in a strategy. Strategies can be replicated and quickly become obsolete. Competitive advantage comes from people and their ability to execute strategies better than others. For this reason, staff learning, practicing the fundamentals of the core business, testing to prevent errors before they occur, evaluating everything, and continuously improving are the tenets that guide day-to-day work. They are ingrained in the organizational culture and have become a part of the organization's DNA.

Thirdly, creating an enrollment management organization that endures fluctuations in enrollment, changes in leadership, budget cuts, technology limitations, political pressures, and the like requires sound underpinnings built on mutual trust and a commitment to stay the course, especially in the midst of adversity. Too many colleges and university leaders panic when enrollment declines, and when we panic, we lose focus. To the contrary, enrollment declines present an opportunity to create a sense of urgency and thus, affect real change. Institutions that have experienced successive years of enrollment victories should be the ones concerned. Success is the quickest road to failure because with success often comes complacency. Comfortable institutions or enrollment management organizations are usually on the brink of self-destruction.

Lastly, on a personal note, to survive in the business, you simply cannot tie your professional success to the decision-making process of an eighteen-year-old or for that matter, a thirty-four-year-old. Moreover, your ability to achieve enrollment goals depends on how the goals were derived, the quality of the educational product you are representing, the perceived value of the institution among its competitors, and the resources you have at your disposal. Your success must be derived from the personal satisfaction of knowing that you have maximized enrollment opportunities given all of these factors that are mostly outside your sphere of control.

11

MAKING ENROLLMENT MANAGEMENT WORK

ROBERT J. MASSA

DICKINSON

The Revolutionary War was winding down when Benjamin Rush, a prominent Philadelphia physician, wrote the charter for Dickinson College in 1783. A grammar school founded in Carlisle in 1773 served as the foundation of the new college, named by Rush in honor of his friend and Pennsylvania Governor John Dickinson, the "penman" of the Revolution. Rush knew that America could only live up to its own expectations if it was a country built of an educated citizenry. So seven years after he met with other members of the Constitutional Congress to add his signature to the Declaration of Independence, Benjamin Rush signed the charter of a new college on what was then the American frontier.

The Revolutionary War was winding down when Benjamin Rush, a prominent Philadelphia physician, wrote the charter for Dickinson College in 1783. A grammar school founded in Carlisle in 1773 served as the foundation of the new college, named by Rush in honor of his friend and Pennsylvania Governor John Dickinson, the "penman" of the Revolution. Rush knew that America could only live up to its own expectations if it was a country built of an educated citizenry. So seven years after he met with other members of the Constitutional Congress to add his signature to the Declaration of Independence, Benjamin Rush signed the charter of a new college on what was then the American frontier. On September 9, 1783, a struggling grammar school in Carlisle was transformed into Dickinson College. Less than a week earlier, the Treaty of Paris had officially ended the Revolution and guaranteed international recognition of the United States of America. Dickinson was the first college charted in these new United States. *

Throughout most of its early history, Dickinson struggled financially and, in spite of the fact that its early graduates included President James Buchanan and Supreme Court Justice Roger Brooke Taney, the college was forced to close twice in the early 19th century due to financial woes. But it was always a place with a creative spirit and a big vision. Dickinson was the first college to establish the pedagogy of "field studies" in its science curriculum in the 1830s (not coincidentally, in 1986, it revolutionized the teaching of physics with its "Workshop Physics" curriculum). It was one of the first colleges to build an athletic field for its students. And its founder encouraged all Dickinson students to take time from their day once a week to see how America was functioning in the courthouse downtown. A tradition of engaging the world was nurtured even in those early days. To this day, Dickinson faculty embrace curriculum-enhancing wider world experiences as valuable and useful components of the liberal arts.

STATEMENT OF THE PROBLEM

By the 1980s, Dickinson was flying high as one among thirty or so top liberal arts colleges in the nation. It had devoted significant resources, in part from what was then the largest grant ever given to a liberal arts college by the National Endowment for the Humanities, to develop a global education program with twelve Dickinson study centers world-wide. As recently as 2002, Dickinson was cited by the Association of International Education as having done the most thorough job among all liberal arts colleges in internationalizing its campus. By 1988, Dickinson was receiving close to 4,500 applications for a class of 550, accepting under 40% of those who applied and adhering steadfastly to need-based financial aid and need-blind admission. It was that admirable commitment, plus a reluctance to promote its premier programs over others, that would eventually lead to a precipitous decline in Dickinson's position and its perceived quality. Financial aid was viewed as a budget item to be capped, and although college administrators did not talk about "discount rates," that cap represented a tuition discount rate in the mid-20s. Need was not met fully, and some students who needed aid were offered none. Applications dropped to a low of 2,800 in 1996, and the college was forced to admit over 80% of its applicants. It missed its class target of 550 students in five of the eight years between 1990 and 1998. SAT averages declined to a low of 1,141 in 1996.

To address this problem, the board of trustees in 1996 authorized a massive infusion of financial aid by raiding the college's "quasi-endowment." As this strategy played itself out over the next five years, over $15 million of the college's reserves were consumed by heavy discounting in order to enroll students. Initially, the strategy paid off. Applications increased in 1998 and 1999 to over 3,400. In 1997, the first year of the "new" financial aid policy, seventy more students enrolled than in the previous year at a tuition discount rate of 52%. In 1998, however, the class target was not met using a 50% discount rate; there was under-enrollment of twelve students. As a result, the administration hired a consultant to leverage aid for the class entering in the fall of 1999. A record enrollment resulted (130 students over the class that entered in 1996) but the tuition discount rate climbed again to 52%. Until 1999, net tuition revenue had declined or had remained flat, but even in that year increased only marginally. The discounting strategy increased numbers, but it had a negligible effect on net revenue. Students, in fact, were coming to Dickinson because of the lower price, not because of the fit. This would have implications for retention and certainly for alumni relations down the road.

Dickinson College experienced a 36% decline in admission applications from 1989 to 1996, an actual decline in net tuition, room and board revenue of 6.5% from 1993 to 1999 in spite of a 31.5% increase in gross revenue, a six point drop in the one-year retention rate from 1991-1996, a 4-year graduation rate in 1995 that was nine points lower than in 1991, and a declining percentage of alumni participation in the annual fund during those years to a low of 38%. Significant change had to take place.

A DESCRIPTION OF STRATEGIES AND RESULTS
A new administration arrived in the summer of 1999 and immediately recognized this as the first challenge. Marketing was to be a part of the equation in a way that was

absent before when no one program was singled out for promotion. Value, not price, needed to be emphasized. And financial aid had to be drastically reduced, while at the same time increasing selectivity, diversity, and the measured academic quality of the class. This was no easy task!

There is no single "best" model of enrollment management, but understanding the scope and complexity of the challenge, Dickinson's new administration quickly created a comprehensive "cradle to grave" model encompassing the traditional EM areas as well as Institutional Research, Athletics, Student Life, Alumni Affairs, and Communications. The goal was to integrate these functions to improve the enrollment stream, net revenue, retention and graduation, and alumni participation. Four years later, the results are clear.

Results: Applications for admission were at an all-time high in 2003, jumping 35% since 1999. Net tuition, fees, room, and board (TFRB) revenue was up almost 50% during the same period. While improvements in one-year retention (two points) and four-year graduation rates (three points) were modest, these typically take longer to achieve. The number of entering freshmen met the budgeted target each year, and minority enrollment doubled. Alumni participation, due to the efforts of a new development staff with assistance from the communications and alumni affairs team, increased five points to its highest level in history. With all of this, the quality of the incoming class as measured by SATs increased almost eighty points.

Of course, with success comes even greater expectations. The scope of this enrollment management organization is broad, and that presents coordination and communication challenges daily. To make certain that the staff in Financial Aid understands the experiences of those in Residential Life, to assure that the Admissions Office knows what actually happens in the classroom and on weekends, and to have the Student Affairs staff understand the impact of student experiences on alumni satisfaction, and their participation in fund raising and in recruiting students for the college, the senior directors in each department meet twice per month around important, shared issues, and the professional staff meets twice a semester. In addition, planning sessions are held twice a year. This helps to keep all informed and tuned in to the "systems thinking" that needs to occur to maximize success. Concrete goals are formulated and staff are evaluated on their ability to achieve them. And risk-taking is encouraged, even if goals are not met in the short term.

Before the enrollment management team could function as a coordinated unit, the college had to undertake a strategic plan. It had inherited in 1999 more than 1,200 pages of planning documents from the '80s and '90s that had seen varying degrees of implementation. Those were reviewed thoroughly by a college-wide task force that understood the need to move quickly. The task force also went back to the college's roots, examining the charter carefully and identifying the founding principles of the college from 1783. Within six months, the mission, vision, environmental analysis, and strategic objectives were identified. The Enrollment Management Division had the tools it needed to operationalize the vision, moving the college forward, positioning the college to the public (especially prospective students), establishing programs to enhance retention and graduation, and reconnecting alumni. Once the community agreed on the college's identity and its purpose for being, once it was able to identify its distinctive elements of the liberal arts, once it understood its mission clearly, then it was able to embark on an integrated marketing campaign that sought to attract the students for whom the college was the right fit, to provide them with the experiences they expected while enrolled, and to keep them connected as alumni to help the college in the future by sharing this vision.

Marketing: In order for marketing to work for a college, it must be integrated. Sevier (1998) claims that most of marketing as it functions today in higher education is "promotion." Rarely does it go beyond addressing marketing from a "single perspective: public relations, recruiting, or fundraising. It is not integrated marketing." He continues, asserting that a marketing plan must be consistent with the institution's mission and vision. This is key, because it requires the institution to characterize itself in a way that is consistent with reality. Otherwise, the students attracted will not remain to graduate and those who do will be disconnected alumni.

In accordance with Sevier's theory, Dickinson formed a marketing and communications committee that evaluated all of its current publications. It engaged an independent higher education consulting firm (Neustadt Creative Marketing in Baltimore) to assess its current position and evaluate its strengths and weaknesses. And it used the results of the consultant's study to reshape its admissions publications, its communication with current students and alumni, its internal marketing (which was non-existent), its development pieces and its alumni magazine. The college also understood that the way the campus looked conveyed its position. Colorful banners, sporting a bold, newly designed logo, appeared all over campus. Red Adirondack chairs were placed randomly on the academic quad to promote conversation and reflective moments, posters highlighting successful alumni were strategically placed in the student union, and messages that engaged the student body and alumni were regularly sent, either by e-mail or posted on the college's Web site. A professional Web manager was hired to coordinate the Web presentation with the college's position and its publications. Admissions publications were completely overhauled to concretely demonstrate what was "Distinctively Dickinson." A new Media Relations staff was hired to promote college experts to the community, the nation and the world, aggressively positioning key administrators and faculty to comment in the national and international spheres on issues that mattered.

Marketing Theory and Practice: Do not underestimate the power of integrated marketing. Understanding your institutional "story" and communicating it effectively to all constituencies, will give an institution an advantage over the competition, most of which do not realize the power of a consistent and accurate message across the entire institution. At Dickinson, staff across the EM Division from Admissions to Athletics to Media Relations to Alumni Affairs understand the power of consistent thematic communication, as do the faculty and the senior management team. EM staff are constantly reminded in training workshops on image and branding that they must "connect the dots." They must see relationships between and among various institutional, student, faculty and alumni accomplishments and must organize these for public consumption in a way that supports the college's position. This is what has made the difference at Dickinson.

The Audience: The most well conceived integrated marketing initiative will not achieve institutional objectives unless it is targeted. Dickinson knew it had to increase its applications in order to enhance diversity, geographic representation, the academic quality of the student body and their willingness to pay for the value added to the college's program and environment. With the message in place, new publications designed and written to attract the type of student the college needed, a defined and distinctive position and an integration of this throughout the college, the EM staff set about the task of identifying students that would "fit," and more of them. Among the strategies employed were:

1. Studying student search trends and eliminating candidates with marginal records while increasing geographically and racially diverse candidates.
2. Identifying key market areas and increasing travel, programs, and communication in these areas.
3. Developing relationships with college counselors in key areas by volunteering to

speak on selective college admission to junior and seniors and their parents, and by also inviting these counselors to campus for specialized programs at our expense.

4. Communicating constantly, though not excessively, with prospects that fit the institution profile, using mass print, Web messages and personal messages from current students, alumni, parents, faculty and staff to "hot prospects" in their regions.

5. Evaluating the promotion and content of on-campus visit programs and structuring the content to demonstrate Dickinson's distinctiveness rather than simply "telling" students and parents about the college.

6. Conducting thorough training of all volunteers on- and off-campus to assure, to the maximum degree possible, a consistency of message and an accuracy of factual information.

7. Initiating strategic partnerships with urban foundations and organizations to help get more underrepresented students in the pipeline, and doing the same with regional community colleges to bolster transfer applicants.

8. Opening secondary and tertiary markets with targeted and repeated visits and counselor contacts.

9. Communicating with teachers who wrote recommendation letters for enrolled students and asking them to nominate similar students.

10. Employing a media relations strategy in Philadelphia, Baltimore, and Washington, DC (three relatively "local" regional areas within two hours from campus) to get Dickinson more exposure through responding quickly to media requests for experts and by writing op-ed pieces on major higher education issues. National press coverage in the *New York Times*, CNN, the *Wall Street Journal* and in local papers throughout the country through the wire services was also pursued successfully.

11. Reducing non-need based aid and targeting it to the top 10% of the pool.

This list is not exhaustive, and there is little that is new or unique. But executing all of this simultaneously, and evaluating the results as each year concluded, helped Dickinson to achieve the dramatic results stated earlier, chiefly by allowing it to significantly increase applications from qualified students nationally (which gave enormous flexibility in the selection of candidates) and then executing yield strategies to impact their enrollment decision. Note also that this approach to student recruitment is indeed integrated—throughout the college, to prospective students and their parents and to the public at large through the media.

Pricing and Aid Strategies: The new administration inherited a tuition discount rate in 1999 at Dickinson of 52%, meaning that only $.48 of each dollar charged in tuition went back to running the college. This was an intolerable position, and one that would clearly bankrupt the institution within a matter of years. Within one year, the staff had reduced the tuition discount rate to 37%, and within four years to 32%, with a TFRB discount of 25%. At the same time, the average SATs of the entering class increased by almost eighty points, the percentage of underrepresented students in the class doubled, and the size of the entering class, which had fluctuated for years, stabilized at the targeted number, thereby significantly boosting net revenue (a low discount rate with low enrollment does little to help the institution financially). The key to making this happen was three-fold, based upon:

1. Understanding the demand and value position of your institution to students of various academic backgrounds, geographic locations and academic interests.

2. Basing a portion of the admission decision at the margin of qualifications on a simple question: "Is the admission of this student worth the investment in financial aid that the college will need to make?"

3. Searching for those students, working to convert them to applicants, and enrolling those for whom the college's environment and programs would be the best fit.

The informed use of predictive modeling, combined with professional "instincts" of the enrollment manager and the staff, can guide decisions toward achieving these ambitious goals. Using a faculty member in statistics and the talents of the director of Institutional Research, a model was developed to help predict the impact of admission decisions on the enrollment: quality, male/female distribution, minority students, geographic representation and net revenue. By adjusting admission decisions at the margin, all of these factors could be impacted by running "what if" scenarios through the model. While this did not guide the EM division in individual admission decisions, and exceptions were made frequently for a variety of reasons, it did provide a road map to shape the class in terms of quality, distribution, and aid. The results were very effective. Minority enrollment was up, geographic distribution was greater, quality increased as did net revenue. Of course, an integrated marketing plan and an understanding of how to communicate the college's distinctive position was also critical in achieving net tuition revenue goals.

Dickinson's results from the freshman survey (CIRP), administered by the Higher Education Research Institute at UCLA, indicated that an increasing percentage of freshmen place Dickinson as their first choice—demonstrating that the marketing efforts and pricing/aid strategies were working.

Pricing, of course, is a related but separate issue from discounting or aid. Most institutions will want to price themselves to cover costs minus aid and other income. In addition, the "list price" at one institution is related to the "list price" at its competitors. A college that is really competing with a peer group may not want to lower its price and risk being disassociated with that group. On the other hand, if a healthy majority of students are benefiting from discounts, a college may wish to reduce its price to increase enrollments (if it has excess capacity) and thereby revenue. This is a risky proposition, because the unintended result could be to move the college out of the competitive sphere it is currently in, and down a notch to another set (which will ultimately influence the quality of the students it attracts). In recent years Muskingum College in Ohio and Bethany College in West Virginia experimented with this paradigm. The Muskingum College case study is described in Chapter Two.

Loomis Hubbell, Massa and Lapovsky (2002) tell us that all but a handful of colleges are tuition-dependent. As such, the management of tuition rates and discounting is critical. The simple theory of discounting, they say, is that "by offering a discount to selected students enrollment could be increased to capacity" and revenues could be maximized. Of course, the use of discounting, or financial aid, should also be targeted to influence the enrollment mix (e.g., diversity in all of its dimensions) as well as academic quality. What has happened, of course, is that discounting has become a competitive tool, pitting one school against another. A subject for another paper, discounting gone wild can handcuff a college (as it did at Dickinson in the 1990s) where it either does not have enough revenue to cover expenditures, and/or it reduces expenditures and thereby threatens the quality of the educational experience for students.

Done appropriately and related to institutional mission, discounting can be used as a strategy to manage the composition of the student body while increasing revenue and remaining true to institutional objectives. The setting of price, also, must position the institution on level with its peers. This is a part of marketing strategy, and while price is not totally unrelated to cost, it is, in part, determined by the number of enrolled students who pay a majority or all of the price. It is therefore related to market strength and the perception of value discussed earlier.

Academic and Co-curricular Programs: Aside from the ability to continue to afford a college (assured by an adequate aid package at the time of admission, which is why the practice of "gapping" is counterproductive since it costs more to recruit a student than to retain a student), there is nothing more important to retaining a student to graduation than delivering on the promise made during admission regarding academic programs and student life experiences. Sevier (2002) tells us that a brand is a promise, and that we must deliver that promise in order to continue to attract students to our institutions and to graduate grateful and committed alumni.

At Dickinson, the administration talks about how the college helps students to "Engage the World." The phrase has been trademarked to highlight its position as central to the character of the institution. Aside from using (some may say "over-using") the phrase on posters in the student union, on the Web site and in some admissions publications, the senior management team strives to ensure that directors, staff and faculty understand this "promise" as they make decisions about academic and student life programs that impact students.

Study abroad programs are expensive to run, but Dickinson manages thirty-five programs in twenty countries on six continents. These are programs in non-tourist cities where students, under the supervision of a Dickinson faculty member, truly experience the culture of another country as they are studying in major universities across the globe. An aggressive program of international internships supports this. So when a faculty member proposes a new program that fulfills this promise, it is likely to be approved even though it may not contribute financially to the college's bottom line.

"Engaging the world" does not simply mean on foreign soil. "The world" consists of the campus, its community and the nation, as well. Volunteer programs are on the rise, for example. During my first year at Dickinson, a part-time volunteer coordinator "managed" a fledgling program. Students that year volunteered about 8,000 hours in our community. To fulfill the promise, a full-time director was hired to provide opportunities for students. In 2002-03, Dickinson students devoted over 38,000 hours of community service. Putting dollars behind the promise is essential, and viewing all of this as contributing to long-term enrollment and financial stability helps to justify expenditures today.

A student cannot "engage the world" unless he or she is a citizen and a leader. Student activities programs, and residential life policies were revised to reflect this. Students set community standards in the residence halls and hold each other accountable. The college "says what it means and means what it says" with regard to student conduct and discipline. Students understand that there are consequences to behavior, and while they may not like it at times, they have come over the last four years to accept it.

Students are also given a great deal of autonomy, under the watchful eyes of the student activities staff, to plan their own programs and to even create new clubs that meet student interest and demand. Last year, for example, a group of students approached the EM Division with a well thought-out proposal to start a TV station. The college had the infrastructure to support this and a good relationship with the local cable company for public access. Their proposal was to broadcast an original show each month, "On Second Thought," that would pit two teams of two students each debating a significant issue such as gay marriages, affirmative action and censorship on the Internet. In addition, they proposed to televise certain lectures given by invited guests on topics of major interest. Engaging the world? You bet. But Dickinson had to find a way to afford the equipment, to find space to house the equipment and provide a "set," and to allocate the time of a faculty or staff member to advise the group. The campus was able to do all three, with the help of an alum and a parent in the "business" and with an understanding on the part of staff not in the EM Division that this was indeed important to fulfilling the promise.

At the most basic level, living the promise has to do with how students, parents, alumni and the public are treated on campus. As with many small liberal arts colleges, part of the promise is "personal attention." Staff who answer questions at the initial point of contact rather than transferring calls, for example, understand this. Faculty who are willing to spend part of their evenings or weekends helping a student or assisting in recruitment activities understand this as well. Through periodic HR training, and through an effective faculty committee structure where faculty (rather than the EM staff) can communicate this promise to their colleagues, staff, and faculty are frequently reminded, often in subtle ways, of the need to fulfill the promise.

Effective enrollment management does not stop here. If part of the promise is quality, it must be reflected in intrusive academic and career advising. This had been weak at Dickinson for some time, and was not fulfilling the promise. Recently, the provost and EM leader teamed up to combine under one roof a new Academic Advising unit and the Career Center. Though the directors report to two different senior officers, the synergy created by this union will have a significant impact on students and outcomes.

This service was relocated to the center of the campus (they had been on different ends of the campus before) and hired new directors to make it work. To symbolize the relationship between academic advising and career/graduate school planning, the staff in these two offices will in fact be integrated. There is no Academic Advising Office separate from the Career Center. A campus culture that embraced the college's mission and vision allowed two departments in different divisions to work together to deliver on the promise.

Finally, the characteristics of the campus community are defined not only by the quality of the relationships but also by the physical space. I spoke earlier of colorful banners sporting the college's new logo and the red Adirondack chairs placed on campus to promote conversation. In the same vein, the physical appearance of the campus speaks volumes to the promise that this institution cares about the student. A campus with overgrown grass and weeds, cracked sidewalks and tiles, chipping paint, etc. indicates to the visitor and the resident alike that the college simply does not care. The enrollment manager typically does not supervise the director of Physical Plant, but the campus-wide education necessary for understanding the college's position, its brand and its promise will pay dividends in many different areas that ultimately impact on the ability to attract and retain students.

Data and Technology: With the current generation tuned into the latest conveniences of technology, enrollment managers must be aware of the recruitment advantages available (without being obvious about it; students do not want to be bombarded with glitz), and they must also understand how the use of technology in registration, course work, and communication can enhance the quality of the educational experience and the connection to the institution.

Dickinson's computer system to support admissions was, in 1999, more of a records system than a recruitment tool. The EM staff moved quickly to evaluate stand-alone systems and selected one that would allow admission counselors to identify students and communicate with them by region, high school, gender, race, activity (including athletics), SAT score, legacy status, academic area of interest and the need for financial aid. It also provided staff with a powerful tool for data sorting and analysis. One lynch pin to successful enrollment management, therefore, is having the right technological power available to evaluate the market and to target institutional messages to students in a strategic way.

Recognizing the power of the Web, the college moved from a half-time Web master with only "on-the-job" experience, to a full time director of Web Services (who was a registrar at another institution and understood the academic mission of the institution) and an assistant. These positions report through the College Relations unit that is a part of the Enrollment Management Division. They work closely with the director of Admissions, with Alumni Affairs and Development, and with the faculty to assure a uniform, accurate, up-to-date and vibrant Web presence that reflects the college's image and position. They designed a special site for admitted students and their parents, and one for enrolled students as well. One feature on the admitted site allows parents to e-mail parents of enrolled students from their area for feedback on the college, and permits accepted students to do the same with Dickinson students from their area and/or in their intended major.

Chat rooms and the like are becoming increasingly popular with students, and Dickinson has just started experimenting in this area. What is more important, though, is giving students the ability to access their data on the Web: admissions application information, course registration, room registration, making appointments, etc. Students expect that today, and a successful enrollment manager will ask the tough questions of IT and Web staff to make sure the institution is at least up-to-date and preferably ahead of the curve in its services.

Johnson (2002) says that communication creates and sustains relationships and that a good communications plan relies on technology to support (though not replace) personal contact with one another. When using print, e-mail, the Web and contact by phone or in person, the most critical element, of course, is consistency of message across all contacts. There also must be a relationship among various contacts. Institutions, for example, have successfully drawn students to the Web through their printed materials and by Web-based e-mail. This is all part of an integrated communications plan that must be supported by technology. At Dickinson, this plan lists in a sequential calendar all communications including those that are Web- and e-mail-based, their purpose and their relationship to other forms of communication. An outline of the communication flow helps to identify the purpose of each contact and aids in the evaluation of each program. It also guards against the inevitable "great idea that we have to do now" syndrome, in that it forces staff to look at the impact of an additional piece of communication on the entire program and sequencing of messages. In addition to the use of technology to recruit students and to provide prospective and enrolled students with necessary services, technology must be used to support research that will guide policy decisions, the creation of new strategies and the evaluation of present efforts. The data, of course, must be integrated at the student record level. Dickinson collects as much data as possible on prospective students (often a challenge), and of course on admitted and enrolled students. Along with demographic and academic data, the college tracks contact responses, the need for aid and the percentage of need met by grant, legacy or "VIP" status, athletic interests and student activity participation and leadership. By doing this, the college is able to model the class prior to final admissions decisions and to make adjustments if enrollment results are projected to fall short of goals. The logistical regression enrollment projection model, designed by a statistics professor and the director of Institutional Research, is an invaluable tool for staff as they refine the characteristics of the class: diversity (race, gender, geographic), academic and financial. The model will not guide the staff at the individual level. In other words, it will not tell them who to admit based on the likelihood of enrollment. It simply projects the class in the aggregate by adding all of the enrollment probabilities and the proportion of each characteristic that is appropriate to that probability (e.g., if there are 100 admitted minority students, and the addition of their individual enrollment probabilities is .33, the model will predict thirty-three minority students in the class, but it can not predict who will enroll).

The data collected and analyzed by different institutions will depend upon individual needs and what looks to have a significant impact on the enrollment decision. The model at Dickinson has been an essential tool in crafting the class in the right number, distribution, quality and net revenue.

At Dickinson, data elements were divided into six areas in order to understand students, competitors and how work was accomplished:

1. **Trends.** The admission funnel from suspect to prospect to admit to enrolled, by sex, race, major, feeder school, aid, contact; total enrollment over time by the same variables; job and graduate school placement rates by the same variables plus major.
2. **College selection.** What is important to prospective students; how is the institution seen relative to others; how do applicants and matriculants differ from non-applicants and non-matriculants; where do admitted students enroll if not here?
3. **Enrollment.** Student ratings of the institution on factors important to them; program demand changes over time; factors that influence student persistence; what distinguishes completers from non-completers.

4. **Post enrollment.** Alumni ratings of experiences and preparation for career or graduate/professional school; employer ratings of graduates; parent ratings of their child's experience and outcomes; differences in ratings among majors.

5. **External.** National demographic trends, supply of high school students in a specific market (Resources: www.nces.ed.gov/stats.html, Postsecondary Education OPPORTUNITY by Tom Mortenson in Iowa City, Student Poll by the Art and Science Group in Baltimore).

6. **Operations.** Track volume to assess staff, supply, budget and computer needs at various points in the cycle which can be used to justify the support required to achieve institution-wide objectives.

This matrix has helped the EM Division to understand how its programs, policies, and practices affect demand and student experience, and has provided Dickinson with the necessary information to make appropriate adjustments. Of course, survey data on the admissions process and on the perceived "quality of life" on the campus can help enrollment managers assess the impact of programs on student decisions and experiences. The most popular national instruments are The College Board's Admitted Student Questionnaire; the Higher Education Research Institute's (CIRP) freshman and senior surveys and their relatively new College Student Survey (the latter measures student satisfaction with quality of life, while the freshman survey gives a baseline of student characteristics compared to national norms; the senior survey allows an institution to see differences over the four years, including student post-graduate plans); and the National Survey of Student Engagement (NSSE) that attempts to give a college information on the degree to which students feel engaged with their education in and out of the classroom. Dickinson has participated in all of the above. It is currently assessing the characteristics of campus "social life" in an effort to understand why only two-thirds of its students are satisfied (compared to a 95% satisfaction rate with the academic program), and to take "corrective action" if that is deemed necessary. This is a strategic retention issue and one that the college is addressing as a result of survey data and analysis.

Finally, other data must be collected to help in the assessment of enrollment management strategies. First year academic performance on an individual level should be compared to academic indicators at the time of admission to determine whether different standards should be applied during the selection process. Data on current academic performance must also be used by academic advisors for early intervention to help students succeed. On the other end, students with high grades should be identified and cultivated for major national and international post-graduate fellowships. Dickinson is beginning to do this with new academic advising/career center program described earlier.

Budget: All of the ambition in the world, with appropriate planning, will not be achieved unless the institution realizes how much it will cost and provides the necessary resources. The EM Division head arrived at Dickinson in the midst of a three-year deficit, with five more years projected. When he said that Dickinson may have to go a little further into deficit in order to come out of it, the president and the chairman of the board did not blink. In fact, more money was spent than in the past, but the college came out of deficit in three years rather than in five, and, as all now conclude, the investment in staff, equipment, marketing studies and student and alumni program refinement was well worth it.

A budget is a spending plan and a means to help staff fulfill the vision of the strategic plan. Once the college community agreed on the institution-wide strategic objectives, divisions and departments began to assemble strategies to achieve the objectives. Each strategy had attendant tactics that, for the most part, required either additional financial support or a re-direction of resources away from non-strategic initiatives. It is always preferable to seek the latter, but in Dickinson's case, because it had been under-funded and under-capitalized through most of the '90s, much new financial support was required. The adage, "You have to spend money to make money," was not a hard sell considering the college's deficit position and enrollment weakness in 1999. Obviously, the college could not fund every tactic that could be suggested by the plan, so funding priorities were set at the divisional level and then negotiated among the senior officers of the college.

Earlier, while describing the impact of academic and co-curricular programs on enrollment management, I discussed Dickinson's top-rated global education program. A strategic objective of the college is to infuse a global perspective throughout the curriculum, acknowledging that the leaders of tomorrow must know and understand a complex world. As a major objective of the college, programs that support this objective should be funded. Those that do not contribute to this, though perhaps worthy in their own right, should have a lower funding priority.

It is easy to identify additional funding needs. Everyone could use more money. It is more difficult to identify areas to cut, and these tend to come slowly and over time.

Without buy-in to the strategic direction, the vision and the promise of the institution, cuts can rarely be made. But trade-offs are indeed necessary in order to sustain a strategic position. At Dickinson, programs in wellness were scaled back in favor of a push in community volunteerism; a program in public speaking was eliminated in favor of a program in journalism to train student reporters (and to save a dying student newspaper); and an expensive program that awarded future teachers $20,000 after four years of teaching (and that was unfunded) was first reduced and then eliminated when its marginal impact on admission and retention was revealed.

LESSONS LEARNED

Enrollment managers must be at the table to help set institutional spending priorities in conjunction with campus-wide objectives. Without this high level of participatory decision-making, the staff in Enrollment Management, Student Life and College Relations could not have accomplished what they did in a period of just four years. Chief enrollment officers must help set realistic revenue targets including net tuition, endowment earnings, government appropriations or grants, annual gifts and auxiliary income. Ideally, revenues should be set in the budget before expenditures. Of course, external factors such as the stock market, state budget deficits, federal student aid programs and health insurance premiums for faculty and staff all impact on the process. Dickinson has a Planning and Budget Committee with faculty and student representation that meets weekly throughout the academic year on which all the senior officers (except the president) sit. This promotes an institution-wide understanding and helps to secure buy-in with all constituencies. It consumes a great amount of time, but it seems clear that Dickinson could not have achieved what it did as quickly as it did, while coming out of deficit in three years rather than five, without the support of the entire campus community. The Planning and Budget Committee was a critical link in this success.

Divisional and department budgets must be related to institutional priorities because again, we cannot do everything. For example, if the objective is to be a global campus, what should be funded in admissions—an outreach to Department of Defense schools, American schools abroad and Governor's schools for international studies in the U.S., or the extensive development of secondary and tertiary markets to increase the geographic distribution of our students? At Dickinson, both were important, but it was clear that the former would be funded before the latter based on the strategic objective. Enrollment managers must have a thorough knowledge of institutional budgets. They must understand what drives the budget and they must share with their senior colleagues how their competitors fund similar items, particularly staff and programs. With a clear understanding of how costs relate to capacity (excess classroom, library, residence hall space) and quantifying the cost of enrolling an additional student on the margin in below- and at-capacity scenarios, enrollment managers can help their institutions see revenue opportunities and secure the resources necessary to achieve their objectives.

This author found it absolutely necessary to build strategic alliances with other senior managers, communicating the importance of the promise we make to students and alumni and considering the impact on that promise before any decision is made to spend resources, develop new programs or change institutional policies. Enrollment managers must be coaches in the best sense of the word. They must be able to rally staff in different offices toward common goals, they must hire excellent managers and give them the resources and tools necessary to do their jobs, and they must be careful themselves to see relationships between seemingly unrelated areas to leverage these to the benefit of the institution. They must also share information frequently, with staff and senior managers in order to maximize the chances of success.

Enrollment managers must be data-driven but human-relations oriented. They must be compassionate and ethical, but demanding of evidence and pragmatic. They must possess a future orientation in their thinking, while at the same time concerning themselves with how current systems will affect the institution in the next fiscal year.

Forming the necessary foundation with trend data analysis from the institution overlaid with competitor data, understanding what "could be" if the institution made some strategic decisions and provided the funds to achieve these, and communicating this effectively to staff, faculty, students, alumni, trustees, senior management and the public at large is vital. These are the building blocks of successful enrollment management.

Beyond this, however, and particularly true in Dickinson's case, is a firm grasp of historical mission and how it relates to today and to the future vision of the institution. Dickinson had a strong academic foundation with dedicated and creative faculty. It had built an extraordinary global network and had integrated an international perspective throughout the curriculum. It had crossed disciplinary borders to produce award-winning curricula in the sciences, social sciences, humanities and the arts. Yet applications fell throughout the '90s as did revenue. Understanding and applying historical mission, and communicating a clear identity and applying strategic enrollment management tools proved a successful formula indeed for the re-emergence of Dickinson as a top, national liberal arts college in the 21st century.

* *The first paragraph in this case study was borrowed liberally from "A History of Dickinson College" at www.dickinson.edu*

REFERENCES

Johnson, R.E. (2002, May). Marketing synergy: Merging publications, the Web, direct mail, and telemarketing. Paper presented at the CASE Institute for Integrated Marketing & Branding, Boston, MA.

Loomis Hubbell, L.W., Massa, R.J., & Lapovsky, L. Using benchmarking to influence tuition and fee decisions. In Bender, B.E. & Schuh, J.H. (Eds.), Using benchmarking to inform practice in higher education. New Directions for Higher Education (No. 118), San Francisco: Jossey-Bass.

Sevier, R.A. (1998). Integrated marketing for colleges, universities, and schools: A step-by-step planning guide. Washington, DC: Council for Advancement and Support of Higher Education.

Sevier, R.A. (2002). Building a brand that matters. Hiawatha, IA: Strategy Pub.

EPILOGUE

The University of North Carolina at Greensboro recently began a capital campaign with a theme of, "The Impact of One/The Power of Many." As I reflected on the writings in this book, it occurred to me that this theme is personified in the stories told. Presidents with vision, enrollment managers who were not afraid to take risks, ordinary people who did extraordinary things—they all demonstrated "The Impact of One."

They made a difference on their respective campuses, but in all of the case studies, they did not do so alone. They were savvy enough to understand "The Power of Many." Together with faculty, staff, students, alums, senior leadership, board members, consultants, and others, they moved mountains—they changed the culture; they altered existing paradigms; they reconfigured structures; they reengineered processes; they reshaped institutional image; they reinvented their colleges and universities and themselves in the process.

Among the many and the few described in this book, there are true heroes or perhaps, as close to a hero as one can expect to find inside the walls of the academy. These people took chances. They made sacrifices. They faced dire situations. And, ultimately they emerged victorious.

If the reader takes one thing from the pages of this book, let it be hope. The authors have inspired me to go beyond my comfort zone—to explore "the art of the possible." My hope is that you have been inspired as well.

APPENDIX 1
BELMONT UNIVERSITY LEADERSHIP STRUCTURES

Senior Leadership Team—president, provost, vp of Finance and Administration, special assistant to the president, general counsel, vp of Church Relations, vp of Development, director of Special Initiatives; meets weekly to guide the university.

Provost's Council—all the direct reports of the provost (academic deans, associate provost, dean of Students, dean of Enrollment Services, and director of Institutional Research); meets weekly to guide the day-to-day operations of student life: curricular, co-curricular, and administrative; carries out strategic initiatives and planning.

Enrollment Services Division—headed by the dean of Enrollment Services; includes the offices of Admissions, Student Financial Services, Belmont Central, the University Registrar, Call Center, and Enrollment Information; the dean reports directly to the provost.
* Enrollment Services Council (ESC)—includes the department heads for all offices within the division, as well as the director of Residence Life. Meets bi-weekly to direct and coordinate the work of the division.
* Expanded Enrollment Services Council (ESCX)—includes all members of ESC as well as representatives from all colleges and schools in the university (including graduate and undergraduate program representatives) and representation for other academic programs (the Honors Program, Undeclared Students, the Library) and a representative from Data and Information Services. This group meets biweekly, alternately with ESC, to detail work issues related to student administrative processes and to resolve issues, develop processes, and brainstorm ideas.

Flywheel Team—the university's leadership team for marketing; includes the dean of Enrollment Services, staff from the Office of University Marketing and Communications, representatives from all academic areas, Development, Web development staff; led by the director of Special Initiatives; responsible for coordinating university marketing efforts.

Enrollment Leadership Team—president, provost, dean of Enrollment Services, director of Special Initiatives, and senior associate to the president; meet bimonthly to review enrollment growth plan strategically—to address progress, funding needs, development of new programs, etc.

APPENDIX 2
KEY EVENTS AT EVCC

1980s	Low enrollment, fiscal distress
1988	Administrative Council and Portland Committee generate initiatives for improved enrollment and services.
1980-96	Low and unstable enrollment patterns
1997	Implementation of "Building Image, Building Enrollment" plan
1997	Re-engineered separate services to form Enrollment Services
1998	Advising and institutional research staff added
1999	New president initiates strategic planning effort
1999	Environmental scan generated
2000	Small SEM committee formed to generate enrollment forecast to support capital growth
2001	First SEM plan produced
2002	Initial SEM goals reached

The Office of Admission & Orientation supports the mission of Oregon State University by bringing to the university students who will benefit from and contribute to OSU's educational goals. In serving our many customers, the overriding mission of our office will be to exceed persons' expectations in meeting their needs and requests. In carrying out our mission, we will operate according to the following principles:

1. The OSU Office of Admission & Orientation will be service-driven and results-oriented. Our primary operating principle will be "We can and we will."

2. We will work to build and maintain a sense of community that promotes open communication, mutual trust, cooperation, and respect among our staff and with other campus departments. To maintain and develop community within our own office, we will participate in workshops and staff development opportunities throughout the year and as new staff are hired.

3. By working cooperatively with every campus department, we will play a leadership role in enrolling the number and types of students, which will enable the university to reach its goals.

4. We will be proactive in honoring and enhancing the diversity of Oregon State. In every facet of our operation we will encourage openness and sensitivity to persons of varied cultural, racial, and ethnic backgrounds.

5. We will always strive to be positive about ourselves, our colleagues, our office and the university, and to translate that energy into positive behaviors and outcomes.

6. Regardless of our specific responsibilities, we will be available to assist in any area where help is needed. We will be ready to do whatever it takes to meet our customers' needs and requests. We will never say, "That's not my job."

7. We will strive for professional excellence. Individually and as a group we will seek to be the best in our field. Our goal is to make a significant contribution to our office, our university, and our profession.

8. We will value creativity and encourage risk-taking. We will learn from our mistakes and encourage constructive criticism as we seek to continuously improve everything we do.

9. While holding ourselves to the highest professional standards, we will seek to be well-rounded persons. We will respect the personal dimensions of our lives and take steps to ensure that we have fun working together.

APPENDIX 4
PROPOSAL FOR ESTABLISHING ENROLLMENT MANAGEMENT STRUCTURE

With our recent enrollment success, OSU has created an opportunity to gain further prominence both in Oregon and nationally. This has important implications under the new state funding model and for our ability to influence legislative decisions in the coming years. Even more importantly, we have the chance to realize our goals for the type of institution we want OSU to be, as defined by the goals we have established for the range and characteristics of students we wish to enroll.

Whether we achieve our enrollment goals, or continue the historical pattern of fluctuating enrollments, will be determined by decisions we make in the next few months. In the near term, turnover in the vice provost for Academic Affairs and director of Undergraduate Academic Affairs positions puts the university's positive enrollment momentum at risk. Over the longer term, fulfillment of OSU's enrollment potential will be diminished, should we choose to retain our current administrative structure. This is true for the following reasons:

* OSU's primary enrollment-related functions are grouped with myriad other responsibilities under the vice provost for Academic Affairs. This limits the amount of focused, cabinet-level attention that can be devoted to these functions and reduces the degree of coordination among them that can and should occur.
* The vice provost role as currently configured virtually assures that the individual in the position will not have expertise either in central university administration or in managing university enrollments.
* Responsibility for new student orientation and the First Year Experience (FYE) program currently is split between Admission & Orientation and the Coordinator of FYE, who report to the associate vice provost for Academic Affairs. This resulting structure is redundant and wastes staff resources. Bringing these functions together could eliminate these negative effects.
* Responsibility for graduate student admissions is spread among three areas—the Graduate School, academic units, and Admission & Orientation. This results in tremendous inefficiency and dissatisfaction for all involved, and hinders our ability to improve graduate enrollment.

These issues can be addressed by reorganizing the departments primarily involved with undergraduate enrollment within an enrollment management model. This would result in a new administrative unit headed by an enrollment professional. Functions to be included in the Enrollment Management unit would include Undergraduate Admissions, New Student Orientation, Financial Aid and Scholarships, First Year Experience, Registrar, Summer Session, and Pre-college Programs. The new unit would be responsible for undergraduate recruitment and retention. Graduate admissions, currently a responsibility of Admission & Orientation, would move to the Graduate School in coordination with academic units.

Benefits of this reorganization would include:

* Providing upper-level leadership to undergraduate enrollment by an individual with training and experience in dealing with enrollment issues from a university-wide perspective.
* Greater coordination of activities among enrollment management units and with other OSU departments.
* Cost savings resulting from the elimination of redundant functions among units.
* Enhanced ability to maximize revenue under the new state funding model.
* The ability to respond more quickly to enrollment opportunities and challenges.
* Stronger continuity of programs to assist undergraduates as they move through the enrollment process from recruitment to retention to graduation.
* More focused attention on graduate admission issues.
* Creation of a more realistic portfolio of responsibilities for the vice provost for Academic Affairs.

APPENDIX 5
OREGON STATE UNIVERSITY

ENROLLMENT MANAGEMENT DIVISION MISSION AND VISION

MISSION
To promote, enhance and safeguard the integrity of the educational mission of the university.

VISION
The Enrollment Management Division leads the university in two primary areas:
* Promoting higher education to students at all levels of the educational system in the state of Oregon and beyond.
* Developing and fulfilling goals for the number and characteristics of students enrolled.

Using comprehensive enrichment, recruitment and admission strategies, we will attract students who meet OSU's standards of excellence and diversity, and will coordinate effective student transitions to the university through responsive scholarship and financial aid programs, orientation, course registration and first year experience opportunities. As students progress in their educational experiences we will support them by coordinating the university's financial aid and scholarship opportunities, assisting with retention through our support of advisers, offering student programs which promote academic success, and providing specific expertise to university committees. Further, we will assist academic departments and the faculty by coordinating the planning of course offerings, the recording of students' educational achievements, and the implementation of degree and academic standards. We will maintain for the former student their one true lifetime link to the university and for the university its history of educational activities. In each of its many roles and activities, Enrollment Management staff will strive for excellence by keeping current with best practices, being active in professional associations, and implementing programs that are recognized both within and outside the university for their effectiveness.

Enrollment Management: Establishing and Meeting Enrollment Goals

Overall responsibility for the process : Strategic Enrollment

Reporting to the Provost's Office **TIMELINE PROCESS** initiated in February/March 2002

STRATEGIC ENROLLMENT PLANNING GROUP

Dean, Extended campus, *Co-chair* • Dean, College of Liberal arts, *Co-chair*

Dean, Graduate school • Professor, ATHM • Assistant Provost for Enrollment Management

Director of Budget and Fiscal Planning • Director of Institutional Research • Director of Marketing

CONSULTATION /APPROVAL	ACTIVITY	TIMELINE
	Develop enrollment targets and mix that meet OSU's enrollment and academic goals, and optimize revenue	February - March 200(X-1)
	Develop resource projections for: • Recruitment and marketing • Financial aid • Academic programs	April-May 200(X-1)
Vice President for Finance and Admin Chief Financial Officer OSU Foundation Vice President for Advancement Provost	Specifying of E&G and private dollars required for financial aid, recruitment/ marketing and program access	June 200(X-1)
	Enrollment targets discussed by University Cabinet and approved by the President	June 200(X-1)
Director of Marketing	Develop (additional) marketing and outreach plans to meet enrollment targets	June 200(X-1)
Enrollment Management Units Director of Development	Regular assessment of admission and financial aid trends	October 200(X-1) to May 200(X)
Vice President for Finance and Admin Chief Financial Officer, OSU Foundation Vice President, Advancement Provost	Evaluate progress and plan mid-course corrections	December 200(X-1)
Administration Enrollment Management Units	Evaluate projected enrollment. Feedback loop to next cycle.	May 200(X-1)
	Share outcomes with University Cabinet, Provost's Council, Faculty Senate	May-June 200(X)

INDEX

ESSENTIALS *of*
ENROLLMENT MANAGEMENT
CASES IN THE FIELD